Assassin!

Also available by Ian Hernon:

Riot!
Civil Insurrection from Peterloo to the Present Day

'His account of the build up to Peterloo and the aftermath is stirring stuff
... written with the pace and detail you would expect from an experienced
journalist.'

Sarah Williams, *BBC History*

'This fascinating history of riots includes the reform riots of 1831, the
violence of the Chartists and the Suffragettes, the lawlessness that occurred
during the bizarre police strike of 1919. It ends with the Stop the War
march in London in February 2003, Britain's biggest ever demonstration
and, in Hernon's view, one of the most futile protests of modern times.'

Ian Pindar, *Guardian*

'Hernon's book is a useful primer on the civil insurrections which helped
Britain lumber towards equitable political representations. He has picked
out key and often overlooked episodes in working class history.'

Tribune

Assassin!

200 Years of British Political Murder

IAN HERNON

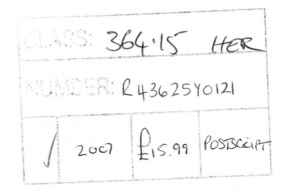

Pluto Press

LONDON • ANN ARBOR, MI

First published 2007 by Pluto Press
345 Archway Road, London N6 5AA
and 839 Greene Street, Ann Arbor, MI 48106

www.plutobooks.com

British Library Cataloguing in Publication Data
A catalogue record for this book is available from the British Library

Hardback
ISBN-13   978 0 7453 2716 7
ISBN-10   0 7453 2716 8

Paperback
ISBN-13   978 0 7453 2715 0
ISBN-10   0 7453 2715 X

Library of Congress Cataloging in Publication Data applied for

This book is printed on paper suitable for recycling and made from fully managed
and sustained forest sources. Logging, pulping and manufacturing processes are
expected to conform to the environmental regulations of the country of origin.

10   9   8   7   6   5   4   3   2   1

Designed and produced for Pluto Press by
Chase Publishing Services Ltd, Fortescue, Sidmouth, EX10 9QG, England
Typeset from disk by Stanford DTP Services, Northampton, England
Printed and bound in the European Union by
CPI Antony Rowe Ltd, Chippenham and Eastbourne, England

Contents

List of Illustrations

1
Introduction

'Stealth and fanaticism'

It is an uncomfortable fact that in Britain's much-vaunted democracy the spectre of the assassin has always haunted our political leaders, and continues to do so. The gunman and bomber, or the perceived threat they pose, have changed the way this country is governed and has been a frequently repeated excuse for repressive measures. How that fear, rather than the actual act of assassination, has played a part in the making of modern Britain is the principal theme of this book. The shadow of the assassin has led to the overhaul of mental health laws, contributed to the expansion of the security services and immeasurably widened the surveillance society. That shadow has undermined our cherished freedoms of movement, dissent and judicial fairness. I have aimed to chronicle the most extreme forms of protest and to nail the myth that Britain, unlike so-called banana republics, has somehow escaped the political assassin.

It is also intended as a companion piece to my earlier book, *Riot! Civil Insurrection from Peterloo to the Present Day*. In the political context, assassinations may have been an underlying part of British political life, but as a tool of real reform, unlike riots, strikes, public protest and mass insurrection, they have been a dismal failure. The random nature of assassination, at least in terms of effect and state reaction, makes it an essentially irrational act.

In Britain assassins have tended to fall into two distinct categories – the lone 'nutter' and the terrorist. In dealing with the latter I have had to write a digested history of the IRA, the partition of Ireland and the bloodshed on both sides of the Irish Sea since 1969, inevitably

going over some well-trodden ground. But here I have focused on the
motivation, character and background of the assassin. There is some
crossover between the mentally disturbed and the most hard-line of
terrorists. But, as with *Riot!*, I aim to illustrate the grievances – real
and imagined – which push a person towards extreme violence. The
motives and ideologies of such killers are, even in the narrow context
of Ireland, varied and complex, but their personal view of history and
their assumed or imagined place in it are a factor in all.

*   *   *

The term 'assassin' was coined during the Crusades from the belief
that a fanatical Syrian and Persian sect, which terrorised the region for
200 years and, legend had it, took hashish to have visions of Paradise
before setting out on their missions. The sect was an offshoot of the
Shia branch of Islam and for each member an act of murder was a
sacred duty inspired by the teachings of Hasan-i Sabbah. From the
eleventh century they waged a war of individual mayhem against their
Sunni rivals and other more conventional military forces. According
to Paul Wilkinson:

> Instead of previous hopeless attempts at insurrection they perfected
> techniques of systematic terrorism which certainly wrought terror not only
> amongst the Muslim potentates (whose personal style of rule made them
> extremely vulnerable to the Assassins), but even amongst Christian princes
> who had been regaled by tales of the Assassins' stealth and fanaticism.[1]

During the Crusades the great Muslim leader Saladin was a target of
the sect which opposed the established Islamic faith. In 1175 the rulers
of Aleppo, under siege by Saladin, hired the Assassins to kill him, but
the murderers were recognised and slain. The following year a second
attempt was made, but Saladin was saved by his body armour. Saladin
now decided to strike at the important Assassin citadel of Masyaf, but
withdrew when, according to some versions of the story, he dreamt of
the Assassin Grand Master, Rashid al-Din Sinan, known as the Old
Man of the Mountains. A poisoned dagger was found on his bed with
some hot cakes and a written threat.

> This episode illustrates perfectly the mystique possessed by the Assassin
> leader: his reputation as a sorcerer and conjuror had spread to every
> kingdom, both Christian and Muslim. Sinan was considered able to charm

any man or woman and was said to possess the powers of telepathy and clairvoyance. To contemporaries [he] was a magical evil genius leading a cult of fanatical killers ... He was thought of as presiding over a sinister web of informants and agents, bound together by dark conspiracies and evil schemes.[2]

The motivation was their religious faith, albeit a 'heretical' offshoot of conventional Islam:

Faith and belief went unchallenged and kept alive the cult's spirit of absolute dedication and self-sacrifice. Western writers went to great lengths to try to explain this mesmeric grip that [Sinan] was supposed to have on his followers. The most popular explanation was the use of hashish to instil the calm killing mind and cold-blooded obedience, but the drug actually has the opposite effect. Hashish created intoxication and a feeling of quiescence. It is unlikely to have been used by Assassins just about to murder someone. Faith was likely to be a stronger drug.[3]

Further stories told by Marco Polo and other travellers spread across Europe and assassination came to mean the murder of the rich and powerful as a political tool or as a means of personal advancement.

In Britain prior to the nineteenth century assassination was largely the preserve of the rich and powerful. The poor, weak and dispossessed turned to riot and rebellion rather than individual slaughter. Henry II set a pattern when he ordered the murder of that 'turbulent priest', Thomas à Becket, in Canterbury Cathedral in 1170. During the Middle Ages and beyond the stiletto and poison phial were features of court and political etiquette. From the slaying of the young princes in the Tower to the judicial alibis of the block, murder was part and parcel of royal succession.

During the cruel and paranoid Tudor era treason was the *bête noir*, and alleged plots typically involve supposed attempts on the life of the monarch. Between 1532 and 1540 alone 308 convicted traitors paid the ultimate price. One observer wrote in 1541: 'To tell the truth, it is now no novelty among us to see men slain, hanged, quartered or beheaded ... Some for one thing and some for another.'[4] The list of the high-born butchered was impressive: Edward Stafford, third Duke of Buckingham, in 1521; Lord Montague and Henry Courtney, Marquess of Exeter, in 1538; Henry Howard, Earl of Surrey, in 1546; Sir Thomas Seymour, the uncle of the young King Edward VI, in 1549; John Dudley, Duke of Northumberland, in 1553; Thomas Howard, fourth Duke of

Norfolk, in 1571; Robert Devereaux, second Earl of Essex, in 1601. In most cases the plots were puerile and doomed from the start. Lacey Baldwin Smith writes: 'Tudor traitors, great and small, performed so clumsily that their sedition reads more like a series of bad historical novels than real history. Almost without exception they behaved in an unimaginably irrational and infantile fashion as if they were seeking to be destroyed; and understandably the verdict of history has been "of unsound mind".'[5]

The spy wars of the Elizabethan era took the English assassin's art to new heights – plots, real, imagined and fabricated, provided a constant backcloth to the age as the new Protestant England outlawed Roman Catholicism.

The ultimate spymaster, Sir Francis Walsingham, in 1586 successfully infiltrated a group of Catholics plotting to incite a Spanish-backed uprising to kill Elizabeth I and place Mary, Queen of Scots on the English throne. The ringleaders, including Anthony Babington, were betrayed by intercepted letters and condemned. The conspirators were hanged, disembowelled and quartered, a fate which awaited hundreds of traitors. One of the Babington plotters, John Savage, was fully conscious when cut open and the agonies he suffered shocked even Elizabeth. The Babington Plot was a classic 'sting' operation by cynical government manipulators. More unusual was the case of Lady Margaret Lambourne. Shocked the following year by the beheading of Mary Stuart, this aristocrat in her mid-thirties decided to kill Elizabeth. Disguised as a man and with two muskets hidden under her top coat – one primed for Elizabeth, the other for herself – she penetrated the royal gardens and approached the queen. But one of the guns was jarred and discharged prematurely; Lady Margaret was swiftly seized. Face to face she told Elizabeth that she was moved by love and asked for her pardon. Astonishingly, the queen gave it. She was not so forgiving that same year to the Irishman Michael Moody, who plotted to put gunpowder under her bed. Once again, the conspiracy had been infiltrated by government agents and Moody paid the ultimate price.

In 1589 a Catholic exile in Prague, Robert Hesketh, was sent to England to deliver plans for a *coup d'état* to the Catholic Lord Derby, picking up a sealed note at the White Lion tavern in Islington. Derby, appalled at the plot, handed Hesketh over to the authorities. There was no need: the letter was a forgery and had been planted by government agents to tempt exiles back from abroad. Hesketh was executed in St Albans.

The execution of Elizabeth's former favourite, the Earl of Essex, for a demented, bungled insurrection was the inevitable endgame for those who saw conspiracies everywhere in court circles. Lacey Baldwin Smith writes:

> As much as Essex and his breed might wriggle and squirm and cry out in anguish, they could never free themselves from the script that society demanded that they recite or from the misconceptions, fears and 'black poison of suspect' which religious and social; training had indelibly implanted upon their minds. Each enacted a destiny, beset by paranoid delusions, which was peculiar to himself; but each traitor's maladjusted response to the normal rhythm of politics was shaped and delineated by a concatenation of cultural, educational, economic and political impulses that gave to Tudor England its distinctive signature and that set the fatal tempo of his life, guaranteeing that treason would never prosper.[6]

Elizabeth's reign was punctuated with such plots and counter-plots, but it was believed that the coronation of James VI of Scotland as James I of England would herald a new age of pragmatic tolerance. Such hopes were shattered when James, under pressure from all sides, announced: 'Nah, we'll no need the papists noo.' The Catholic aristocracy responded with a conspiracy, the 'Treason of the Main', which aimed to kill him and put Lady Arbella Stuart on the throne. Some alleged plotters, including Sir Walter Raleigh, were reprieved or had their sentences deferred, but several Catholic priests were executed. Such plots, including an earlier one known as the 'Treason of the Byre' which had aimed to imprison James in the Tower of London until he abandoned persecution of Catholics, were small beer compared with the most famous of all.

Guido Fawkes was born in 1570, the son of a notary of the ecclesiastical courts. Although his family were not overt Catholics, he was educated in York where he discovered his faith. On receiving his inheritance he enlisted as a soldier of fortune with the Spanish army in Flanders. He was present at the capture of Calais, where his 'nobility and virtue' were noted. On the death of Elizabeth I the English Catholic Sir William Stanley, a senior officer in the Spanish ranks, ordered him to visit King Philip of Spain to secure relief for their fellow Catholic countrymen. Returning to England he was drawn to a group centred on Robert Catesby who, at a meeting in the Duck and Duke Tavern in central London, drew up a plan to rid England not just of its king, but also of the upper ranks of the Protestant nobility, the bishops and the structure of government. The conspirators ordered Spanish swords engraved with words 'The Passion of Jesus' in readiness for the coup.

After a year of delays and false starts Fawkes and his co-conspirators packed a rented vault under the Palace of Westminster with enough gunpowder, modern engineers have calculated, to blow up not just the House of Lords during the 5 November 1605 state opening of Parliament, but much of the surrounding, densely populated area. If it had succeeded it would have dwarfed any single act of terrorism before or since. However, Robert Cecil, the Earl of Salisbury and Walsingham's successor as spymaster-general, got wind of the plot. In this he was helped, unwittingly, by Catesby himself, who not only confessed the plan to his priest, but also warned aristocratic friends to stay away from Parliament. A watch was placed on Westminster and Fawkes, who had volunteered to light the fuse, was arrested. Fawkes declared that had he been in the cellar when the officers approached he would have blown himself up along with Parliament. He regretted nothing but that he had failed. When questioned about his readiness to kill the royal family he asserted that a desperate disease required a dangerous remedy and that his objective had been to 'blow the Scots back again to Scotland'. He refused to name his fellow conspirators, even after a day suffering the tortures of the rack.

Catesby and the others went on the run but were cornered at a country house at Holbeach, near Shrewsbury. Two hundred men laid siege and the conspirators were shot down as they tried to break out with pistols and swords. The dead were decapitated and the wounded sent to London. Fawkes, while being racked, was told of their death or capture and finally confessed. On 27 January 1606, he and the surviving plotters were tried in Westminster Hall. Their not guilty plea was rejected and on 31 January they suffered the bloody ritual of hanging, drawing and quartering. Fawkes was the last to mount the scaffold opposite Parliament House. He was 'weak and ill' from the torture he had already suffered. He briefly asked forgiveness of both king and state.[7] Their heads, daubed with preservative tar, were displayed on spikes along the length of London Bridge. 5 November has been 'celebrated' ever since, with the burning of effigies of Fawkes and, in some places, the pope and other figures of hate among the bigoted.

The aftermath of the English Civil War witnessed many assassination plots as Protestant Republicans battled with Catholics and Fifth Monarchists for supremacy. In 1666, just months before the Great Fire of London, John Rathbone, a former colonel in the parliamentary army, plotted with a handful of veterans to kill Charles II and his brother, James, Duke of York, confine the Horse Guards to barracks, capture the Tower of London and set it ablaze. The conspirators were captured and executed. In 1683 Anglicans met at Rye House, a large manor house near Hoddesdon, in Hertfordshire, owned by Richard Rumbold, to plan a *coup d'état*. The house stood on the edge of a marsh which the king and his brother would have to cross while riding back to London from the Newmarket races. At a narrow point in the road a cart would be overturned, the royal party ambushed and slain, and James, Duke of Monmouth, Charles's ultra-Protestant illegitimate son, would be proclaimed king. The plot was foiled when a fire at Newmarket cancelled the racing that day and the royal brothers returned home early. The plot was uncovered and for 18 months the conspirators and their associates were hunted down, tried and executed. The Earl of Essex cut his own throat in the Tower. Rumbold himself escaped to Holland.

Catholics became the scapegoats for most plots whatever their origin, when William of Orange ascended the throne in 1689. Most were fabricated. By the reign of George III, the increasing accessibility of monarchs to the people threw up a new phenomenon which would feature in the nineteenth century – the subject with a personal grievance.

A well-dressed woman approached George as he stepped out of his carriage at St James's Palace on 2 August 1786. She held out a rolled-up petition and as the king bent to receive it she drew a knife which she aimed at his heart. The king instinctively pulled back and the blow missed. The woman struck again, but the blade was incapable of penetrating his waistcoat and she was disarmed by a Yeoman of the Guard. Enraged onlookers tried to tear her apart but the king roared: 'The poor creature is mad! Do not hurt her! She has not hurt me!'[8] He showed himself to the mob as proof and the woman was bundled away. The novelist Fanny Burney later wrote: 'There is something in his whole behaviour upon this occasion which strikes me as proof indisputable of a true and noble courage.'[9]

In custody the woman refused to utter a word, but when she was brought before the Privy Council she was identified as Margaret Nicholson, a forty-something, unmarried domestic servant from Stockton-on-Tees. She told the Council that she had a right to 'property due to her from the Crown of England'. She had carried out the assault, after many petitions had failed, not to kill the king, but 'merely to shew the Cause'. Medical examination found that she 'appeared to have a consciousness of what she had done, but did not seem sensible of having committed any crime'. Dr Munro, of the Bedlam lunatic asylum, said that he had rarely seen such a clear case of insanity. The Council agreed and Nicholson was committed to Bedlam, where she died in May 1828.[10]

George, before he went mad, displayed further personal courage as his reign was hit by the political turmoil around the turn of the century. In autumn 1895 he told the Attorney General, Lord Eldon, that it was 'not improbable' as revolutionary fervour mingled with war fatigue that he would be the last king of England. On 29 October, while being driven to the State Opening of Parliament, his coach was surrounded by an angry mob shouting 'Peace and Bread! No War! Down with George!' Lord Onslow, who was accompanying the king, wrote:

> Nothing material happened till we got down to the narrowest part of the street called St Margarets where a small ball, either of lead or marble, passed through the window glass on the King's right hand and, perforating it, passed through the coach and out the other door, the glass of which was down. We all instantly exclaimed, 'This is a shot!' The King showed, and I am persuaded, felt no alarm; much less did he fear, to which indeed he is insensible.

George calmly read his speech to Parliament, setting out the Government's legislative programme, but on his return to St James's Palace he ran the gauntlet of a larger, even angrier mob. Every window in his coach was broken and several stones struck the king. Onslow recalled: 'The King took one of the stones out of the cuff of his coat, where it had lodged, and gave it to me saying, "I make you a present of this, as a mark of the civilities we have met on our journey today".'[11] At a critical moment a Mr Bedingfield leapt in front of the coach door and threatened to kill anyone who came closer. He was rewarded with an invented state appointment worth £650 a year.

   That was possibly the last time a ruling British monarch came close to falling victim to a politically motivated mob, as opposed to an individual assassin or lunatic. Five years later when George was reviewing the Foot Guards in Hyde Park a bullet struck and wounded a Navy Office clerk standing a few yards from him. That evening he was watching a performance of *She Would and She Would Not* at the Theatre Royal, Drury Lane, when a shot was fired at him from the pit. He reassured the queen: 'It's only a squib. We shall not stir. We'll stay the entertainment out.' He was wildly applauded. The would-be assassin was a former soldier, James Hadfield, who was declared insane.[12] By the end of the performance the theatre's manager, Henry Sheridan, had composed an extra verse to the National Anthem which began:

> From every latent foe,
> From the assassin's blow,
> God Save the King.

*   *   *

My main problem in choosing to cover British assassinations in the 200 years from the dawning of the industrial age to the present has been one of definition. There is a case, for example, for saying that most of the 3,350 slayings since the 1969 Northern Ireland outbreak of violence were assassinations motivated by political, geographical and religious concerns. That is why I have not simply covered the most high-profile murders, but have also included snapshots of 'ordinary' lives lost. They are just as valuable to their families and friends, and in some instances, have had wider implications than the headline grabbers. There is also the question of whether a killer labelled insane (or close to it), as happened in most of the attempts on Queen Victoria, can properly be labelled an assassin. It is a grey issue, and one which I have been unable fully to resolve. I have taken as my definition a murder or attempted murder of a person as a planned strategy to change either the killer's personal circumstances or that of the society in which he or she lives. That incorporates both those with a personal grievance or sense of social injustice and those ordered or hired to kill as part of a wider conflict or process of social change. In doing so I have attempted to paint a composite portrait of such assassins, including their motivation and sense of guilt or lack of it.

Another key motivation in writing this book is, as I tried to do in previous books on colonial wars and home-grown riots, to disprove the notion that we live in an essentially peace-loving country. We may not have been the banana republic of caricature, with presidents being popped as soon as they step on a balcony, and it is true that other countries have suffered more major assassinations – three presidents in the United States, a tsar in Russia, a whole aristocracy in France. But the last 200 years have witnessed a prime minister assassinated, attempts on at least three others, numerous attempts on members of the royal family – one of them successful – the killing of four MPs, several ambassadors, a Lord Lieutenant of Ireland, a Minister Resident in the Middle East, a Governor-General, a Chief of the Imperial General Staff, a defence attaché, senior civil servants, prison governors, generals, soldiers, informers, police and prison officers, writers and opinion-formers.

This book is dedicated to their families.

2
The Despard Plot

'I have weighed the matter well, and my heart is callous'

Madame Marie Tussaud, newly arrived in London from revolutionary France, was given permission to take a plaster cast of the face of the severed head before the coffin was closed. From that she created a waxwork which was to grace her new museum in the Lyceum Theatre. Within a few years the star exhibit would be Lord Nelson. In a separate room, later dubbed the Chamber of Horrors, was her waxwork of Colonel Edward Despard, the last man in England to be sentenced to death by hanging, drawing and quartering. In one room, a national hero, in the other a convicted traitor.

Despard had been condemned for an alleged plot to murder the king and foment a revolution. The *Newgate Calendar* described the scheme as 'the most vain and impotent attempt ever engendered in the distracted brain of an enthusiast'. It continued:

> Without arms, or any probable means, a few dozen men, the very dregs of society, led on by a disappointed and disaffected chief, were to overturn a mighty empire; nor does it appear that any man of their insignificant band of conspirators – Colonel Despard excepted – was above the level of the plebeian race, and not a few of them were Irish. Yet a small party of this description, seduced to disloyalty by a contemptible leader, brooding over their vain attempts at a mean public house, alarmed the nation.[1]

For almost two centuries history has treated Despard as a deluded fool whose assassination attempt was risible, or as the hapless victim of government spies and *agents provocateurs*. The truth was rather different and reflected the growing radicalisation of the age. Indeed, Thomas Paine's clarion call for social justice was a key motivation in the

Etched by Barlow, from a Sketch taken at his Trial.

COL. DESPARD.

1. Colonel Despard (engraving from an 1804 pamphlet)

first truly 'modern' assassination plot. Despard showed that the whiff of revolutionary fervour could cross class divisions and traditions.

* * *

Edward Marcus Despard was born in Queen's County, Ireland, in 1751, the youngest of six sons. His family were Protestant landowners with a strong military background and all but one brother were groomed for the army. After schooling at the military academy in Dublin Castle his father bought him a commission as an ensign in the 50th Infantry and Despard served as a foot soldier until he was posted, at the age of 21, to Jamaica with the rank of lieutenant. There he soon displayed a talent for engineering, working tirelessly to strengthen the island's fortifications against the Spanish.

The expedition which was to make his reputation as a gallant and industrious soldier came in 1780, when Governor Sir John Dalling hatched an ambitious plan to defend British interests on the Mosquito Coast by sending a force upriver to take the Spanish fort of San Juan, continue to Lake Nicaragua and cut Spain's New World colonies in two. From the lake it was only a few miles to the Pacific and his scheme envisaged a waterway joining two great oceans and under the control of Britain. Despard and 21-year-old Captain Horatio Nelson, in command of his first ship, enthusiastically joined the expedition. It was a disaster: the invasion was repeatedly delayed awaiting reinforcements and local levies; the Mosquito Coast was no paradise but a disease-ridden swamp; and the organisation was chaotic. Despard and Nelson were among the few to distinguish themselves. After a slog up-river the fort was taken with minimal casualties after a bombardment. One officer reported: 'There was scarcely a gun fired but was pointed by Captain Nelson of the *Hinchinbrooke*, or Lieutenant Despard, the chief engineer, who has exerted himself on every occasion.' But the fort, rather than offering shelter as the rainy season began, proved to be a death trap. Men died from every form of tropical disease – the 'bloody flux' (dysentery) in particular – and supplies were lost in the labyrinth of waterways. The expedition was abandoned. Despard was the last to leave, setting alight the charges to blow up the ramparts. Nelson was taken back to his ship in a delirium of fever. But he was one of the lucky ones. Of over 2,000 who took part in the adventure, only around 380 survived.

Despard was promoted to captain and put in charge of the island of Roatan, and shortly after that the Bay of Honduras, defending English logwood cutters against the Spanish. Dalling then recalled him to oversee Jamaica's defences, threatened at the time by a fleet commanded by the Comte de Grasse. Admiral Rodney's famous naval victory removed the imminent threat, and in August 1782 Despard commanded a force of settlers at Cap Gracias a Dios which took Spanish possessions on the Black River. The king gave his special thanks and Despard was promoted to colonel by the new Governor of Jamaica, Sir Archibald Campbell.

Under the 1783 peace treaty Spain permitted British settlers in the Yucatan peninsula to cut logwood, but do little else. The following March Despard was directed to administer the new territory. He was warmly welcomed by the settlers, many of whom had served with him in the previous administration, and at their insistence Despard was made superintendent. The relationship soured, however, and Despard, once the hero, was now referred to as a 'despot'. At issue was his determination to give equal rights to an influx of shoremen, including mulattoes, former slaves, ex-convicts, shipbuilders and Irish labourers. The earlier settlers, known as the Baymen, complained that Despard favoured the incomers. Despard insisted they had rights too, including the right to tend property and to vote. The Baymen levelled numerous accusations at him, including illegally usurping the powers of local magistrates. By sticking to the Spanish treaty and wringing many concessions from the Spaniards, Despard was branded a traitor. He in turn responded with counter-claims that the Baymen were simply defending their vested interests at the expense of the new pioneers. He called a snap election, a vote of confidence, which he won by a landslide. The settlers were outraged that blacks and Irish were given the same voting rights as themselves – arguably the first time the concept of 'one man, one vote' had been exercised anywhere in the growing British Empire. The Jamaican Assembly gave short shrift to Despard's critics, and the Colonial Secretary in London, Lord Sydney, dismissed them as frivolous. However Sydney's successor, Lord Grenville, was swayed enough by the Baymen's accusations to order Despard back to England. He arrived in May 1790, deeply stung by the claims of impropriety, accompanied by his black wife, Catherine. He demanded an immediate investigation to clear his name. He expected to return to Honduras within months. Instead he was kept hanging about the Secretary of State's office, a political embarrassment, for two years. He was then told that there were no real accusations against him, his reputation was unblemished and, although his old post had been abolished, employment would be found for his undoubted talents. There was plenty of work for a proven military engineer and administrator as Britain and Napoleonic France prepared for war, but none was found for him. He fumed and petitioned and launched legal action for payment of his meagre £500 annual salary in Honduras, much of which had been spent carrying out Crown duties. His own finances dwindled, and he spent some time in debtors' prison.

Gradually Despard's fight for the rights of the Bay settlers and justice for himself became entwined with the wider battle for electoral reform and social justice. They came together when Despard read Paine's *The Rights of Man* soon after its publication in early 1792. Elegantly written and passionately argued, it stirred republican and revolutionary sentiments in the disgruntled former soldier and colonial administrator. Paine vehemently attacked the monarchy, the principle of heredity, the system which preserved the vote for the wealthy properties class, warmongering and taxation without representation. He demanded a general revolution and the creation of a new state in which taxes would be spent for the benefit of all, rather than on war and propping up the old, class-based society. His proposals included pensions, free education and much of what would later be called the welfare state. Sixpenny editions flooded the nation and the 200,000 copies sold within two years were read by many more than those who bought it.

Within weeks of publication of *The Rights of Man* a 40-year-old cobbler, Thomas Hardy, and eight other artisans formed a society to agitate for political reform. After some dispute they called it the London Corresponding Society and advertised for members under the slogan: 'Are you thoroughly persuaded that the welfare of these kingdoms requires that every adult person, in possession of his reason, and not incapacitated by his crimes, should have a vote for a Member of Parliament?'

Despard, newly released from debtors' prison, responded to the call and soon became one of the Society's most prominent members. Mike

Jay, Despard's biographer, maintains that his conversion was dramatic but not puzzling:

> He had always been a practical man. Now, politics had become an urgent practical problem. His particular experience in diplomacy in a society patched together from disparate worlds of military rank, social class and ethnic origins made him well suited for bridging the alarming divides that were opening up in British politics. His interest in electoral representation had developed because it was the most effective tool for demonstrating that the system he had set up in the Bay was based on consent, and was thus practical. His extended stay in London had edged him across an invisible divide he had not even known existed; he had looked for support in the places he expected to find it, and it had not been forthcoming. Now, his insistence that authority should be based on consent – which he had, like many Britons, held as an unquestioning assumption – was indeed being echoed, and powerfully, from every quarter of society. Another British revolution seemed to be stirring, and his experience since his return had left him in little doubt as to which side he was on. There was a new force in politics, with a powerful manifesto and a massive weight of numbers behind it. This was no lost cause – at least, not yet.[2]

By 1794 the Society had been infiltrated by government spies who reported on the well-dressed gentleman of military bearing who mingled with working men and Irish labourers. The Government of William Pitt regarded such men as the enemy within, especially after the outbreak of war with France, and all efforts were made to crush the movement. Hardy and several other high-ranking Society members were arrested, and with habeas corpus suspended the prisoners were held without trial. The authorities colluded with 'King and Church men' to break up reformist meetings brutally. Several gentlemen who joined the movement were charged with sedition or libel and transported to Botany Bay. Pitt's purges became known as the 'Reign of Terror' – an ironic nod to events on the other side of the Channel. In 1795 the 'Two Acts' made it a treasonable offence even to contemplate the use of force 'to make the King change his counsel', and banned reformist meetings of more than 50 people. Despard, both orator and organiser, frequently moved lodging houses to avoid arrest. But as the Government trumped up treason charges against Hardy and the other prisoners, Despard's convictions became more militant. With a growing number of others, he began to see agitation by legal means and parliamentary process as powerless against the repression of the state.

The same period saw the growth of the United Irishmen movement
(see chapter 7) determined to use force to overthrow the 'tyranny' of
British rule which denied the vote to three million Irish Catholics and
the majority of one million Protestants. It was inevitable that the two
movements would converge to some degree. Spies reported increased
fraternisation, and Despard, an Irishman, was named in several secret
reports. Government hysteria was generated by a failed French bid to
land a fleet in Bantry Bay and the 1797 Spithead naval mutiny over
pay and conditions. In February 1898 a Catholic priest was caught red-
handed carrying a message to the French urging an invasion to liberate
the masses. It was the first solid piece of evidence of a conspiracy,
and the Government swooped on every suspected plotter that could
be found. Despard was arrested and placed in solitary confinement,
though he was released when it emerged that his brother John, a
distinguished general, had also been arrested, suggesting a failure of
intelligence-gathering. But in April Despard was re-arrested and held
without trial with 16 others who had met at a Drury Lane pub.[3]

Despard was incarcerated in the new, purpose-built Coldbath Fields
gaol in Clerkenwell when the United Irishmen rose up in 1898 in a
rebellion which left 30,000 dead (see chapter 7). Reprisals were vicious,
and the Home Office Committee of Secrecy found that secret societies
were behind a 'systematic design to overturn the laws, constitution
and government of Britain and Ireland'.[4] Government spies reported
that Despard was a key member of one such society, the United
Britons, which was building a paramilitary structure akin to the United
Irishmen. But the evidence against him was flimsy and contradictory
– one revolutionary said by informers to be Despard's main contact
with the United Irishmen had been in America for several years, for
example. Further doubt was cast on the ability of the United Britons
to raise a single pike, never mind an army.

Despard was held in a seven-foot square cellar with no glass in the
window and which flooded when it rained. His diet was bread and
water, and his wife Catherine was refused visiting rights. She campaigned
against his harsh treatment, recruiting Opposition MPs to her cause.
These included Sir Francis Burdett, who confirmed Catherine's accounts
of the squalor of a prison fast becoming known as England's Bastille.
Despard's incarceration was seen as indicative of wider injustices, but
to the Government he was a dangerous man. After the restoration of

habeas corpus, however, they could no longer detain him and Despard was finally released in April 1801.

After being feted by reformers, Despard and Catherine largely disappeared from public view, though the secret service found them in February 1802 living in lodgings in Lambeth and kept them under surveillance. Reports filtered through that the United Britons and United Irishmen had not been smashed, but had gone to ground, setting up cells which could not be penetrated. Most worrying for the authorities, there were reports that soldiers deployed in London to guard public buildings were being recruited for an armed rebellion. Intelligence reports suggested that several hundred might be involved, although Despard's role in this was shadowy. One report stated, 'he does not feature very prominently', although a soldier who reported clandestine approaches to the police said that he was introduced in a pub to 'the Colonel who was confined so long in the Bastille'.

More evidence of a conspiracy was provided by Private Thomas Windsor of the Third Battalion who signed up with the Home Office as an agent in return for an honourable discharge. He approached Despard in a pub in Tower Hill and said he could bring more volunteers to the cause. Despard suggested a further meeting in the Oakley Arms, Lambeth. Windsor claimed that Despard referred directly to a plot to assassinate the king on his way to Parliament, and thereby spark a general uprising to give the people their liberty. Two other informants who had also been in the pub at the time could not corroborate Windsor's story, but the authorities determined to act. On 16 November 1802 three Southwark policemen and numerous Bow Street Runners raided the Oakley Arms and burst into an evening meeting of the high command of the United Britons in the first floor club room. There they found 40, mainly working men, but others in regimental uniforms. Despard, dressed as a gentleman and carrying his trademark green silk umbrella, shouted, 'One and all, follow me!' but found the exit blocked by more officers coming up the stairs.[5] Despard was searched, under protest, but nothing incriminating was found. However, in the pockets of three men were found 'unlawful oaths', each headed: 'Constitution: The Independence of Great Britain and Ireland. An Equalisation of Civil, Political and Religious Rights; an ample Provision for the Heroes who shall fall in the Contest.' Despard was again thrown into a gaol cell.

*   *   *

Despard was first interrogated by Sir Richard Ford, the chief magistrate and principal spymaster, who had built up a massive dossier on the London Corresponding Society and its associated organisations. Over the following two days he was examined by the Privy Council in conditions of utmost secrecy. These early sessions left the authorities with concerns that they might have acted too soon before the plot was fully formed, and that Despard might have become involved only latterly. Ford was also reluctant to blow the cover of his informants by calling them to testify. But after ten days the prosecutors felt confident enough to allege that Despard was at the centre of a dastardly conspiracy which from then on bore his name. He and a dozen confederates were charged with high treason.

The Crown's case shocked the nation. According to the charges the Oakley Arms meeting was convened to put the finishing touches to a plot to assassinate the king the following week. Members of three Guards regiments had been recruited and were to act together with many divisions of the United Irishmen and the United Britons who had been secretly assembling across London for several weeks. The king's coach was to be blasted, according to some accounts, with a Turkish cannon captured from the French and on display in St James's Park, as he rode to Parliament in his carriage. That would be a signal for the Guards to take control of the Houses of Parliament, the Post Office and the Tower of London. All messages out of London would be halted, and the sudden disruption of the mail service would itself be a signal for revolutionaries in other regiments and civilian groups to rise up across the country.

However, the scale of the alleged plot and the seriousness of the charges raised suspicions. Despard had already spent years in prison without being convicted of any crime, there was little real evidence of mutiny in army ranks and the grandiosity of the scheme appeared laughable. Sir Francis Burdett and Catherine Despard formed a defence committee funded by a small group of wealthy sympathisers. They accused the Government of using the charge of treason to stifle serious debate about the guilt or innocence of the accused. But the Government was determined to make an example of Despard, in part to dissuade any other well-bred sympathisers of the 'mob'. The pre-trial commission

opened in Horsehanger Lane on 10 January 1803, with the sessions
house surrounded by hundreds of police and soldiers. The hearing was
presided over by the Lord Chief Justice, Lord Ellenborough, a man who
believed that 'criminal laws could not be too severe'. Prosecuting was
the Attorney General, Sir Spencer Perceval, a future prime minister.
Defending was Sergeant William Draper Best, a barrister and Whig
MP. Ellenborough read the charge of high treason and announced
that Despard would be tried alone, with the trials of nine confederates
following. Three more soldiers had agreed to turn king's evidence in
return for immunity from prosecution. The main charge was that the
accused 'maliciously and traitorously with force of arms, did conspire,
imagine and intend to put our Lord the King to death'. Among the
many secondary charges was that they did 'traitorously conspire,
combine, consent and agree, and attempt and endeavour to seduce
divers soldiers and persons serving in the forces of the King by sea and
land, from their duty and allegiance to the King'. From the initial list of
100 potential jury members the Home Office weeded out all but a few
who might have been in favour of electoral reform, or other pernicious
ideas. The eventual jury was clearly biased against Despard, although
not as much as the prosecution had hoped.

The trial proper opened on Monday, 7 February. To justify the treason
charge Spencer Perceval had to show that Despard was at the centre
of a plot to kill the king. The trouble was that much of the evidence
was tainted by self-serving informers and was, at best, contradictory.
Perceval aimed to prove that by a series of 'overt acts' Despard had
to be guilty. Those included his attendance at the Oakley Arms where
persons were found with illegal oaths in their pockets, his meetings
with disenchanted soldiers and his well-known views in the cause of
political reform. He made much of the fact that Despard was the only
'gentleman' present in the company of men 'planning a most desperate
act of treason to be executed the very next week, by the lowest and
basest of society'. It was a logical assumption, Perceval said, that such a
man, with such a distinguished background, must be the leader of this
band of ill-educated desperadoes. Perceval had the grace to admit that
Despard might have been trying to exercise a moderating influence, but
argued that that did not diminish his guilt. His very presence proved
his complicity. Even if, as some witnesses suggested, Despard wanted
to abandon the plot, that was only because 'the time was not yet ripe'.

More impressive was the evidence of Private William Francis of the Foot Guards who claimed that Despard had called on him to swear an oath to 'take the Tower'. According to his evidence, Despard had also talked of waiting for money and support to arrive from France.[6]

Francis was easily discredited on the witness stand by Sergeant Best, but Despard's defence had trouble dismissing the evidence of Thomas Windsor, the Home Office informer who had triggered the raid. He testified that over a jug of brandy and water at the Flying Horse, Stoke Newington, Despard had told him: 'I believe this to be the moment. The people, particularly in Leeds, in Sheffield, in Birmingham, and in every capital town in England, are ripe. I have walked twenty miles today, and the people are ripe everywhere I have been.' Despard, according to Windsor, continued: 'His Majesty must be put to death. The mail-coaches must be stopped as a signal to the country, that they had revolted in town.' When asked whether it might be simpler to shoot the horses rather than destroy the king's coach with the great cannon, while another conspirator warned that they would be cut down by the Life Guards, Despard was alleged to have snapped: 'If no one else will do it, I myself will.' Windsor was asked whether he remembered any other expression used by Despard. He replied: 'He said, "I have weighed the matter well, and my heart is callous".'[7] This was dynamite, and the phrase stuck, even though the defence denied throughout that Despard had ever uttered it. Windsor detailed plans, discussed with Despard, to seize the Bank with 600 muskets in its arsenal, and then the Tower of London. More weapons would be seized from the East India Company's premises in Bishopsgate, and rebel divisions would then converge on Parliament. Despard allegedly said: 'If we have the Bank and the Tower, we have everything.' The prosecution then rested its case.[8]

The prosecution had proved no link between Despard and the plot which bore his name, apart from circumstantial evidence and the testimony of liars. Best argued that someone of the stature of his client would never have become involved in such a 'ludicrous' conspiracy. Despard, a man himself much injured, had merely attended the meeting to hear the grievances of others, 'especially from those of the army rank and file whose interests he had always defended'. Contemporary reports praised Best's performance. He addressed the jury 'in a speech replete with ingenious argument, clothed in elegant diction, and delivered with persuasive energy'. He asked how it was possible that '14 or 15 men, at a common tap-room, with no firearms but their tobacco pipes, men of the lowest orders of society, without mind or intelligence, were to seize the King, the Bank, the Tower, and the Members of Parliament'.[9] It may have been discussed, in the way that men talked over ale, but there was not one iota of proof that it was a genuine plot.

Despard's supporters were surprised when he exercised his right not to take the stand and made no testimony in his own defence. The best explanation for this is his sense of honour. In excusing his own actions he might incriminate the eight working men due to stand trial later. He would offer no explanation which might save his own life but condemn others. And that, despite the flimsiness of the prosecution case, despite the loading of the justice system against him, despite the vindictive aspects of a political show trial, is the best indication that Despard, in his own mind and by the standards of the day, was indeed guilty of conspiracy to commit treason. He was also a brave and honourable man.

The next sensation, in a sensational trial avidly followed by all classes, came when Best called a series of character witnesses. First up was Lord Nelson, the most popular man in Britain, a national hero, recently ennobled, whose personal endorsement was second only to the king's whom Despard was accused of plotting to kill. Nelson could not resist speaking on behalf of his friend and war-time comrade, even though his appearance in court had the potential to do him great political and social harm.[10] Nelson told the court that Despard's desire to help the downtrodden was understandable and did not amount to treason, even if he had been swayed by tavern talk. 'Want of loyalty is not among his faults,' Nelson said. The great hero was interrupted by the judge when Nelson began to detail Despard's military record, and told to limit his comments to the defendant's 'general character'. Nelson replied:

> We went on the Spanish Main together; we slept many nights together in our clothes upon the ground. In all that period of time no man could have shown more zealous attachment to his sovereign and his country than Colonel Despard did. I formed the highest opinion of him, as a man and as an officer. If I had been asked my opinion of him, I should certainly have said ... he is certainly one of the brightest ornaments of the British army.[11]

It did no good. The prosecution forced Nelson to admit that he had not seen Despard for 23 years, a point Lord Ellenborough stressed in his summing up. A military hero could, it appeared, turn traitor. The jury returned a guilty verdict after 25 minutes, but with an earnest recommendation of mercy due to Despard's 'former good character and eminent services'.

The following day nine of Despard's confederates were also found guilty, and six were sentenced to death. They were 53-year-old Arthur Graham, a slater; a stout Irishman and carpenter John Macnamara, 50; a shoemaker, James Sedgewick Wratton, 35; the carpenter Thomas Broughton, 26; and two soldiers, Private John Wood, 36, and John Francis, 23. All six were married and had children. Despard was recalled to the court where he made his only statement: 'I have only to say that the charge brought against me is one which I could not have the most distant idea of. I have now nothing further to say than what I said at first: I am not guilty.' Ellenborough pronounced the sentence of death by hanging, drawing and quartering for all seven. Calling each by name he declared:

> After a long, patient and, I hope, just and impartial trial, you have been all of you convicted, by a most respectable jury ... Such disclosures have been made as to prove, beyond the possibility of doubt, that the objects of your atrocious and traitorous conspiracy were to overthrow the Government, and to seize upon and destroy the sacred persons of our august and revered Sovereign and the illustrious branches of his Royal house.

After a pause Despard said: 'Your Lordship has imputed to me the character of being the seducer of these men. I do not conceive that anything appeared in the trial or the evidence against me, to prove that ...'

Despard was taken to Surrey county gaol with his fellow condemned, where he spent much of his time writing a petition to the king. Catherine was distraught on hearing the verdict, but swiftly recovered and visited him daily. She also visited Nelson, who later recalled that she was 'violently in love with her husband'.[12] Nelson wrote to the Government pleading for clemency, but to ministers and law officers Despard was an unrepentant traitor who deserved to die. They were, however, deeply concerned about the reaction of the populace, especially given the barbaric nature of his sentence, a form of execution not used for half a century. Public pressure for clemency was growing by the day, but the awful authority of the law was implacable. The executions were scheduled for 21 February. On the night of the 20th Catherine said farewell to her husband. According to contemporary reports, she was 'almost sunk under the anticipated horror of his fate', but he 'betrayed nothing like an unbecoming weakness'. That same night the prison chaplain offered Despard improving Christian texts to read, but he declined and asked the cleric 'not [to] attempt to put shackles on my mind and body'. Unlike most of the other condemned men, he also refused to attend chapel or receive the sacrament. Despard said that he believed in God and understood that worship was useful for political purposes, but was equally indifferent to the opinions of churchmen, dissenters, Quakers, Methodists, Catholics, savages and atheists. Despard spent the night pacing the cell muttering, according to his gaolers, 'Me? No, never! I'll divulge nothing! No, not for all the treasure the King is worth!'

At seven the next morning Despard, calm and composed, shook hands with his solicitor and was led, bound, with his fellow prisoners into the prison yard.

Outside there was a vast multitude of working men, the 'lowest of the vulgar', according to one official report.[13] Given the sensational nature of the trial and widespread sympathy for the condemned, the authorities had every right to fear massive disorder or a rescue attempt. The execution of Despard could even precipitate the revolution he desired. Horsehanger Lane was surrounded by uniformed police, while plainclothes officers infiltrated public houses where the 'disaffected' might gather. Newspapers stoked up passions, reporting rumours that the prisoners were being tortured to exact their confessions. Gaol officials had trouble finding men willing to build the scaffold. Tensions rose to such a pitch that magistrates remitted the mutilation part of the death sentence – the condemned men's bodies were no longer to be disembowelled and quartered. That still left the 'drawing', a device whereby the condemned was secured to a griddle and dragged to the place of execution while being abused by the crowd. But such a spectacle would only inflame the crowd, not entertain them, so the authorities came up with a bizarre solution: Despard and the others were to be dragged in a wheel-less cart drawn by two horses within the walls of the prison yard. When Despard saw the contraption he laughed and said: 'What nonsensical mummery is this?' The prisoners were placed on straw within the cart and driven around the cobbled yard several times followed by a robed priest, officials and police with drawn swords. The spectacle was so ridiculous that no court would ever pass the sentence again.

By now the crowd outside the walls packed the carriageway of Horsehanger Lane and filled every window and rooftop within sight of the scaffold belatedly erected on the prison roof. Seven coffins were brought up while the execution team tested the equipment. Bags of sawdust were strategically placed to catch the blood when the heads were severed. At 8.30 the prisoners ascended the gallows. John Macnamara looked down at the crowd and said: 'Lord Jesus, have mercy upon me', Arthur Graham looked 'pale and ghastly' and James Wratton 'ascended the gallows with much firmness'. Next came Thomas Broughton and the two soldiers, John Francis and John Wood, followed finally by Despard. The colonel's face was impassive as he helped the executioner adjust the noose. Macnamara muttered: 'I am afraid, Colonel, we have got ourselves into a bad situation.' Despard replied: 'There are many better and some worse.'

Despard asked permission to address the crowd. The Sheriff of Surrey agreed, but warned that if he uttered anything 'inflammatory or improper' he would order the gallows platform immediately dropped to cut fatally short any sedition.

It was to be a carefully balanced gallows speech in every sense. Despard began with the words 'Fellow citizens', a phrase with republican overtones fully appreciated by the 100 officials on the gaol roof and the thousands of hushed onlookers within earshot. The speech which followed rivals any of the era for its integrity, courage and assumption that all men, of all nations, religion and race, should be protected by the law, not crushed by it. Despard continued:

> I come here, as you can see, after having served my country faithfully, honourably and usefully, for thirty years and upwards, to suffer death upon a scaffold for a crime of which I protest I am not guilty. I solemnly declare that I am no more guilty of it than any of you who may be now hearing me. Though His Majesty's ministers know as well as I do that I am not guilty, yet they avail themselves of a legal pretext to destroy a man, because he has been a friend to truth, to liberty, and to justice, because he has been a friend to the poor and oppressed. But, Citizens, I hope and trust, notwithstanding my fate, and the fate of those who no doubt will soon follow me, that the principles of freedom, of humanity, and of justice, will finally triumph

over falsehood, tyranny and delusion, and every principle inimical to the interests of the human race.[14]

That was going perilously close to the incitement the authorities feared. The sheriff leaned over and whispered his final threat. Despard nodded, and concluded: 'I have little more to add, except to wish you all health, happiness and freedom, which I have endeavoured, so far as was in my power, to procure for you, and for mankind in general.'

Despard's egalitarian views were successfully spoken through the thinnest of veils. Robert Southey later wrote: 'This calm declaration of a dying man was so well calculated to do mischief.' But, apart from an occasional cheer, the crowd listened in silence. John Francis, standing next to Despard, said: 'What an amazing crowd', to which Despard looked up and observed: ''Tis very cold; I think we shall have some rain.' They were his final words.[15]

At seven minutes to nine, as the crowd removed their hats, the signal was given to drop Despard's trapdoor first. His hands contracted in spasm as the rope jerked taut, but he made no sound or any sign of struggle. The other six swiftly followed him. After 37 minutes Despard's body was cut down and laid over the block. A surgeon stepped forward with his dissecting knife to sever the head, but botched the job and was reduced to hacking at a neck vertebra. The executioner pushed him aside and began twisting Despard's head in an attempt to wrench it off. He was finally successful and carried the head by the hair to display it to the crowd waiting below. He proclaimed: 'This is the head of a traitor: Edward Marcus Despard.'

Freezing rain poured down as the people silently took their leave.

*   *   *

Cheap pamphlet copies of Despard's gallows speech were sold across the nation. *The Times* and assorted clerics condemned its contents, but among working people it struck a loud chord. People who damned the jury which found him guilty were arrested, along with those who sold the pamphlets. The *Morning Post* was not alone in fearing a backlash when it editorialised: 'Shall Despard's headless corpse walk into every tap-room, to make proselytes an hundred fold?'

Catherine Despard discovered that the family's male line had a right to be buried in the parish churchyard of St Faith's, now within the walls of St Paul's Cathedral. With Burdett's help, and probably that of Nelson, she petitioned the prime minister. He concurred, feeling it unwise to stir up further controversy. The funeral was delayed until 1 March to allow Despard's son James time to travel from Paris, where he was serving as an ensign in the French army. Despite the fears of the authorities, the funeral was a modest affair. The large crowd that gathered along the route from Despard's home in Lambeth across Blackfriars Bridge was quiet and sombre as the hearse and three mourning-coaches passed by. Police and soldiers called to quell any disturbances were not needed. Despard was interred near the north door of the cathedral. The remains of the other six were earlier buried in one grave, in the vault of a chapel in St George's Fields.

Catherine and James were cared for initially by Burdett and other moneyed supporters, but faded from British life. According to some accounts Catherine settled in Ireland. The Despard family, gentlemen and ladies that they were, never accepted her or James as their relatives.

Colonel Despard had not died an ignoble death, but a hero's. He was, and remains, an exception, especially compared to the rag-tag of assassins and would-be assassins who followed him as the nineteenth century progressed. Some had heroic visions, some were motivated by a desire to change society for the better, others were deluded fools, vainglorious or just vain, dupes and vagabonds. Some were simply mad.

3
Death of a Prime Minister

'... the pelting of the pitiless storm'

Henry Burgess, a Mayfair solicitor, told the coroner that he had been in the lobby of the House of Commons when he heard a pistol's report: 'In less than half a minute I saw a gentleman coming forward towards the door of the House, staggering, and at the same time I heard a cry of "Murder, murder." This gentleman had his hand on his breast, and exclaimed "Oh!" faintly, and fell forward on his face.' Another witness claimed that the gentleman cried: 'I'll have one of Bellamy's veal pies!' before he fell.

The gentleman was the prime minister of Great Britain. His assassin stood by mildly, waiting to be arrested, another loaded pistol in his pocket. This was a time of turmoil and the victim was widely detested for his suppression of the Luddites but, unlike the Despard Plot, this was not a political assassination. It was personal.

* * *

Spencer Perceval was born on 1 November 1762, the second son of the second Earl of Egmont, the scion of an ancient Irish family. The young Spencer grew up with eight siblings and a further nine half-brothers and sisters from his father's first marriage. Educated at Harrow and Trinity College, Cambridge, where he excelled in English, Perceval took to the law and practised on the Midland Circuit from 1786. He became Deputy Recorder of Northampton and married Jane Spencer-Wilson, by whom he had six sons and six daughters. He became MP for Northampton in 1796 and advanced up the governmental ladder, becoming in turn

Solicitor-General, Attorney General and Chancellor of the Exchequer. He was the Princess of Wales' chief legal adviser during her misconduct hearings in 1806, and was instrumental in effecting a reconciliation between her and George III. Perceval was deeply Conservative and anti-Catholic, but also supported William Wilberforce's anti-slavery campaign. He was considered an able and efficient finance minister during the turmoil of the Napoleonic Wars.[1]

In 1809 the prime minister, the Duke of Portland, was taken ill. The administration swiftly split into factions and George Canning, the foreign affairs minister, emerged as the frontrunner to take over. But 47-year-old Perceval was also a strong candidate, and on 4 October the king, wishing to avoid a war-time election, appointed him to the post, describing Perceval as 'the most straightforward man I have ever known'. However, given the bitterness of Canning and other disappointed rivals, Perceval had difficulty filling his Cabinet, and remained Chancellor as well as premier.[2]

His premiership was turbulent. War taxes fell short of the costs of fighting Napoleon's army, and the 1809 Walcheren expedition, in Flanders, was a disaster – thousands of lives were lost, not in battle but to malaria. During 1810 his administration was defeated four times in parliamentary divisions on the conduct of the war. Rioting in April greeted the arrest of Sir Francis Burdett after he supported the right of the press to report Commons proceedings. And the year's end saw the return of the king's apparent insanity. Perceval steered through a Regency Bill which restricted the powers of the Prince of Wales. By July 1811 the cost of the war had sent inflation spiralling, but Perceval solved the immediate crisis by making bank notes legal tender. Perceval's Government moved to suppress the Luddites, working men who were protesting at the mechanisation of their craft skills and the resulting unemployment, and introduced the Frame-Breaking Act which made industrial vandalism a capital offence. His troubles continued into 1812 when key ministers began to resign. Perceval survived, but another crisis quickly followed in the wrangles which would lead to the American War of 1812–14. Perceval was loathed by Catholics, social reformers, anti-war activists, the Opposition in Parliament and many within his own party. But though an adept political operator, he would see his leadership terminated, not by a political assassin, but by a disgruntled businessman.[3]

John Bellingham was a 41-year-old insurance broker and shipping merchant who bore a deep grudge. He was born in Huntingdonshire, the son of a land surveyor and miniature painter; his mother was the daughter of a respectable St Neots squire. The family moved to London where his father became deranged and was committed to St Luke's Hospital. After twelve months he was sent home as an incurable and died shortly afterwards when John was not yet ten years old. At 14 Bellingham was apprenticed to a Whitechapel jeweller of excellent character, but he was regarded as 'perverse and troublesome' and ran away from his master. His mother pleaded with her sister's husband, a man of means called William Daw, for help. In 1786 Daw fitted Bellingham out for the East Indies and the following year he sailed as a subaltern in the service of John Company. His ship was wrecked on the outward journey and Bellingham was one of the survivors who got back home. Daw, who had already spent a considerable sum on his nephew, was now pestered for a large loan to set Bellingham up as a tin-plate worker in Oxford Street. Soon Bellingham's shop caught fire in mysterious circumstances and Bellingham told his creditors that a large quantity of banknotes had been destroyed in the blaze. In 1794 he was bankrupt. Bellingham next managed to get a job in a merchant's counting house, where he convinced his employers that his destiny lay overseas. They sent him to Archangel, in Russia, where he stayed for three years. During that time he went into partnership with a timber firm and contracted to supply Hull merchants with timber worth £12,000. They paid in advance, but the cargo which arrived was valued at just £4,000. Bellingham blamed his partners, who had themselves gone bankrupt, and was thrown into prison after foolishly returning to Hull. There he spent several months, steadfastly declaring his innocence, before he was freed.

On his return to Russia, he was suspected of sending intelligence to Lloyds of London that a ship sunk in the White Sea had been scuttled. The underwriters refused to pay out and Bellingham became embroiled in complex litigation which resulted in his imprisonment in Archangel. On his release he went to St Petersburg where he complained bitterly to the Russian Government. He was again gaoled on what he claimed was a trumped-up charge of debt. His 22-year-old wife was obliged to return to England with their infant child, while Bellingham was treated like a common criminal. He applied to Lord Leveson Gower, the British representative at the Imperial court, for help but, he later claimed, to no avail. After some months (which he later inflated to six years) a sympathetic Russian succeeded in getting his case reviewed and Bellingham was released, but received no redress. He joined his wife in Liverpool where he set up as an insurance broker, while she worked as a well-respected milliner.

From Liverpool Bellingham bombarded officials and ministers with demands for compensation. He wrote to Perceval directly, but got no satisfaction. He now moved to London lodgings, where fellow tenants viewed him as deranged. He became obsessed with the notion that he would make the Government understand the depths of his despair by inflicting despair on them.[4]

Bellingham sought out the MP for Liverpool, General Isaac Gascoyne, at his Mayfair home where he spoke for an hour about his sufferings under false arrest. Gascoyne said there was nothing he could do, and later recalled: 'During our conversation he was as calm and collected as any man could be, and had not the least appearance of a man insane.' Bellingham spent four guineas on the purchase of two small iron pistols, which he tested on Primrose Hill, and added an extra pocket on either side of his coat to carry them. For three weeks he hung around the lobby of the Commons, mingling with petitioners and the general public, awaiting his opportunity.

It came on 12 May 1812, at five in the afternoon. Perceval left the Commons Chamber with Lord Osborne and descended the stone stairs. Bellingham was waiting behind a pillar, a sheaf of case papers in one hand, a pistol in the other. There was a knot of people gathered in the lobby and Bellingham approached his prey from behind them, extended his arm over another's shoulder and fired slightly downwards into the left of Perceval's chest. The ball drilled through his heart. In the rush to attend to the stricken man, his assailant was momentarily forgotten. Perceval was raised still breathing, taken to the Speaker's drawing room and placed on a sofa. There he was declared dead.[5]

In the meantime a vote office official shouted: 'Where is the rascal that fired?' Bellingham stepped forward and said coolly, 'I am that unfortunate man.' He was surrounded by members of the public and MPs who had spilled out of the Chamber after hearing the shot. Joseph Hume, MP for Weymouth, said that Bellingham 'appeared to be forcibly pulled on every side by the bystanders'. They placed him on a bench near a fireplace and all the doors were closed to prevent any accomplices leaving or rescuers entering. Bellingham insisted there was no need. When asked who he was and why he had fired, he replied: 'My name is Bellingham; it is a private injury. I know what I have done. It was a denial of justice on behalf of the Government.' He was searched by the solicitor Henry Burgess, who found a still warm pistol close to his hand. (Later General Burgoyne would claim to have disarmed Bellingham after a short but determined struggle.) A second pistol was found, loaded, with a bundle of folded papers. Still not formally under arrest, Bellingham was taken into the Chamber where 'the utmost confusion and anxiety prevailed'. Order was restored and General Gascoyne, peering intently, said: 'I think I know this villain.' Walking up to him he said: 'Is your name not Bellingham?' The culprit stood motionless, apparently composed, resting his hands on the bar of the House and looking directly at the Speaker's chair. The Speaker ruled that a contingent of MPs should escort the prisoner to a cell, from which he could be handed over to Magistrate Watson, the Sergeant-at-Arms in the House of Lords. Bellingham offered no resistance and made no complaint.

News of the murder spread rapidly, and crowds gathered at the closed doors of Westminster Hall, while constables were posted at all exits. Only MPs and witnesses were allowed to enter or leave. Mrs Perceval was visiting the wife of the Home Secretary in nearby George Street at the time of the murder, and was told of her husband's death when she returned to Downing Street. She and her twelve children were plunged into 'inexpressible grief' and every window in No. 10 was closed. Outside, the crowds thronged until midnight, rendering Parliament Street and Palace Yard almost impassable. In those jittery times the thoughts of the remaining ministers turned to revolution and riot rather than to the idea of a lone gunman. A Cabinet council was summoned and the mail was delayed until despatches could be sent to civil and military authorities across the country with orders to preserve the peace. The orders were particularly stringent in 'those districts where an inflamed and infatuated multitude have committed the most savage barbarities'.[6] The Earls of Derby and Stamford rode to their respective counties to exercise their authority as lords lieutenant. Certainly, there was cause for concern. A Colonel Fletcher was appalled at how the news of the assassination was greeted by the populace of

Bolton: 'The people expressed joy at the news. A man came running down the street, leaping in the air, waving his hat round his head, and shouting with frantic joy, "Perceval is shot, hurrah! Perceval is shot, hurrah!"'[7]

By 9 o'clock that evening, however, it was clear to all at Westminster that Bellingham was no instrument of insurrection. He was taken under a strong escort of troopers to Newgate Gaol, where the keeper was given instructions to watch him closely to prevent any suicide attempt. Two wardens were ordered to sit up all night with the prisoner.

Perceval's body was taken to 10 Downing Street, where it was viewed the following morning by the coroner's jury. The inquest was held nearby at the Rose and Crown. William Smith, MP for Norwich, was one of several parliamentarians to give evidence:

> Yesterday afternoon, about a quarter past five o'clock, passing through the lobby to go to the House of Commons, I stopped to speak to a gentleman, and while in conversation with him, I heard the report of a pistol. I immediately turned my head, and observed some confusion at the end of the room. Several voices called out to shut the door to prevent any person escaping. There might have been present in the lobby some 30 to 40 persons. In an instant I observed a person rush from the cluster of people who were standing about the door, and come staggering towards me; he reached about the spot where I was first standing, and then fell on his face on the floor. I walked around him, not immediately recognising his person, and not supposing he was mortally wounded, but observing that he did not stir. I stooped down to assist him, and on raising his head I perceived him to be Mr Perceval.[8]

A Westminster surgeon, William Lynn, testified that he was called to the Speaker's secretary's room and found Perceval supported by two men, his body partly on a table:

> His shirt and white waistcoat were bloody. I found a wound over the fourth rib, on the left side, near the breastbone. On examining his pulse, I found he was quite dead. I then passed a probe to ascertain the direction of the ball, and found that it had passed obliquely downwards and inwards in the direction of the heart. The wound was at least three inches deep, and I have no doubt but it caused his death.

A verdict of wilful murder was delivered. The prisoner wrote to his landlady, Mrs Roberts of 9 New Millman Street, expressing a certain pride at being escorted by a 'noble troop of light horse' to his cell at Newgate, where he was treated as 'a state prisoner of the first class'. He told her: 'For eight years I have not found my mind so tranquil as since this melancholy but necessary catastrophe; as the merits and demerits of my particular case must be regularly unfolded in a criminal court of justice, to ascertain that guilty party, by a jury of my country.' He asked her to send him 'three or four shirts, some cravats, kerchiefs, night-caps, stockings etc., out of my drawers, together with comb, soap, tooth-brush, with any other trifle which you might think I may have occasion for, also my great-coat, flannel gown and blue waistcoat ...'[9]

*   *   *

Bellingham was put on trial just three days after the murder, on 15 June. There was never any doubt about the outcome. This was a period of war abroad and social unrest at home. Killing the prime minister set a bad example. The only real issue was Bellingham's sanity. Affidavits from neighbours and colleagues in Liverpool declared him to be mad. However, the Attorney General, prosecuting, quoted precedents which showed that 'though a person be insane from his childhood, if he be capable of distinguishing right from wrong when committing the crime, he is criminally answerable'. The prisoner had shown competence in managing his own affairs, and had even been entrusted with the affairs of others. The preparations he made to carry out his horrible crime gave further proof of that. The crime was even more wicked because Perceval, if he had breathed after receiving the death wound, would certainly have prayed to God for the forgiveness of his murderer.[10]

In his defence, Bellingham addressed the court for nearly two hours in what an observer described as a 'collected and fluent manner'. He denied bearing any personal ill-will towards Perceval, but said that a denial of justice had obliged him to take redress into his own hands. He described his tribulations at length, and when recalling Lord Gower's refusal of assistance in his distress, burst into tears. He told the jury: 'Lord Gower saw and permitted so much misery. Oh, my God, what must his heart be made of! Gentlemen, I appeal to you as men, as fathers, as Christians, if I had not cause of complaint!' There was an intake of breath in the court when he regretted that he killed Perceval instead of Gower. Bellingham said that he regarded his treatment in Russia as a national affair which deserved a ministerial response. He had given due notice that he would go to any length to seek remedy. He argued that he was not insane but should be acquitted because he had shown no wilful malice. He had been robbed of his property, seen his family ruined and his mind tortured by government agents. He would sooner suffer 500 deaths than suffer again the torments of the last eight years. He concluded: 'If I am destined to sacrifice my life, I shall meet my doom with conscious tranquillity. I shall look forward to it as the weary traveller looks for the promised inn, where he may repose his wearied frame, after enduring the pelting of the pitiless storm.'

Much to his chagrin, Bellingham's counsel refused to call several witnesses he had listed because they could only confirm that he had preferred claims against the Government, which was not contested, and they could be used to show his lucidity of mind. Bellingham fiddled with the carvings of the bar as instead his counsel brought forward witnesses to his insanity. Anne Billet told the court that she had known the prisoner from childhood. His father had died mad, and Bellingham had followed him into a world of delusion. The jury was not impressed. After a trial lasting eight hours they retired for just ten minutes before delivering a guilty verdict. Bellingham asked for a glass of water and listened to the death sentence pronounced in 'extreme awe'.

That weekend, languishing in Newgate, Bellingham continued to protest his innocence, but insisted he had 'no vain regrets'. He wrote a final letter to his wife, Mary, saying:

> It rejoiced me beyond measure to hear you are likely to be well provided for. I am sure that the public at large will participate in and mitigate your sorrows. I assure you, my love, my sincerest endeavours have ever been directed to your welfare. As we shall not meet any more in this world, I sincerely hope we shall do so in the world to come. My blessing to the boys ... With the purest of intentions it has been my misfortune to be thwarted, misrepresented and ill-used in life; but we feel a happy prospect of compensation in a speedy translation to life eternal. It is not possible to be more calm or placid than I feel; and nine hours more will waft me to those happy shores where bliss is without alloy.

He asked for a crust of bread and gave his last shilling to the warder who brought it to him, saying he wished it was a guinea. He slept soundly until six the following morning. On being woken he dressed with great composure and read his prayer book for 30 minutes. Told that the sheriffs were ready, he replied: 'I am perfectly ready also.' He was taken to the press-yard to have his fetters hammered off where, looking up, he exclaimed: 'Ah! It rains heavily.' An observer said that he displayed the same character as he had done at his trial just three days before: 'No emotion of fear or compunction were visible.'[11]

Bellingham was taken for a final interrogation. Sheriff Birch asked him whether anyone else had been involved in the assassination. Bellingham replied: 'Certainly not!' Questioned further he said that he regretted Perceval's fate, but the Government had to take responsibility for shunting him from office to office. 'It was my own sufferings which caused this melancholy event,' Bellingham added. 'I hope it will be a warning to future ministers to attend to the applications and prayers of those who suffer by oppression. Had my petition been brought into Parliament, this catastrophe would not have happened. I am very sorry for the sufferings I have caused to Mr Perceval's family and friends.' He was asked whether he felt contrition. Bellingham replied, with emphasised dignity, 'I hope so, sir. I feel as a man ought to do.' He grew tired of further questioning, and asked if the proceedings could be speeded up, but was told there was still ten minutes to the appointed hour.

He was taken to the scaffold in a cart. Crowds of the 'lower classes' shouted 'God bless you!' As the executioners bound his hands, he said to one of them: 'Do everything properly, that I may not suffer more than necessary', and to the other: 'Draw the cord tighter; I wish not to have the power of offering resistance.' An onlooker recalled: 'He ascended the scaffold with a cheerful countenance, and a confident and calm air; he looked about him a little rapidly, but he had no air of triumph. Some of the mob huzza-ed him, but it escaped his notice.' Bellingham first objected to the black hood, but swiftly agreed and began to pray. The crowd fell silent. The clock struck eight, and on the seventh stroke the internal slab of the platform was struck away.

Bellingham's body hung until nine o'clock and was then taken by cart to St Bartholomew's Hospital for immediate dissection. It was rumoured that when it was opened up the heart continued to beat for four hours. The *Annual Register* reported: 'The expanding and contracting powers continued perceptibly till one o'clock in the day – proof of the steady, undismayed character which he preserved to the last gasp. It is said of some men that the heart dies with them; but here the energies remained when life was extinct.'[12]

*   *   *

The day after the execution Spencer Perceval was buried in the family
vault in St Luke's Church, Charlton, while Parliament voted a generous
annuity to his wife and children. The following month a memorial was
placed in Westminster Abbey. Stuart Wortley told fellow MPs: 'Mr
Perceval had great talents. He was anxious to see an administration
formed upon a liberal basis, calculated to comprehend the talents and
influences of the country, and to promote its security and honour.'

The obituaries of the two victims of this tragedy were very different.
Perceval's spoke of his 'impeccable character, skill in debate, and the
broad appeal of his conservatism and humanitarianism'. Later historians
acknowledged his political acumen and his financial stewardship at
the height of the Napoleonic Wars, while condemning his refusal to
adopt real social reforms and the terror tactics he sanctioned against
the Luddites.

Another obituary writer recorded:

Bellingham was a mere adventurer. He never had any capital of his own;
and when in Russia drew upon British merchants for £10,000 but never
made any shipments. He lived upon indifferent terms with his wife, who
still keeps a milliner's shop in Liverpool, and is much respected. He has
several times been on the point of separating from her; and seldom visited
her but for the purpose of possessing himself of the little money she had
gained by her industry.[13]

One was considered by many as a great man, the other as a failure.
But murder proved the great leveller and both went prematurely to
their graves.

4
The Cato Street Conspiracy

'the reluctance of the soul'

On 16 August 1819 workers from across Manchester and neighbouring towns gathered peacefully for a mammoth meeting in St Peter's Fields to hear Henry ('Orator') Hunt speak on the need for electoral reform. Panicky magistrates summoned the Manchester Yeoman Cavalry and the 15th Hussars. The troopers charged the crowd and within a quarter of an hour at least 15 people, including an infant, were dead or dying, and many hundreds wounded. The Government of Lord Sidmouth followed the carnage with the infamous Six Acts, which banned public meetings of more than 50 people, effectively outlawed freedom of the press and massively increased the powers of the police and courts to curb sedition. The vast majority of the population remained without the vote. It was repression on a scale rarely seen before or since.

The 'Peterloo' Massacre and its aftermath continued to enrage long after the victims were in their plain board coffins. Its name – an ironic play on the battle of Waterloo – was invoked by public speakers across the country. They included 45-year-old Arthur Thistlewood, the illegitimate son of a prosperous stockbreeder, who declared: 'High Treason was committed against the people at Manchester. I resolve that the lives of the instigators of massacre should atone for the souls of murdered innocents.'

Also active at protest meetings during those impassioned times were George Edwards, a statue-maker who had been raised in extreme poverty; James Ings, a failed butcher; William Davidson, the mixed-race son of a lawyer; Richard Tidd, a shoemaker and army deserter;

and John Brunt, also a shoemaker. Their lives would shortly be fatally entwined. One of them was a spy.

*　　*　　*

In September 1814 the Radical speaker and pamphleteer, Thomas Spence, died and was buried by 40 followers who vowed to keep his spirit and ideas alive. Spence was a Newcastle schoolteacher who had for over 20 years been a key figure in London agitation politics. He was imprisoned several times for publishing sedition in his inflammatory journal, *Pigs Meat*. He argued that society would be transformed not by a centralised radical body or single political party, but by small groups who could meet in public houses scattered across the country. His message was simple: 'If all the land in Britain were shared out equally, there would be enough to give every man, woman and child seven acres each.' Followers chalked his slogans on walls – 'The Land is the People's Farm' and 'Spence's Plan and Full Bellies' – and caused considerable alarm among property owners. He and his followers were blamed for sparking bread riots in London in 1800 and 1801, but on those occasions there was insufficient evidence to charge him.[1]

After his death, his followers formed the Society of Spencean Philanthropists, which met in the Cock, Soho, the White Lion, Camden and the Nag's Head in Carnaby Market. The Government employed an agent, John Castle, to infiltrate the Society and the reports he sent back became increasingly alarming. In October 1816 he reported that their objective was nothing short of the total overthrow of the British Government and monarchy. On 2 December, the Spenceans organised a mass meeting at Spa Fields, Islington, inviting Henry Hunt to speak. London magistrates and John Stafford, the chief clerk of Bow Street police station and supervisor of Home Office spies, employed 80 constables to break up the meeting. During the mêlée one constable, Joseph Rhodes, was stabbed. The four Spencean leaders, James Watson, Arthur Thistlewood, Thomas Preston and John Hopper, were arrested and charged with high treason.[2]

Watson was the first to be tried, but the case against him collapsed because of a distaste for state subterfuge. Castle was the main prosecution witness and the defence was able to point to his own criminal record. The jury agreed that Castle was an *agent provocateur* and refused to convict Watson. The three others awaiting trial were also released.

Following the trial the Society fell out over strategy. Watson was essentially a moderate and was increasingly sidelined by Thistlewood, who argued that violent revolution was not only possible, but inevitable. His powerful rhetoric was seductive and he became the effective leader. Thistlewood was a disappointed Establishment man, possibly soured by his illegitimacy. Born in Tupholme, Lincolnshire in 1774, he was educated at Horncastle grammar school and trained as a land surveyor before obtaining a commission in the army. His second wife, Susan, was the daughter of a butcher who helped him buy a farm. When the enterprise failed he moved to London in 1811. He joined the Spenceans and soon became a leading committee member. Police spies described him as a 'dangerous character' who believed in revolution.

By 1817 they were right: at one meeting he was reported to have boasted that he could raise 15,000 men in 30 minutes. Stafford immediately recruited more spies to infiltrate the organisation. For several years, however, it seemed that Thistlewood's words were mere bluster. His comments after Peterloo were certainly incendiary, the authorities concurred, but he was hardly alone in expressing his disgust. The Spencean meetings were closely monitored by government agents. One reported that at a meeting at the White Lion, Camden, on 21 July, a member blurted out: 'You are all cowards, let us try what can be done with physical force.' To which James Watson replied: 'It is no use till the country is ready. I will lose my life as well as the rest, but till the time comes it is only exposing ourselves.' Thistlewood added: 'We shall all be hanged!'

The men who gathered round Thistlewood were a mixed bunch. The statue-maker George Edwards was born in Clerkenwell in 1788 but was raised by his father in Bristol; his mother was an alcoholic and his childhood had been spent in destitution. During the 1790s he sold plaster-of-Paris busts of the famous on street corners, before renting a small shop in Windsor. At Spencean meetings he said that ministers should be killed. The butcher James Ings was born in Portsea, Hampshire in 1785 and for several years made a good living until his shop failed. In 1819 he opened a coffee-shop in Whitechapel, where he also sold Radical pamphlets. That business failed also and, unable to find work, he sent his family to stay with friends in Portsmouth while he took lodgings in Bishopsgate. He was horrified at the Peterloo Massacre.

William Davidson was born in Jamaica in 1781, the illegitimate son of the island's Attorney General. At 14 he was sent to Glasgow to study law and there became embroiled in the cause of parliamentary reform. He took to sailing and was impressed into the Navy. On his discharge his father sent him to study mathematics in Aberdeen but he grew restless and moved to Birmingham where he opened a cabinet-making business and fell in love with a local heiress. Her father suspected he was after her £70,000 dowry and arranged his arrest on a false charge. That did not stick, but his business collapsed and Davidson moved to London where he married a widow with four children. For a time he taught at a Wesleyan Methodist Sunday School, but was discharged after it was claimed that he had tried to seduce a female student. The truth of the matter will never be known, but Davidson was certainly the victim of racial prejudice when it came to his dealings with women. Peterloo reawakened his interest in radical politics. After Richard Carlile was imprisoned for blasphemy and seditious libel, Donaldson told a friend that those events had caused him to lose his faith in God.

The shoemaker Richard Tidd was born in Lincolnshire in 1775 and moved to London where he did good business from a slum alley near Gray's Inn Lane. That ended when the war with France created a slump and, now the desperately poor father of eight children, he enlisted in the army under a false name. He deserted as soon as he received his bounty payment and later claimed that he repeated the fraud several times. In 1806 he voted for the Radical Sir Francis Burdett by falsely claiming he was an enfranchised freeholder. He was charged with perjury but fled to Scotland. He returned to London in 1814 and joined the Spenceans as a fervent revolutionary.

His fellow shoemaker, John Brunt, was born around 1790 and also enjoyed initial success in his trade. At one time he was earning nearly 50 shillings a week, but in the post-war depression his weekly income dropped to 10 shillings. Brunt, his wife and their child were forced to move to the squalid Fox Court where he met Tidd and was recruited to the Spenceans.

The clandestine debates in the back rooms of London pubs grew more desperate as the Government's Six Acts, instigated by Lord Sidmouth and introduced in Parliament by Lord Castlereagh, began to bite. On

22 February 1820 George Edwards showed Thistlewood an item in *The Times* announcing that several Cabinet ministers would be dining at Lord Harrowby's house, 39 Grosvenor Square, the following night. Thistlewood agreed that this was the opportunity they had long been waiting for. They decided that a group of Spenceans would break into the house and kill the lot. The heads of Sidmouth and Castlereagh would be stuck on poles and carried in triumph through the London slums. Thistlewood argued that such action would be the opening shot for an armed uprising which would overthrow the old order. A period of turmoil would end with the creation of a Spencean administration. Over the next few hours Thistlewood tried to recruit people to the plot and 27 agreed. Among them were Edwards, who had provided the key information, Ings, Davidson, Tidd and Brunt. Fortuitously, Davidson had previously worked for Lord Harrowby and knew some of the servants at the Grosvenor Square mansion, so he was sent to get more details of the Cabinet dinner. Surprisingly, he reported back that Harrowby was not in London and so *The Times* report must be false. Thistlewood for his part insisted that Harrowby's staff were lying and declared that the mass assassination should proceed.

An operational base for the attack was required. Another gang member, John Harrison, knew of a small stable with a hayloft available for rent in Cato Street, a short distance from Grosvenor Square. The following morning sabres, pistols and a hand grenade were delivered there by Brunt. His co-conspirators first gathered at his house and agreed that the killing of the Cabinet was to be immediately followed by an attack on nearby army barracks and other public places. Thistlewood wrote two proclamations. One was addressed to the people declaring: 'Your tyrants are destroyed – the friends of liberty are called upon to come forward – the Provisional Government is now sitting'; the other promised serving soldiers full pay and a life pension if they join the revolution. Thistlewood and the nucleus of the force committed to do murder in Grosvenor Square reconvened in the hayloft later that afternoon in a state of high anticipation. Ings stood look-out in the stable below.

Shortly after 7.30 pm Ings was silently overcome by constables and George Ruthven, a former spy who knew most of the Spenceans, shouted: 'We are police officers. Lay down your arms.'[3]

* * *

The informant was George Edwards. One of the customers at his Windsor shop selling plaster busts of Wellington and other worthies was Major-General Sir Herbert Taylor, who recruited him as a Home Office spy. He befriended John Brunt solely to infiltrate the Spenceans and sent a steady flow of reports written on narrow strips of paper which were folded into tiny squares and passed on to the spymaster, John Stafford. Thistlewood regarded Edwards as a true friend and made him his *aide-de-camp*, but others had their doubts. On one occasion Edwards offered William Tunbridge a pistol to use against the Government. Tunbridge replied: 'Mr Edwards, you may tell your employers that they will not catch me in their trap.' Such doubts were suppressed by his closeness to Thistlewood, his revolutionary ardour and his success in attracting new recruits to the Society. At least two months before the Spenceans read of the Cabinet meeting in Grosvenor Square he had been preparing the ground for the plot. *The Times* notice was a ruse – there was never any dinner planned for ministers.

Edwards naturally lost no time in telling Stafford of the assassination plot, and the Bow Street magistrate Richard Birnie was put in charge of the operation. Lord Sidmouth made available men of the second battalion Coldstream Guards. Birnie sent Ruthven, the spy-turned-police officer, to the Horse and Groom which overlooked the Cato Street stable. He watched the gang gather from 2 pm and in the early evening he was joined by Birnie and twelve Bow Street policemen. When the Coldstream Guardsmen failed to arrive at the agreed time, Birnie decided he had enough men to capture the gang.

Ruthven led the way, climbing a ladder to the loft. After his opening yell Thistlewood and Davidson drew their swords while the other conspirators began to load their pistols. Thistlewood used his sword on the constable Richard Smithers who gasped 'Oh God, I am ...' before losing consciousness. He died soon afterwards. Some Spenceans surrendered without resistance but Davidson and others were only taken after a struggle.

Thistlewood, Brunt, Robert Adams and John Harrison escaped through a back window. Edwards, however, furnished a complete list of those who had taken part in the conspiracy and they were soon captured.

Eleven men were eventually charged. Sidmouth had learnt the lesson of the previous Spencean trial and neither Edwards nor any other spies were called to give evidence; by then they were secure on Guernsey, protected from reprisals. Ings told the court that Edwards had originated the murder plot, but to no avail. The police offered to drop charges against certain low-ranking gang members if they gave evidence against their co-conspirators. Robert Adams and John Monument agreed and their statements were damning. The Attorney General, Sir Robert Gifford, said: 'Arthur Thistlewood had for some time conceived the wicked and nefarious plan of overturning the Government so long established in this country; and it will appear to you that several, nay, all of the persons mentioned in the indictment, were participators in the same design.'[4] On 28 April 1820, Thistlewood, Davidson, Ings, Tidd and Brunt were convicted of high treason and sentenced to death. James Wilson, John Harrison, Richard Bradburn, John Strange and Charles Copper were also found guilty, but their death sentences were commuted to transportation for life.

In his cell Thistlewood's mood swung from self-pity and depression to vainglory to defiance. Several visitors doubted his sanity. In one outburst he said: 'If it is the will of the Author of the World that I should perish in the cause of freedom – his will, and not mine, be done! It would be quite a triumph to me!' John Brunt said: 'When I found my income reduced ... I began to look around. And what did I find? Why, men in power, who met to deliberate how they might starve and plunder the country. I looked on the Manchester transactions as most dreadful. I joined the conspiracy for the public good. I will die as the descendants of an ancient Briton.'[5] James Ings said: 'I consider myself murdered if Edwards is not brought forward. I am willing to die on the scaffold with him.' On the eve of his execution Ings wrote to his wife, Celia: 'I must die according to the law, and leave you in a land full of corruption, where justice and liberty have taken their flight from, to other distant shores. Now my dear, I hope you will bear in mind that the cause of my being consigned to the scaffold was a pure motive. I thought I should have rendered my starving fellow-men, women and children a service.'[6]

On 1 May the condemned men faced the scaffold at Newgate Prison. *The Traveller* reported: 'The executioner, who trembled much, was a long time tying up the prisoners; while this operation was going on a dead silence prevailed among the crowd, but the moment the drop fell, the general feeling was manifested by deep sighs and groans.'[7] One witness, George Theodore Wilkinson, wrote:

> Thistlewood struggled slightly for a few minutes, but each effort was more faint than that which preceded, and the body soon turned around slowly, as if upon the motion of the hand of death. Tidd, whose size gave cause to suppose that he would pass with little comparative pain, scarcely moved after the fall. The struggles of Ings were great. The assistants of the executioner pulled his legs with all their might; and even then the reluctance of the soul to part from its native seat was to be observed in the vehement efforts of every part of the body. Davidson, after three or four heaves, became motionless; but Brunt suffered extremely, and considerable exertions were made by the executioners and others to shorten his agonies.[8]

The government minister John Hobhouse wrote in his diary that night: 'The men died like heroes. Ings, perhaps, was too obstreperous in singing *Death or Liberty*, and Thistlewood said: "Be quiet, Ings; we can die without all this noise".'[9]

* * *

George Edwards became a figure of hatred and disgust. Questions were raised in Parliament about his role in the sordid but deadly affair. One MP, Matthew Wood, stated that he had evidence that Edwards had instigated the conspiracy and betrayed his comrades for blood money. Joseph Hume claimed that Edwards was one of many in the Government's employ recruited to incite rebellion and smear the campaign for parliamentary reform. Edward Aylmer wrote: 'Edwards was not merely an informer, who appeared to accede to the plots of others for purpose of revealing and defeating them: he was a diabolical wretch who created the treason he disclosed, who went about – a fiend in human form – inflaming distressed and desperate wretches into crimes, in order that he might betray them to justice and make profit of their blood.'[10]

After a short period in hiding on Guernsey at public expense, Edwards was given a new identity and, like several other former government agents, sent to start a new life in South Africa. Under the name of George Parker he worked as a model-maker at Green Point until his death in 1843.

The Cato Street Conspiracy gave Sidmouth and Lord Liverpool's Government the excuse they needed to justify the Six Acts and impose even more stringent repression. It may have been a crazy, doomed enterprise from the start; it may have been encouraged by *agents provocateurs*; it may even have been a complete set-up. But in the minds of many the plot was of murderous intent and the threat of armed insurrection, even revolution, behind the guise of Radicals and Reformers had been exposed. Nevertheless, their lordships were disappointed in the wider outcome. For although Thistlewood and some of the defendants had been well known Radical agitators, others were clearly motivated to join such a sorry adventure by genuine outrage over Peterloo. Furthermore, the repression and executions failed to tackle the fundamental causes of unrest – an economic recession and the inequality which the ruling classes refused to address. No bungled assassination designed by the rulers to crush dissent could disguise that or halt the onward march of Reform, although it would take many years and more lives to achieve.

There was one more casualty of Cato Street, this time in the Government's ranks. Lord Castlereagh, the gang's chief intended victim, was made of more sensitive stuff than Sidmouth. He was deeply hurt by Shelley's poem in response to Peterloo, which included the lines: 'As I saw death along the way / He had a mask like Castlereagh.' He was jeered every time he appeared in public and fell into a depression. His doctor advised him to retire to his estate at North Cray Place, Kent. There, on 12 August 1822, Castlereagh cut his throat with a penknife in his dressing room. He was aged 53. His family mourned him. Few others did.

5
Queen Victoria – The First Attempt

'I might as well shoot at her as any one else'

At 6.15 pm on Wednesday, 10 June 1840, Queen Victoria, 21 years old and four months pregnant with her first child, left Buckingham Palace in a low, open carriage drawn by four bays, sitting alongside her beloved husband, Albert. A good-sized crowd greeted them as it was well known that on a fine summer evening the royal couple liked to ride in Hyde Park before dinner. It was part of Victoria's façade of normality that their carriage was unescorted by soldiers or armed guards. She savoured the warm applause of her subjects, unhindered by intervening security. On this occasion she planned to combine the customary ride in the park with a visit to her mother, the Duchess of Kent, in her house in Belgrave Square. The carriage had travelled barely 100 yards from the palace gates when Albert noticed 'a small disagreeable-looking man leaning against the railings of Green Park only six paces away'.

Edward Oxford was the 18-year-old son of a mulatto jeweller. He was small – 5 feet 4 inches tall and slightly built – with a nervous giggle, unprepossessing and looked younger than his years. He alternated between pacing up and down outside the railings and lounging against them. In his pockets he carried two recently obtained pistols with which he intended to kill the queen. Again, these were turbulent times, riven by social unrest and the fear of revolution, but Oxford's aim was not political. Victoria's crime, in his fevered imagination, was her celebrity. And, as we have seen since, celebrity breeds jealousy and mania.

*   *   *

2. Queen Victoria in her open carriage (*Illustrated London News*)

The subsequent trial would hear much about insanity in Edward
Oxford's family. His grandmother, Sophia, told the court that her
husband, who had died at Greenwich Hospital eleven years earlier,
was during 35 years of marriage 'always very unsettled in his mind,
particularly when he took liquor'. Their son, Edward's father, was just
12 months old when his father caused such a disturbance he was placed
in a straitjacket for two weeks. During his later years at Greenwich
Edward's grandfather was treated by Sir Richard Dobson for 'an
attack in his head'. Edward's father, was a prosperous gold-chaser in

Birmingham, where he had a reputation for a hot temper and erratic behaviour. He met his wife, Hannah, in that city's Hope and Anchor public house when they were both 20, and they married six weeks later. Hannah's family and friends were horrified at his mixed-race origins, his drinking and low habits, but she ignored their advice. She told the court: 'Both before and after I was married to him he acted very strangely, and previous to our marriage he attempted to draw a razor across his throat, and threatened to shoot himself with a double-barrelled pistol, which he said was loaded with slugs.'[1] Days before the wedding Hannah had had second thoughts, whereupon her future husband flew into a rage and threw a bundle of bank notes, meant to purchase furniture, into the fire. He was later found in the street with an open razor in his hand and was led home by the local watchman, crying uncontrollably. Hannah recalled: 'After we were married he did not mend in the least and during my pregnancy with my second child he used to make all sorts of faces and grimaces at me, and when the child was born it used to distort its face in the same way, and never showed any indication of sense or reason.' That child died aged two years and nine months and Hannah's husband, rather than show pity, remorse or kindness, continued to torment Hannah. 'I never did anything to vex him,' she said, 'but, on the contrary, was too kind and attentive to him. He bought a horse on one occasion, and used to lead it about the parlour. When I was pregnant [with Edward] my husband threw a quart pot at me, and hit me on the head. I fell down from the effects of the blow, and was insensible for some time.'[2]

Edward was born on 9 April 1822. As a young child he witnessed many of his father's rages and suffered manic beatings. The elder Oxford got into financial difficulties and fled to Dublin, selling every stick of furniture in their Birmingham home to finance a drunken binge. He returned penniless some weeks later, unrepentant. 'He pushed me from him,' Hannah said, 'and refused to take my hand. He always acted contrary to what he was told to do. When I was in distress for money he used to laugh, and had a sort of supernatural look with him.' He was seen taking laudanum on several occasions and died in June 1929 when Edward was seven. The family moved to London and the lad attended school in Lambeth.

The evidence given at Edward's trial by his mother and grandmother must be seen as part of an insanity plea, and Edward did indeed appear to replicate his dead father's behaviour. Hannah attested:

> When he was seven he used to burst out crying for no cause. He would sometimes get into a violent rage without any cause, and he would knock and destroy anything he might have in his hand. The first day he brought pistols home he pointed one of them at me, and on another occasion he levelled a loaded gun at me. When a child he burned his face with gunpowder, and he was very fond of firing off little cannons. After his fits of passion he would burst out into fits of laughter, which appeared to be quite involuntary. When he was not under such excitement he was very reserved, and would not speak, and used to be very angry with me if I spoke to him.

When Edward was about ten his mother, unable to cope, put him in the care of a man called Salmon, while she went into the service of a banker as a 'confidential housekeeper'. Edward returned, apparently improved, but was soon throwing missiles at passers-by from the roof of their home. He was once taken to a police station 'for getting up behind a carriage and alarming a lady'.

Edward began work as a pot-boy in his aunt's public house in Hounslow. He learnt the business and was soon working as a barman at another pub in the city. Although generally well regarded, his temper got the better of him and he attempted to stab a fellow barman during a fracas in another hostelry at Marylebone. He moved to the Hog-in-the-Pound on the corner of Oxford Street and South Molton Street where he was given responsibility for the day-to-day running of the establishment. The landlord later spoke well of him, but four weeks before the incident which was to make Oxford's name, he was sacked for laughing in the faces of customers. Until then he had been earning 20 shillings a week and living in lodgings at 6 West Street. He had taken to visiting shooting galleries and on one occasion showed his mother a pistol. She asked him why he spent his money on such foolish things. He claimed he was simply holding it for a friend. Hannah decided to return to Birmingham, but a few days before her departure Edward struck her across the face. The landlady told him that if she had struck her mother she would expect her hand to drop off. Oxford 'appeared ashamed and became very sullen'.

Left alone, Oxford began to fantasise about guns. He appears to have conjured up a phantom organisation called Young England in which he

would 'make his mark'. Just when that turned into a fantastical plot to
murder the queen was never made clear, but Oxford became obsessed
with the idea of celebrity through notoriety. On 4 May he bought a
pair of pistols from a man called Hayes of Blackfriars Road for £2.
He practised at shooting galleries in Leicester Square, The Strand and
elsewhere in the West End. On 3 June he went to a shop in Lambeth
run by an old school friend called Grey and bought 50 copper caps used
to fire pistols. He got directions to another shop that sold bullets, and
told Grey that he already had gunpowder. On the evening of 10 June
he was seen with a pistol, which he stated was loaded. Asked what he
intended to do with it, he replied: 'Fire at targets.'[3]

*   *   *

Victoria was a new queen and wife. After a cold, unhappy childhood,
various accidents of heredity saw her take the throne when aged just
18. She was small, plain to some eyes, but strong-willed, with a quick,
if basic, intelligence. She was the head of a nation that had grown tired
of the excesses of monarchy after decades under Mad King George, the
profligate George IV and his brother, the lacklustre William IV. Her
infancy saw the aftermath of great political turmoil: the return of troops
from the Napoleonic Wars to a Britain of the New Poor Laws and the
workhouse, the police state created to counter the Luddites, the Reform
movement and the martyrs of Peterloo. Her childhood had witnessed
pitched battles in Bristol, Merthyr and Newport as people fought for
the right to vote in a parliamentary democracy. Approaching puberty
she saw the mass executions and transportations which followed the
rural wars in which farm labourers smashed and burnt the machinery
which was robbing them of their livelihoods. Moreover, the young
queen came under the influence of her prime minister, Lord Melbourne,
who persuaded her that calls for reform were the work of political
agitators and criminals. While he gave her much-needed support and
friendship, and instilled in her the idea of the duties of a constitutional
monarch, Melbourne cynically manipulated her. She knew very little
about the real hardships and inequalities suffered by millions of her
subjects. He also convinced her that a figure from her childhood, Lady
Flora Hastings, was pregnant with an illegitimate child. When the
unfortunate woman died of stomach cancer soon after, the resultant

scandal – the so-called Bedchamber Crisis – saw Victoria's personal popularity plummet. She was heading for the same level of public contempt achieved by her uncles. She needed a strong man to channel her passions and her maternal uncle, Leopold of Saxe-Coburg, King of the Belgians and another major influence, hatched a plan to marry her to one of his nephews.

The first meeting with Prince Albert, the younger of the two, was frosty, but she came to covet his manliness. She proposed to him and many years later recalled the day of their engagement: 'Albert had been out hunting and looked so beautiful in a green coat with top boots, and that heavenly expression in his eyes.' They married on 10 February 1840 and she quickly became pregnant. With Albert she discovered the joys of sex and thrilled to their bedchamber athletics, an ardour which was only to cool after many difficult pregnancies. Victoria revelled in the role of adoring wife, while Albert came to terms with having a queen who loved him. He returned that love, although he found her gossipy late nights and openly passionate nature at odds with his Teutonic upbringing. Despite such difficulties, both took pleasure in creating as close an approximation to 'normal' family life as possible. The afternoon or early evening drive in the park was one of their most cherished routines. It also brought them closer to the people – or so Victoria believed.

That afternoon Edward Oxford, who no longer regarded himself as one of her loyal subjects, arrived in Hyde Park at about 4 o'clock. He saw Prince Albert return from a visit to Woolwich and enter the palace. He then walked to Constitution Hill to await the arrival of the queen's carriage.

Victoria and Albert emerged in their open carriage, with two equerries, Colonel Buckley and Sir Edward Bowater, seated opposite. Unusually, the queen was sitting on her husband's left. That meant she was skirted to her left by a long brick wall instead of by the railings of Green Park to her right. One schoolboy who raised his cap to her as she passed was the future renowned painter John Everett Millais. A contemporary account recorded:

> The carriage had proceeded a short distance up the road when a young man, who had been standing with his back to the Green Park fence, advanced to within a few yards of the carriage, and then deliberately fired, pointing towards the Queen. The ball did not take effect; and her majesty rose from

her seat, but was instantly pulled down by Prince Albert. Some say she uttered a loud scream; this is contradicted; it seems true that she turned deadly pale, and appeared excessively alarmed, but made no exclamation.

The queen certainly heard the first explosion as the horses came to a halt. Albert called out: 'Don't be alarmed.' They both turned as Oxford shouted: 'I have got another!' and levelled his second firearm. Victoria later told the Home Secretary, Lord Normanby, that 'it was not at all pleasant' to see the assailant take aim. Albert ordered the postillion to drive on as the second shot was fired. It too missed and Albert later told his step-grandmother, 'the ball must have passed just above her'.[4] The *Annual Register* gave a slightly different account:

> When the carriage approached Oxford turned around, nodded, then drew a pistol from his breast, and, as the carriage was nearly opposite him, he discharged that pistol. The providence of God averted the blow from Her Majesty, the ball whizzed by on the opposite side, and in all probability Her Majesty was quite unconscious at that moment that any attempt had been made on her life. The carriage proceeded. Oxford then looked back, as if to see whether any person was standing near enough to see him, and drew another pistol, although whether with his right or left hand seems uncertain, he aimed it, however, at Her Majesty. It would appear that Her Majesty saw him aiming at her, for she stooped down. Again the providence of God saved her. Oxford fired; the ball was heard to whiz along, but it missed its object. The Queen immediately drove along to allay any alarm that might arise in the heart of her august mother on hearing the perils to which Her Majesty had thus been exposed.[5]

Oxford made no attempt to escape. Instead, he lounged against the park railings, his pistols, still smoking, in plain view. Immediately, he was surrounded by an outraged crowd shouting: 'Kill him! Kill him!' Several men rushed to seize him, including Millais's father. Another man, called Low, screamed at Oxford: 'Why, you confounded rascal, how dare you shoot at our queen?' to which Oxford replied: 'It was I who shot at her.' Oxford was bundled away from the furious mob to the police station house, where he asked: 'Is the queen hurt?' He was asked whether his pistols had been loaded, and replied in the affirmative. An officer was immediately sent to search his small back room at the West Place lodging house. There he found a box containing a sword and scabbard, a powder flask with 3 oz of powder, a bullet mould, five lead bullets, some percussion caps and various papers setting out the regulations of a seditious club, later to prove fictitious, called New England.[6]

Victoria and Albert themselves continued on their way to visit the Duchess of Kent, for whom Victoria harboured few affections, then proceeded to take their planned drive in Hyde Park. There, according to one report, 'an immense concourse of persons of all ranks and both sexes had congregated. The reception of the royal pair was so enthusiastic as almost to overpower the self-possession of the queen; while Prince Albert's countenance, alternately pale and crimson, betrayed the strength of his emotions.' They returned to Buckingham Palace through more wildly enthusiastic crowds and at the gates a multitude cheered them. Victoria, 'although pale and agitated', repeatedly bowed and smiled in return. On reaching her private apartments she burst into floods of tears, but recovered enough to join Albert and guests at dinner. A little later Albert brought Oxford's two pistols to show her. She was clearly unnerved to see the weapons 'which might have finished me off'.

The whole of London, it seemed, was thrown into a state of loyal excitement by the assassination attempt. 'God Save the Queen' was sung with fervour at theatres and public dinners. At the Opera House a grand charity concert was due to end with Mozart's overture to Idomeneo, but the conductor, Sir George Smart, informed the audience of events and substituted the National Anthem.

The following day Oxford was taken to the Home Office for examination as Victoria prepared for the Loyal Address. Under-Secretary Fox Maule was besieged by witnesses eager to attest to what they had seen. Maule refused to admit reporters because it would have been 'contrary to all rule'. Maule, Normanby and two police officers conducted the examination, in the presence of other ministers and law officers. Oxford could not curb the habit that had got him sacked from his previous job: he laughed and giggled. The panel committed him to Newgate to be tried for high treason.[7] To avoid the mob waiting outside he was conveyed though a back corridor, where he embraced his worried sister. His uncle, a publican in Gracechurch Street, called at the Home Office to say he was hiring a professional advocate to defend his nephew. Police combed the dust and gravel at the scene of the outrage, but found no bullet. They did, however, spot a mark on the brick wall which seemed to be the impact point of one shot. Oxford was examined by a surgeon, Mr McCann, who cut a lock from his hair. Several MPs tried to buy some strands, but the doctor instead divided it among his most distinguished patients.

That afternoon Victoria and Albert again took their customary drive in and about Hyde Park, escorted by hundreds of civilians on horseback. The crowds were vast, while a line of carriages queued outside the palace to deliver messages of respect. One report said: 'Buckingham Palace and the approaches to the royal residence presented a most splendid and extraordinary spectacle. The calls of the nobility and gentry in carriages, on horseback and on foot, who entered their names in the visitors' book were incessant ... The crowds of persons in front of the palace, amounting to several thousands, were kept back by a strong body of police.'[8]

At noon the next day, 12 June, the sheriff of London and other city functionaries arrived to deliver the address of the common council. A detachment of the Grenadier Guards, accompanied by their band, marched through the gateway. The royal standard was raised as Cabinet ministers arrived in quick succession. At 2 pm the state carriage of the Speaker of the Commons arrived, followed by a further 100 vehicles filled with MPs. Then the Lords came, the barons first, then the royal dukes, with the Lord Chancellor bringing up the rear. All was a glittering mass of robes, decorations and baubles. Victoria received the address from the throne as the crowds cheered outside. Two gunshots had sent her popularity soaring.

*   *   *

The trial of Edward Oxford began on Thursday, 9 July at the Central Criminal Court and ended the next day. He pleaded not guilty. The judges were Lord Denham, Baron Alderson and Judge Patterson. The Attorney General, Sir Frederick Pollock, opened for the prosecution. The charge was based on the law that where the alleged act of treason was a direct attack on the life of the sovereign, the trial should be conducted as a common trial for murder. That did away with the need for two witnesses to the event and also removed certain rights enjoyed by political defendants in other treason cases. The events were largely uncontested. Instead, the trial hinged on two questions: were Oxford's guns loaded, and was he sane? The jury was warned not to act on the basis of newspaper reports or public indignation.

Pollock outlined Oxford's background, his regular attendance at shooting galleries, his purchase of weapons and ammunition, and his general demeanour as reported by eye witnesses. He detailed the attack on the queen's carriage and Oxford's arrest. He attached little importance to the failure to find the discharged bullets, declaring that the balls had probably gone over the wall. Oxford, he said, was not a skilled marksman and 'in the flurry of the moment he probably directed the pistols unsteadily'. Pollock then turned to the question of his sanity. Oxford was calm and collected when interrogated after the event, had admitted to the act, and, although given several opportunities, had never claimed his pistols were empty. The Attorney General told the jury that 'though they must feel compassion for the unhappy youth now at the bar, they should remember that they had a duty to perform, and they should perform it with firmness'. During the first part of Pollock's speech Oxford appeared careless and indifferent in the dock, but he became agitated and anxious when various forms of madness were mentioned.[9]

The first witness to give evidence was Samuel Parkes. He testified: 'On the report of the pistol I heard distinctly a whizzing or buzzing between my face and the carriage.' Joshua Reeve Low said that the prisoner was within three yards of the carriage when he first saw gun smoke. Oxford took deliberate aim and fired the second shot after the carriage, which had advanced about eight yards. Elizabeth Stukeley, housekeeper to Lord Bexley, also saw the defendant fire and felt the flash of the second pistol as something whizzed past her ear. A policeman, Charles Smith, said he heard Oxford boast, when asked by someone in the crowd whether his guns were loaded, 'If your head had come into contact with them you would have found whether there were balls in them or not.' One of the arresting officers, George Brown, said that he and other policemen had carried out a minute search of the ground on both sides of the garden wall but, despite sifting through earth and dust, had found no bullets. In the police cell he asked Oxford whether his pistols were loaded. The prisoner replied: 'There were balls.' Lord Uxbridge, who saw Oxford at the station house, said:

> At the opening of the cell door, where I addressed him, he addressed me by saying, 'Is the Queen well?' I answered, 'How dare you ask such a

question?' He said he had been in a public house in Oxford Street for about four months, and that he had left it about a fortnight. He said he had been doing a great deal of shooting; that he was a very good shot with a pistol, and a better shot with a rifle.

J. W. Linton, a former playmate of Oxford, said that the prisoner had shown him two handsome pistols, while the perfumer Thomas Lawrence told how he had heard another man tell Oxford that he was 'more fit to fire at a hay-stack than a target'. Fox Maule presented Oxford's signed deposition: 'A great many witnesses against me. Some say I shot with my left, others with my right hand. They vary as to the distance. After I fired the first pistol, Prince Albert got up as if he would jump out of the carriage, and sat down again, as if he thought better of it. Then I fired the second pistol. That is all I shall say at present.'[10]

The lawyer Sidney Taylor spoke for Oxford, warning the jury that the defendant was charged with the gravest crime in the land, subject, on conviction, to the most solemn and appalling punishment. If they found Oxford, a mere boy, guilty he would be drawn on a hurdle, hanged by the neck until dead, beheaded, and the quarters of his body put at the queen's disposal. Taylor insisted that there was no proof that the pistols had been loaded and witnesses disagreed on the distance of the prisoner from the carriage. If, as Pollock suggested, the bullets had been fired over the 12-foot garden wall, there was no case to answer as Oxford must have aimed high above the queen's head to avoid wounding her. Taylor referred to a recent case in which Lord Abinger had directed a jury to acquit a prisoner who had put a pistol to the head of a prosecutor and threatened to blow his head off because there was no evidence it was loaded. In another case in 1786 a man called Edwards had come up behind his supposed sweetheart whom he suspected of walking out with another and discharged two pistols at her back. The young woman suffered two slight contusions and, on his arrest, the defendant was found to have two more pistols 'loaded to the muzzles' with which to commit suicide. Although the assailant expressed deep regret that he had not succeeded in murder, he was acquitted on the ground that the first pistols were not loaded with balls. Taylor contended that if Oxford's pistols were loaded only with powder and wadding, he must go free. His enquiry as to the queen's health while in custody could easily be construed as concern that she might have been harmed by the wadding.

As to Oxford's sanity, if the jury believed that the pistols were loaded, there was strong evidence that no sane man would have made such an incompetent attempt. No sane man would have drawn such attention to himself, fired from outside the park railings instead of behind them, and then made no attempt to escape. The secret society of which Oxford had boasted membership did not exist. Taylor said:

> He did not take any precautions, but went in the public manner described by witnesses, and committed the mad and desperate act described by the witnesses; and after he had committed the act, what then was his conduct when the excitement of the crime was over, and the natural feeling to preserve his life might be supposed to have induced him to consult his safety by flight? Did he fly? No; he stood his ground ... Might he not have naturally expected that the indignation of the crowd at such an attempt on the beloved queen would have induced those around him to have torn him to pieces on the spot? But no thought of that kind influenced him; he stood firm and surrendered himself up at once to await the consequences of his act, and braved the danger of the inflamed spectators. Would any sane man or boy have acted thus?[11]

Taylor reprised in detail previous attempts to kill the queen's grandfather, George III. All were premeditated and each 'took the surest means of executing their intentions, yet in each case the offender was judged insane'. He added: 'At that time, events in France had excited the public mind, and a motive might suggest itself for acting the part of a regicide; but what motive could any sane person have for killing the Queen of England?' Much had been made of the papers found in Oxford's box, which the prosecution suggested were evidence of a clandestine plot. But the papers were written by Oxford himself and were the product of his own 'foolish fancy'. It was ludicrous to suggest that Oxford was part of a conspiracy. The secret society referred to did not exist but was the product of the 'heated imagination of the stripling at the bar'. It was incredible that any society would seek to recruit as a political assassin such a callow fantasist.

After evidence was heard from Oxford's mother and grandmother about insanity in the family, Taylor called Dr John Connolly, physician to the Hanwell lunatic asylum, who had seen the defendant two days before the trial. He judged him to be of unsound mind. Oxford had answered his questions willingly, but the answers were 'unsatisfactory'. Under cross-examination Connolly said:

When I spoke to him of his trial he said, 'Trial, when?' as if he did not know anything about it. When I asked him if he was not aware that he had committed a very grave crime in shooting at the Queen, he replied, 'I might as well shoot at her as any one else.' I examined the head of the prisoner, and found the upper part of the forehead of such a formation as frequently indicates an imperfect development of the brain.

Dr Chowne, physician to the Charing Cross hospital and lecturer on medical jurisprudence, told the court:

I should consider the conduct of the prisoner as extremely strong indication of unsound mind. I consider doing an act without a motive a proof to some extent of an unsound mind. That state of insanity has been described by the term 'lesion of the will.' From the conversation I have had with the prisoner, I am decidedly of the opinion that his state of mind is a mixture of insanity and imbecility. The laughing and the crying are an evidence of the same state of mind.

A third physician, the surgeon James Clarke, stated that he believed Oxford suffered from imbecility. He described visiting the young prisoner while he was with his mother:

He took no notice of me, and behaved as if he did not see me. His mother said, 'How rude you are, why do you not speak to Mr Clarke?' He appeared absorbed and unconscious. She spoke to him a second time, and still he took no notice. On her speaking to him a third time, he jumped up with great violence of manner, and threatened 'to stick her.' In cases of hereditary insanity, it has been noticed that it frequently showed itself at the period of puberty, between the ages of 14 and 20.[12]

Chief Justice Denham summed up for the jury. He left the question of insanity entirely up to them, but cautioned against the 'dangerous doctrine that the commission of a great crime without an apparent motive was in itself proof of insanity'. He told the jury:

It is for you to determine whether the prisoner did fire the pistols, or either of them, at Her Majesty; and whether the pistols, both or either of them, were loaded with a bullet. Supposing, gentlemen, that you should come to the conclusion that the pistols, or one of them, were levelled at her majesty, and that they or either of them were loaded, then the defence which has been set upon raises the further inquiry whether, at the time the prisoner committed the act, he was responsible for it.[13]

At 6.30 pm, after considering the case for 45 minutes, the jury delivered a special verdict, finding Oxford 'guilty of discharging the contents of two pistols, but whether or not they were loaded with ball has not been satisfactorily proved to us, he being of unsound state of mind at the time'. A fierce argument ensued when Pollock insisted that the verdict meant that Oxford should be detained at Her Majesty's pleasure. The defence claimed it meant that the offence of firing loaded pistols had not been proved. Lord Denham ruled that the jury was mistaken and sent them out again to consider the question of whether the pistols had been loaded. The jury returned after another hour with the legally acceptable verdict that the prisoner was guilty, but at the time insane.

Edward Oxford probably owed his life to Dr Connolly, whom Lord Denham had described to the jury as 'very experienced'. The jury certainly took full regard of his evidence. Oxford was transferred to Broadmoor criminal lunatic asylum, where he spent the next 27 years. He expressed 'deep regret' at his behaviour and, released in 1867, was ordered to quit Britain. On 30 December that year he sailed on the *Suffolk* bound for Melbourne. His fortunes overseas are unknown.

The assassination attempt, if that was what it was, had one significant consequence. As Victoria was expecting a child, Lord Melbourne stressed the importance of appointing a Regent to maintain stability if – heaven forbid – the queen was fatally injured while the child was still a minor. The necessary bill was introduced within days of Oxford's trial.

The queen was determined that her daily routine and official duties should not be affected by Oxford's attack and she continued to ride in an open, unguarded carriage.[14] Well-meaning courtiers, possibly Albert himself, presented Victoria with a green silk parasol. Between its cover and lining was a layer of chain mail. However its 3¼ lb weight made it difficult to hold up, and it is unlikely that the queen ever used it.

The Foreign Secretary wrote to the queen after Oxford's attack: 'Viscount Palmerston humbly trusts that the failure of this atrocious attempt may be considered an indication that your Majesty is reserved for a long and prosperous reign.' During that long reign Victoria came face to face with would-be assassins on another seven occasions. None was driven by even rudimentary political motives.

6
The McNaughton Rules

'a grinding of the mind'

The body was opened by C. Gardiner Guthrie at 1 pm on Thursday, 26 January 1843 in the presence of four other medical men. They found that the ball had entered from behind, 2 inches from the ridge of the backbone, between the eleventh and twelfth ribs, and 3 inches from the inferior angle of the shoulder blade. It travelled erratically through the chest cavity just below the left lung, perforated the diaphragm, grazed the fat of the left kidney, but missed the vital organs of the abdomen, and lodged beneath the skin at the front of the deceased's stomach pit, from where it had been extracted at the scene of the crime. Twelve ounces of coagulated blood were removed. The post mortem report concluded:

> The absence of all that shock and alarm which almost invariably follow the opening into either of the great cavities of the body, together with the great difficulty of ascertaining the spot at which the ball had entered, from its small size, gave rise during the first 12 hours [after the shot] to the anxious hope that it had not passed so directly across. We consider such a wound to be inevitably fatal.[1]

What added to the grief of the dead man's family was the near-certainty that he had not been the intended victim. And paranoia, not politics, was the root cause of this assassination.

* * *

The tragedy brought together the fortunes of three very different men.
Sir Robert Peel was born in Bury in February 1788, the son of a wealthy Lancashire cotton lord and Tory MP and the eldest of

eleven children. After he excelled at Harrow and Oxford, his father groomed him for Westminster and bought him the Tipperary seat of Cashel, one of many he would hold during his career. During Lord Liverpool's administration he was Chief Secretary for Ireland for six years and his arch-Unionist stance won him the nickname 'Orange Peel'. He challenged the Catholic leader Daniel O'Connell – who compared Peel's smile to the silver plate on a coffin – to a duel, but O'Connell was arrested on his way to the venue. Peel resigned in 1817 and five years later became Home Secretary. In that role he softened his sectarian beliefs and pushed the Bill of Catholic Emancipation through Parliament, arguing that civil strife was the greater danger. He also created the Metropolitan Police in 1829, and their nicknames of 'Bobbies' and 'Peelers' stuck. In 1834, after the prime minister, Earl Grey, resigned, he refused the premiership but relented the following year and called for fresh elections. His Tamworth Manifesto set out the definition of Conservatism as support for establishment institutions while permitting gradual, moderate parliamentary reform. He scraped back, but his slender majority was eroded by untimely deaths in the Tory ranks and he quit within months. He was elected prime minister for a second time in June 1841, a period of turmoil and civil strife. Despite his conservatism he took steps to liberalise trade, introduced a permanent income tax and in 1842 passed the Mines Act, which forbade the employment of women and children underground. He wrote: 'It may be that I shall leave a name sometimes remembered with expressions of goodwill in the abodes of those whose lot it is to labour, and to earn their daily bread by the sweat of their brow, when they shall recruit their exhausted strength with abundant and untaxed food, the sweeter because it is no longer leavened by a sense of injustice.'[2]

Whereas Peel came from 'new money', Edward Drummond had grander connections. He was born on 30 March 1792 the eldest son of the Charing Cross banker Charles Drummond; his mother was of the daughter of the first Lord Auckland. He was the cousin of Viscount Strathallen, and his banking and aristocratic connections helped him win a clerkship at the Treasury. His 'assiduity, fidelity and good humour' won him the patronage of government ministers. As private secretary to the Chancellor of the Exchequer he came to the notice of George Canning, Lord Wellington and Sir Robert Peel. Under their patronage for nearly 20 years, he carried out, inconspicuously but effectively, affairs of state at a rank, for those in the know, only just below that of a Cabinet minister. Inevitably, he became Peel's private secretary in Downing Street.

Daniel McNaughton was born in 1805 the eldest and illegitimate son of a respectable Glasgow merchant. He served four years as an apprentice in his father's workshop and continued as a journeyman for three more years, before setting up business in the city's Stockwell Street, where he remained for five years. He was described during that time as 'very steady, industrious and temperate'. He was also 'inoffensive, fond of children and humane to animals'. But around 1834 he contracted typhus fever which left him restless and with insomnia. He was also resentful that his father had not offered him a partnership in the family firm. But his own business seemed to prosper, he built up a local reputation for shrewdness and he took an active part in discussing the affairs of the Mechanics' Institute. However, personal demons seemed to take over and in 1837 his lodgings landlord evicted him because of his bizarre behaviour. He moved into his workshop where friends, neighbours and customers were increasingly shocked by his antics. He would sit for days uttering tortured exclamations and would run out to dip his burning brow into the River Clyde, or even plunge into the river. He saw persecution everywhere and in 1841 tried to sell his business to escape tortures real or imagined. In a rare meeting with his father he spoke of being followed day and night by 'spies' who never spoke but who laughed in his face and shook sticks at him. He shunned family and friends, and a plan to study arithmetic so that he could get a job in a Glasgow counting house came to nothing. Former colleagues occasionally saw him walking the streets, muttering and keeping his eyes firmly fixed on the ground. He told acquaintances that he had suffered persecution during visits to England and France and claimed that one of the 'spies' had popped out from behind the watch-box of the Customs House quay at Boulogne. He complained of persecution to the Sheriff of Lanarkshire, the MP for Kilmarnock, the Gorbals parish minister and the Lord Provost of Glasgow. To each he initially blamed priests at the Clyde Street Catholic Chapel assisted by 'a parcel of Jesuits', but could offer no evidence. He told Hugh Wilson, the Glasgow Police Commissioner, that Jesuits followed him everywhere, even into his bedroom. Wilson later recalled: 'He was perfectly calm and collected when he first came in; but when he began to talk about persecution he became very much excited, and I then thought he was daft.' McNaughton did not appear to have much interest in politics – one former landlady blamed his behaviour on reading 'infidel doctrines' – but over time his obsessions turned from Scots tormentors to the Conservative Party. He complained they were in league with a 'system or crew' who were out to kill him by torment. He said that Sheriff Bell had sneered at him when he made representations and expressed sadness that he had not had a gun to shoot him dead in his own courthouse.

In August 1842, after his repeated complaints of persecution fell on deaf ears, he left Glasgow, sailing in the *Fire Queen* to Liverpool, where he stayed seven days before travelling on to London. At the London Joint Stock Bank he deposited £750 in a draft from the sale of his business, and withdrew £5. He took lodging at 7 Poplar Row, Newington, a house where he was known from previous visits, at a rent of 2s 6d a week. He paid his rent regularly, always ate out and was in the habit of leaving before nine each morning and returning in the evening. His landlady, Mrs Sarah Dutton, tended him during an illness in December. She said that during this time 'he was always very sullen, avoiding conversation and hanging his head'. At night he would moan and groan and she heard him leaving his bed several times. He complained of headaches and a cold. During one walk McNaughton met by chance a brass-founder named David Gordon whom he had known in Glasgow. They passed Peel's house and Gordon said: 'I believe that is where Sir Robert Peel stops.' McNaughton replied: 'God damn and sink it.' Witnesses later claimed that McNaughton was seen for several days loitering by the Treasury. On the morning of 20 January 1843 he left at his usual time but returned an hour later. After two or three minutes he left again. Mrs Dutton noticed nothing unusual in his appearance or demeanour.[3]

*   *   *

That day Edward Drummond called to see his brother at the family's Charing Cross bank. He left shortly before 4 pm and was walking close by the Salopian coffee-house when he was confronted by McNaughton brandishing a pistol and 'decently' clad in a black coat and plaid waistcoat. Drummond turned away and was shot once in the back, the discharge setting his coat on fire. He scrabbled with his left hand to locate the wound as he staggered to the pavement. McNaughton replaced his pistol in his pocket and, very coolly and deliberately, drew another and aimed it from eight paces at the stricken man. PC James Silver, on hearing the first report, dashed across the road as McNaughton cocked his second weapon. Silver seized his right arm, and at the same time tripped him up. The pistol discharged harmlessly into the ground. After a short but violent struggle Silver took both weapons and rushed McNaughton to the nearest station house in Gardiner Street. On the way McNaughton told Silver that 'he or she' – the policeman was not sure which – 'shall not break my peace of mind any longer'. McNaughton was searched and Silver found ten percussion caps, two £5 Bank of England notes, a receipt from the Glasgow and Ship Bank for £750, four sovereigns, four half-crowns, one shilling, a fourpenny piece, some halfpence, a knife and a key. He was charged with attempted assassination. He told officers that he was an object of Tory persecution. Asked if he knew the identity of the gentleman he had shot, McNaughton replied: 'It is Sir Robert Peel, is it not?'[4]

Drummond, with the help of a bystander, staggered back to the bank where he was seen by the St James's apothecary Richard Jackson, who had known him since infancy. Jackson saw that he had been wounded but, instead of examining him, took him by carriage to Drummond's home. There he was attended by George James Guthrie and Bransby Cooper, who initially failed to find a wound. They turned Drummond on his back and found the ball in his front, half an inch below the skin. They removed it with a lancet and declared that it had lodged in the fleshy part of the thigh close to the groin, injuring 'no important part'. Drummond's calm manner appeared to confirm the diagnosis. The following morning, however, his symptoms worsened, inflammation increased and his physicians belatedly realised the extent of his internal injuries. Attempts to bleed the patient failed until they opened the temporal artery. For three days Drummond's condition fluctuated then, on 24 January, took a rapid turn for the worse. His physicians told him that there was no hope. He took the news 'with perfect calmness and remained undisturbed in mind'. He had throughout made no complaint and had shown no fear. That night he suffered considerable pain but remained conscious. His sister and three brothers sat up with him all night. At seven the next morning his pulse was barely perceptible. He lingered until 10.30 am, when he died, surrounded by his relatives.[5]

News of his death was conveyed to a shocked Queen Victoria and Prince Albert at Windsor Castle, and to the Cabinet. Sir Robert and Lady Peel were 'severely afflicted'. A contemporary account said that Peel's grief was understandable 'as there is no connection so close as that which binds the English statesman to his secretary'. Public grief was great, one obituary writer noted, because: 'The man whose qualifications for public duties were prized by Canning and Wellington, whilst the charm of his personal intercourse was no less valued in private circles, could not have passed away for ever without the deep and earnest regret of those to whom he was known, either as an intimate friend, or as a public servant.' Drummond was buried at Charlton, near Woolwich, after a simple, private service conducted by his brother, the Reverend Arthur Drummond. His family vault lay under the chancel window. In a remarkable coincidence the graveyard was also the last resting place of the assassinated premier Spencer Perceval.

The inquest had been held on 26 January, at the Lion and Goat in Grosvenor Street, before the Westminster coroner, Mr Gell, and a jury of God-fearing tradesmen and property owners. PC Silver told them that there had only been a matter of seconds before McNaughton's first and second shots. A 19-year-old carpenter, Robert Hodge, described witnessing the attack before running away 'very frightened'. Charles Guthrie produced his report of the post mortem. The jury unanimously returned a verdict of 'wilful murder'.[6]

McNaughton's trial opened on 3 March at the Central Criminal Court before Lord Chief Justice Tindal, Mr Justice Williams and Mr Justice Coleridge. The prisoner pleaded 'not guilty' in a firm voice.

The Solicitor-General, Sir William Follett, addressed the jury on behalf of the Crown. He said he would be able to show that the prisoner had intended to kill Peel, for whom he had mistaken Drummond. The fact that he had killed the wrong man did not alter the legal consequences. Follett said that the defence would no doubt cite insanity, but he believed that there were 'very few crimes in which the offender was not, at some time, labouring under some morbid affection of mind'. He pointed to the attempts on the life of the queen and the French monarch, crimes for which it was difficult to find any motive other than that of an ill-regulated mind worked upon by political feeling. 'It is not, therefore, the absence of any adequate motive that was in itself to be taken as proof of want of reason in the perpetrator,' he said, adding:

> The whole question will turn upon this – if you believe the prisoner at the bar at the time he committed this act was not a responsible agent – if you believe that when he fired the pistol he was incapable of distinguishing between right and wrong – if you believe that he was under the influence and control of some disease of the mind, which prevented him being conscious that he was committing a crime – if you believe that he did not know he was violating the law both of God and man, then, undoubtedly he is entitled to your acquittal. [But to] excuse him, it will not be sufficient that he laboured at the time under partial insanity, that he had a morbid disposition of mind, which would not exist in a sane person; that is not enough, if he had that degree of intellect to enable him to know right from wrong, if he knew what would be the effects of his crime, and consciously committed it ...[7]

There was little disagreement about the facts of the attack, and witnesses were cross-examined mainly to illustrate McNaughton's apparent frame of mind at the time. The office porter Benjamin Weston, who had turned on the first gunshot to see the second attempt, said: 'The prisoner drew the pistol very deliberately, but at the same time very quickly. As far as I can judge, it was a very cool deliberate act.' Inspector John Matthew Tierney of A Division gave a detailed account of interviewing McNaughton in his cell on the night of his arrest and the following morning. The officer cautioned the prisoner several times and succeeded in winning his confidence. McNaughton talked freely about the boats available from Scotland, Paisley's reputation for making fine shawls and the lineage of the Earl of Perth, whose family name was Drummond.[8]

The prosecution evidence took all day. The following morning McNaughton's defence barrister, Cockburn QC, opened with a four-hour speech. He asserted that modern science had thrown so much light on the organisation of the brain, and its morbid conditions, that earlier convictions and death sentences imposed on John Bellingham and others should be regarded with caution. Indeed, there was a general opinion that Bellingham should not have been convicted. Perceval's killer had been tried and executed within a week of the crime, and witnesses were not given the opportunity to give evidence of his insanity. Cockburn quoted other cases where it was shown that:

a man might be in general conscious that murder was a crime, and yet commit a particular murder under the influence of some unaccountable delusions which does not make him morally responsible for the crime. [Likewise], a man might be as sane as the rest of the world on all points but one, and yet that act committed under that particular delusion was one for which the man was no more accountable than if *all* his mental faculties had been deranged.

Cockburn referred to the case of a lunatic who had brought an action against his own brother and a madhouse keeper for false imprisonment. Lord Erskine, also counsel for the defence, was unable in cross-examination to extract a single answer from the witness which showed that he laboured under the slightest delusion. Before the close of proceedings, however, a medical man told the court that the accused believed himself to be Jesus Christ, his only delusion.[9]

Cockburn reviewed the different periods of McNaughton's life: from the beginning his habits were gloomy; he was given to abstruse studies; he was disappointed that his father did not take him into partnership; he was a 'natural' son and might not have received the same measure of kindness as his siblings. He outlined the many and various symptoms of madness, or extreme eccentricity, which had been noted by family, friends, colleagues and landlords. Cockburn insisted that he would prove that Drummond was not mistaken for Sir Robert Peel, whom McNaughton greatly admired. He castigated the prosecution for not bringing forward eminent medical experts who had reported to the Government that in their view McNaughton was indeed mad. Their evidence was, however, on the record and its absence in court 'spoke trumpet-tongued as to what were their opinions'. Numerous witnesses were called, including John Hughes, a tailor with whom McNaughton had lodged for seven months in 1835. Hughes had slept in the same room as the accused many times and was troubled by his restlessness at night. 'Whilst he remained at my house he never had any person call upon him,' Hughes said.

> I observed that his manner and behaviour were generally very strange. He did not appear to be fond of society, and scarcely ever spoke unless first spoken to, and then his replies were quick and hurried, as if he wished to avoid conversation. I also noticed that when any person spoke to him, if their eye caught his he immediately looked down to the ground, as if ashamed; whenever he asked for anything he appeared confused.

Many more gave similar evidence of behaviour which grew increasingly erratic as time went by. Then it was the turn of the medical witnesses.[10]

Dr E. T. Monro, who had studied lunacy for 30 years, reported a conversation with the prisoner in his cell. McNaughton said he felt 'a grinding of the mind', which left him 'tossed like a cork on the sea'. In Glasgow people pointed at him and called him a murderer. Persons dogged him to Boulogne and would not let him learn French. They wanted to murder him. The man he had shot at Charing Cross was part of that crew and McNaughton believed that it was only by killing him that he would find peace. Dr Monro said he had not a shadow of a doubt that the delusions were real to the prisoner. The killing was the climax of a pre-existing idea which had haunted McNaughton for years. Monro said that he frequently saw insane people who exhibited great cleverness in all matters not associated with their delusions. An insane person might commit a criminal act and be aware of the consequences. This became the hub of the case and Monro was cross-examined on the moral responsibility of lunatics by the Solicitor-General, Sir William Follett:

> *Follett*: What do you mean by insanity? Do you consider a person labouring under a morbid delusion of unsound mind?
> *Monro*: I do.
> *Follett*: Do you think insanity may exist without any morbid delusions?
> *Monro*: Yes; a person may be imbecile: but there is generally some morbid delusion; there are various shades of insanity. A person may be of unsound mind, and yet be able to manage the usual affairs of life.
> *Follett*: May insanity exist with a moral perception of right and wrong?
> *Monro*: Yes; it is very common.
> *Follett*: A person may have a delusion and know murder to be a crime?
> *Monro*: If there existed antecedent symptoms, I should consider the murder to be an overt act, the crowning piece of his insanity, but if he had stolen a £10 note it would not have tallied with his delusion.[11]

Sir Arthur Morrison, who had studied insanity for 50 years, concurred with Monro, as did a succession of other medical men. Doctors, academics and surgeons testified to their belief that McNaughton's morbid delusions consisted of fancying that he was the victim of persecution and that delusion deprived him of all restraint or control over his actions. Cockburn was preparing to call further witnesses when Lord Chief Justice Tindal halted him and asked the Solicitor-

General whether he had expert evidence to rebut the medical testimony given on behalf of the defence. When Follett said he did not, Tindal said that the bench felt that the medical evidence was so strong that they had to stop the case. Follett agreed not to press for a verdict. The Chief Justice than put it to the jury that they must be satisfied that McNaughton was incapable of understanding that his murderous act was wicked and a violation of the laws of God and man. The jury did not hesitate to deliver a verdict of 'Not guilty, on the ground of insanity'. McNaughton was committed to Bethlem Hospital and then to the recently opened Broadmoor Criminal Asylum, to be detained at Her Majesty's pleasure.

But Her Majesty was definitely not pleased. She wrote to her secretary on 12 March: 'Not *Guilty* on account of *Insanity* ... everyone is convinced he was perfectly conscious and aware of what he did!'

*   *   *

McNaughton disappeared into the asylum system and there is no record that he was ever released. But his name lived on. His acquittal on the grounds of partial insanity gave rise to the McNaughton Rules. His case, debated in the House of Lords,[12] established that to succeed with an insanity defence it must be shown that the defendant did not know the full nature of the act he was committing. Alternatively, if he did know, he did not properly understand that the act was morally wrong. In summary, the Rules stated that a person could not be held responsible for a crime if he was 'labouring under such a deficit of reason from disease of the mind to not know the nature and quality of the act; or that if he did know it, that he did not know that what he was doing was wrong'.[13] Despite having no statutory basis, the Rules remained in law until the passing of the Homicide Act 1957, which aimed to iron out some imperfections by recognising the plea of diminished responsibility. That year, in the case of a man who killed his wife during a blackout while suffering from arteriosclerosis-induced automatism which restricted the blood supply to his brain, the judge ruled that brain damage could amount to disease of the mind. And in 1963 Lord Denning ruled: 'It seems to me that any mental disorder that manifests itself in violence and is prone to recur is a disease of the mind. At any rate it is a disease for which a person should be detained in hospital rather than given an unqualified acquittal.'

But that was over a century in the future, and the mental state of assassins and would-be assassins would exercise legal minds many more times during the nineteenth century.

7
Queen Victoria – Further Attempts

'Fool that I was, not to shoot'

On 29 May 1842, Queen Victoria, now 23 and the mother of an infant male heir and a daughter, and her devoted Albert attended Sunday service at the Chapel Royal in St James's Palace, then headed back along the Mall to Buckingham Palace. As they passed Stafford House, the prince spotted 'a little swarthy, ill-looking rascal' standing two paces from their carriage. The man wore 'a shabby hat and was of dirty appearance'. He pointed what appeared to be a pistol at the carriage and then disappeared into the crowd. The queen and their attendants noticed nothing, and Albert began to doubt what he had seen. On their return to the palace the pair did indeed behave as if nothing had happened. Later, however, Albert informed the prime minister, Sir Robert Peel, and several other gentlemen of his suspicions.

The following day the palace was informed that 16-year-old James Pearson, a wood engraver, had seen 'a young man who was standing near him with his back to the rails, pull a pistol out of his breast, and as the Queen's carriage passed, present the weapon at it, but whether he pulled the trigger he could not positively say. At any rate the pistol did not go off, and no sooner had the carriage passed than the individual returned the weapon to his breast.' The man then said: 'They may take me if they like; I don't care; I was a fool not to shoot.'[1] The lad had a severe speech impediment which had prevented him from raising the alarm. He also assumed that the potential assailant was merely 'on a frolic'. There was no policeman in sight and by the time the boy had reconsidered, the man had disappeared. Another man, a well-dressed person of about 50, witnessed the incident. He told Pearson that he would have charged the gunman, 'only it would cause so much trouble'. A respectable woman also came forward to report that she had heard the scruffy man tell another wearing a flannel jacket: 'The queen! Why should she be such an expense to the nation? Is it to support her in such grand style that us poor persons have to work so hard?'

The Times thundered:

> We cannot for an instant suppose that this miserable attempt is anything else than the wild and causeless act of another lunatic. It is impossible – or at least incredibly monstrous – that anyone who is master of his own mind can have found motive for such a crime ... Is a young Queen, so lately married, the mother, so lately become so, of our future King, is she never to leave the walls of her own parks and gardens – never to come freely and openly among her people, without the apprehension that the pistol of some fresh assassin may be waiting for her? Is she, with all the spirits and popularity of a young person entering life, to be driven like the King of the French back from the public resorts of her people behind a file of musketeers, as if she were carrying on war with her subjects, plotting against their welfare, or forcibly subverting their liberties?[2]

The royal couple no longer doubted that a second attempt had been made on the queen's life. Albert told his father that Victoria was 'very nervous and unwell'. The queen insisted she did not want to be 'shut up for days', but was convinced that the assailant would try again. She was right.

*   *   *

John Francis, a cabinet-maker aged about 20, was the son of the stage carpenter at Covent Garden Theatre. The father was of 'irreproachable character' and later claimed that his son had always been 'a very steady lad'. But the proprietor of the Caledonian coffee-house painted a different picture, describing Francis as 'idle and reckless but of a good disposition'. The younger Francis would sit for hours over one cup of coffee. In his teens he fell out with his family and failed in an absurd and under-funded attempt to set up as a tobacconist. He was out of work and in 'straitened circumstances'. His original motives for aiming a pistol at the queen remain unclear. The second attempt may come under the category of 'unfinished business'. The following afternoon Francis again mingled with the crowds, most of whom merely wanted a glimpse of their monarch and her dashing husband.

Victoria and Albert were still badly shaken but determined to stick to their routine. That meant their customary constitutional drive. Victoria saw it as a way of drawing out the assassin-at-large. She told Albert's secretary, George Anson, that she would 'much rather run the immediate risk at any time than have the presentiment of danger constantly hovering over her'.[3] The queen chose not to take her lady-in-waiting, Lady Portman, not wishing to risk her life, but did not tell her the reason for leaving her behind. In another carriage were the queen's mother, the Duchess of Kent, and her uncle, Emanuel, Count von Mensdorff-Pouilly. On horseback 60 paces behind was the Dowager Queen Adelaide's sister, Princess Bernhard of Saxe-Weimar-Eisenach. All scanned faces in the crowds, looking for an unkempt assassin. Albert later wrote: 'Our minds were not easy. We looked behind every tree, and I cast my eyes around in search of the rascal's face.' The postillion was instructed to drive faster than usual and the equerries were told to ride as close as possible to the carriage. Only one of them, Colonel Arbuthnot, was at that time aware of the threat. Plainclothes police officers had, however, been deployed along the route.

The ride to and around Hyde Park was uneventful, but Francis acted on the return journey on Constitution Hill, at almost exactly the spot Oxford had chosen two years earlier. He drew his pistol and fired once. Albert speculated that the shot must have gone under the carriage because Francis lowered his hand at the last instance. No one was harmed and this time Francis was promptly seized by a plainclothes officer and a soldier of the Fusilier Guards. *The Times* reported:

> The royal cortege, when the pistol was discharged, was fortunately passing at a rate rather more rapid than usual, and to that circumstance it is supposed Her Majesty in a great measure owes the preservation of her life ... [Francis] was seen by police-constable Tounce to take a deliberate aim. The act had been noticed by Prince Albert who sat on the right hand of his Royal consort, and who immediately rose from his seat. He pointed out the miscreant to one of the outriders.[4]

Francis made no attempt to escape and showed no regret or symptoms of derangement. Victoria returned, much relieved, to the safety of Buckingham Palace. There she shuddered at her 'reckless decision' to take her normal drive.

The culprit's identity was speedily established. Among the spectators attracted by the commotion was a ticket collector at the same theatre in which Francis's father had worked for 20 years. He had been sitting under a tree with his family and identified Francis to police officers. Francis was bundled away to the Home Office for questioning. After an hour he was smuggled out of a wicker door under guard, giving every sign that he fully understood the danger in which he had placed himself. The operation was so adroitly done that few if any of the angry crowd outside noticed his removal. The warrant of committal charged 'John Francis with shooting at our sovereign Lady Victoria the Queen with a pistol loaded with powder and ball'. Some doubts were expressed over whether Francis had actually fired, but a respectable witness, Mr Fitzgerald, told how from barely 10 yards he had heard the discharge. His evidence was supported by Colonel Wylde and two gunsmiths who examined the pistol and deemed that it had been recently fired. The question of whether it had been loaded with shot remained unanswered. Pearson identified Francis's pistol as the same he had seen pulled out the previous day. Francis was remanded that night to Tothillfields Bridewell where he formally gave his name and address – 106 Great Titchfield Street – and his occupation – carpenter. According to the prison governor he answered questions 'in a firm voice and apparently without excitement'. Asked if his father was a scene-shifter at Covent Garden he indignantly replied: 'No! he's a stage carpenter.' When he was asked if he had money to purchase food while in custody he falteringly said he had none. He meekly submitted to being stripped and put into a common bath like all new prisoners.

The next day the Duke of Wellington moved a humble address of congratulations that Victoria had escaped harm. His petition concluded: 'We make our most earnest prayers to Almighty God that He will confer on your Majesty every blessing and that He will continue to watch over and guard a life so justly dear to us.'[5] Meanwhile the carriages of the nobility and gentry again queued outside the private entrance to Buckingham Palace so that their owners could leave their fawning messages. Outside the main gates a crowd of more common people swelled in anticipation that the young queen would show herself. She did not disappoint them. At 4.35 pm the side gates were thrown open and the royal carriage emerged, drawn by four horses and attended by servants in scarlet livery. Sitting in the open barouche were Victoria, Albert and the Duke of Saxe Meiningen. Victoria and Albert both had an instinctive understanding of what would later be called public relations and political spin. The message was clear: she would not run for cover; she would remain at least within sight of her people; she would ensure business as usual. The crowd responded with cheers, hurrahs and the waving of hats and handkerchiefs. Victoria appeared calm and collected, but somewhat flushed, while Albert acknowledged the crowd with smiles and bows of the head. The route along Constitution Hill to Piccadilly was thronged with well-wishers, while hundreds of civilian horse-riders trotted behind the royal party. 'Throughout the whole of the ride Her Majesty was enthusiastically received by all classes of her subjects,' one report enthused. When told that another attempt had seemingly been made on Victoria's life, Edward Oxford told a warder: 'If I had been hanged there would have been no more shooting at the Queen.'

Francis was tried on 17 June 1842. No proof was found that he had intended to kill or harm the queen, and it was found that his pistol had not been loaded. But he did his case no good by feigning indifference to the proceedings and mocking the judges. When those men found him guilty of high treason and condemned him to death, Francis fainted into the arms of his gaoler.[6]

Victoria and Albert's feelings were ambivalent. When the death sentence was announced Victoria confided in her journal that she felt pain at the thought of Francis's impending execution, but felt it was necessary. Albert had previously told his father that Francis 'was not out of his mind, but a thorough scamp ... I hope his trial will be conducted with the greatest strictness.' But Albert in particular felt that when there was no evidence of insanity, such cases of attempted assassination should be treated as ordinary crimes rather than high treason. Up to now there could be only two punishments for any assault, or intended assault, on the monarch: a horrible death or the madhouse. Since insanity was not necessarily the only motive, logic should apply and the crime treated as any other. He and Victoria privately petitioned for Francis's death sentence to be commuted, especially as her life was not actually endangered. The senior law officers, after consulting with the Cabinet, accepted the royal wishes. On 1 July Francis's sentence was commuted to transportation for life with hard labour, which he served in Tasmania before disappearing in 1855. Albert received a 'deeply moving letter of gratitude' from the elder Francis for sparing his son. Victoria and Albert later succeeded in pushing through a new law making any attempt to harm the queen a misdemeanour. Instead of death, the punishment became transportation for seven years or imprisonment, with or without hard labour, for up to three years, plus whipping. Victoria wrote in her journal following Francis's reprieve: 'Of course I am glad.' But she also believed that it might encourage others to follow suit. Two days later a fourth attempt was made on the queen's life.

*   *   *

'Attempt' is probably too strong a word for the farcical events of 3 July 1842. Victoria was blissfully unaware of the incident until later, as were, initially at least, the police on the spot.

The queen, Albert and their uncle, King Leopold, were driving in the usual open carriage to a service at the Chapel Royal when a hunchbacked youth shot at Victoria. The pistol misfired and was torn from his hands by 16-year-old Charles Edward Dassett. The crowd, thinking it a joke with a toy, shouted: 'Give him back his pistol.' Dassett and his brother dragged the assailant to some policemen who merely laughed at them. PC Hearn, who had been in uniform just three months, said it was a hoax, while PC Claxton said: 'Pooh, pooh, it's all nonsense,' and walked away. In the confusion, as the amused crowd pressed around the brothers, the culprit slipped away. Another officer, PC John Partridge, saw the snatched pistol in the hand of an over-excited youth. He promptly arrested Dassett and took him to the Gardiner's Lane station house, followed by a crowd of 3,000 as the rumour of another assassination attempt swept the streets. Dassett was only released after being proclaimed innocent by his uncle and others who had seen the incident.

Young Dassett's testimony to the hastily convened inquiry was a minor masterpiece of understated outrage:

> I was standing in the Mall, about half-way between Buckingham Palace and the milk house gate, when a hump-backed youth elbowed his way to the front. There was at that time a great number of persons collected, and the line of spectators was two or three deep. The second Royal carriage had passed, and the third, which contained Her Majesty, was coming up, when I saw him pull a pistol from the breast-pocket of his coat. I saw him present it at the carriage – I should say at the back of the carriage, because it was

passing quickly at the time. I distinctly heard the click and saw the hammer go down. There was no flash in the pan and no explosion. I immediately seized him by the wrist of the hand that held the pistol. I made the remark to my brother Frederick, who was standing near to me, 'Here's a young gentleman going to have a pop at the Queen.' Seeing two policemen walking along on the opposite side of the Mall, I took the youth over to them. A showed them the pistol. I showed them the pistol, and said to them, 'This lad has been attempting to shoot the Queen.' They laughed at me and Hearn said that it did not amount to a charge. The greatest portion of the populace sided with the hump-backed youth, and cried out, 'Give the pistol back to the boy'; others said, 'Give it to the policeman'; and some said to the lad, 'Put it in your pocket and run away with it.' I still continued my hold of the hump-backed youth, and had proceeded some distance down the Mall, when the pressure from the crowd became so great that I was obliged to let him go, otherwise my arm would have been broken. Soon after this Partridge, seeing me with a pistol in my hand, took me into custody. Just before this I saw the youth go into Green Park ... The policeman took me to the station-house, and told the inspector on duty that he had found me in the park with the pistol in my hand, and trying to excite the mob. I then said to the inspector that I had taken the pistol from a deformed boy, who had attempted to shoot the queen.

His statement was backed by his younger brother, his uncle and several independent witnesses. Dassett was complimented by Sir James Graham, chairman of the inquiry, for the 'meritous manner in which he had acted'. The hapless constables Hearn and Claxton were called in by the examining body, severely reprimanded and suspended from duty.

The search was now on for the real culprit. Six hours after the pistol's discharge the police issued a description based on that given by Dassett and eight other witnesses:

He is about 16 or 18 years of age, five feet six inches high, thin made, short neck, and humped back, walks a little on one side, long sickly pale face, light hair and dressed in a very long coat of a brown or dark colour, which appeared much too large for him, a dark cloth cap, his nose marked with a scar or a black patch, and he has an altogether dirty appearance.

The notice added: 'The police will make every exertion to apprehend this boy, and convey him immediately to this station.' The police rounded up all the hunchbacked people they could find in London. The assailant was found by nightfall after the surgeon Mr Simpson recognised the description of his former errand-boy. The arrest was made by PC Young who spotted him near King's Cross. The description fitted, apart from the cap, which he had switched for a glazed hat of the type used by coachmen. He spoke to the suspect, who gave his name as John Oxman, and escorted him to Phoenix Street station. By coincidence a *Times* reporter was hovering outside. He reported: 'The prisoner seemed exceedingly agitated and flushed ... He was then questioned as to whether or not he had been out and after a good deal of hesitation said he had been out during the morning, and at length admitted that he had taken a walk towards the parks.' The increasingly distressed defendant was moved to another station before being told of the charges against him.[7]

That evening Victoria, on being told of the alleged attack, wrote in her journal: 'I felt sure an attempt would be shortly repeated.' She noted that the suspect was a boy with a 'pitiable expression' but 'certainly not a simpleton'. He was John William Bean, deformed, a chemist's assistant and the son of a gold worker. Bean had recently and repeatedly been heard to say that he greatly admired the conduct of John Francis in attempting to slay the monarch and regretted that he had not been successful. According to one report Bean regarded Francis as 'a brave fellow, and he wished he had been in Francis's place, for he would do for the Queen; that he had a prime air-gun, and a pistol, and he would use them in the same cause'. Such sentiments had been repeatedly reported to local police officers, who regarded them as immature bravado.[8]

Bean's pistol was an old flintlock with a rusty screw and rifle barrel. It contained very little gunpowder and was filled mainly with paper and a piece of a tobacco pipe, making it extremely unlikely that he seriously intended to kill the queen. His trial on 25 August came a month after the new law championed by Victoria and Albert came into effect. It meant he no longer risked death, a punishment which Albert regarded in such circumstances as 'judicial murder'. During the short trial it became clear that Bean was obsessed with both Edward Oxford, whose name he had come close to adopting on his arrest, and John Francis. He was neither mad nor bad, just somewhat naive, embittered and delusional. Bean was sentenced to 18 months' imprisonment.

* * *

A pattern was beginning to emerge. Real or bogus attempts on the life of the monarch were largely the preserve of the mentally damaged or handicapped, the disgruntled loner or the childish attention-seeker. The bids did, however, generally coincide with a slump in Victoria's personal popularity, which soared after each well-publicised incident. In retrospect it seems bizarre that there were so few genuine attempts. Despite the rosy picture painted by the historians of Empire, Victoria was actively despised or loathed by large sections of the populace during several periods of her reign. She was a true conservative who resisted many of the electoral reforms which were reluctantly introduced during her era. Republicanism went hand in hand with many aspects of the Reform movement. She believed that the early Suffragettes needed whipping. Her stubbornness outraged many, not least during her extended mourning. Her links of blood and marriage to the European royal families raised hackles among those suspicious of anything foreign, while many old families despised her bourgeois family values. Her fondness for the new industries, encouraged by Albert, ignored the very real miseries of the Industrial Revolution. She supported the export of Irish cattle and grain to England at the height of the potato famine. And the growth of the Empire during her 64 years on the throne belied the myth of *Pax Britannica* – a succession of bloody wars left their own legacy of bereavement, disability and the poverty which all too often followed. Yet the next so-called attempt, on 19 May 1849, was motivated by a desire merely to frighten the queen.

William Hamilton, a bricklayer's labourer, was born at Adare in Limerick. He lived rent-free in a Pimlico lodging house owned by a former bricklaying boss but was unemployed and had modest debts of £2 10. He was by no means destitute but was embittered by the pomp and privilege surrounding Victoria, especially when compared with the plight of his homeland. He fostered a desire to give Victoria a 'bit of a scare'. He started to fashion a home-made pistol using 'some bits of wood and a tea kettle's spout', but quickly realised it was hopeless and instead borrowed a small pocket pistol with a flintlock from his landlady, which her husband had bought seven years earlier and which was used by their children as a toy. He told her he wanted to clean it and the woman saw no harm, even when one of her children was sent to buy halfpenny-worth of powder.

Hamilton was next seen shortly before 6 pm inside the railings of the park at the lower end of Constitution Hill, within 100 yards of Oxford's earlier bid. Hamilton approached a woman and asked her what she was waiting for. Before she could explain he said: 'Oh, for the queen. Has she passed yet?' Victoria was returning to the palace from her official birthday celebrations. Beside her in the open carriage were three of her children, Alice, Alfred and Helena, while Albert rode ahead. The woman told Hamilton: 'No, she has not come yet, but if you wait a little time you will see her.' She had barely spoken when the outriders of the royal cortège clattered by, and she cried out: 'Here she comes.' Hamilton answered 'All right', and immediately drew the pistol from his breast pocket. He levelled it and fired at the queen's carriage at a slanting angle because it had just passed him. Another spectator felt the heat of the discharge on his cheek, but none heard the whistle of a bullet. Albert was ignorant of the incident and rode on.[9] Victoria, unaware that the gun was not loaded and concerned about her children, suffered 'a great shock'. Three-year-old Princess Helena stated matter-of-factly: 'Man shot, tried to shoot dear Mamma, must be punished.'

On hearing the loud report the crowd turned on Hamilton and came close to dismembering him. *The Times* correspondent wrote:

There were crowds of people collected along the drive, and on the sound of firearms being heard an instantaneous rush was made towards the spot whence it proceeded. One of the park keepers claimed the merit of having arrested the prisoner, but General Wemyss, one of the equerries in waiting and who acted with great judgement during the emergency, declared that Hamilton was first seized by a gentleman dressed in a brown cloth coat. The prisoner offered no resistance, nor did he even attempt to escape, and so bunglingly did he manage that in returning the pistol to the pocket in his flannel jacket that the handle of it stuck fast. The park keeper and constables who took him in charge had some difficulty in rescuing him from the vengeance of the excited crowd which soon formed around him. On his way to the station-house, whither he was conveyed in a cab, he is said to have stated that he was driven to the commission of the act by poverty, and that he had no accomplices.

Hamilton was described as

rather under than above the middle height, is stoutly built and presents no appearance of emaciation. His expression of face and general manner indicate a sullen, sulky disposition, and it was with great reluctance that he gave his name, address and origin. He wore a dirty flannel jacket, old corduroy trousers, and on his head a greasy cap. In his pocket were found the bowl of a pipe, a small quantity of powder, and a few halfpence. There was nothing about him to indicate insanity, and he seemed to have perfect use of his faculties, such as they were.[10]

3. William Hamilton firing at the Queen's carriage, 19 May 1849 (*Illustrated London News*)

4. William Hamilton snatched by an angry crowd (*Illustrated London News*)

Hamilton was charged by Wemyss and left in the station house lock-up. That night the National Anthem was sung in London's theatres, great clubs and the grand mall in St James's Park. Again, the carriages of the nobility queued outside Buckingham Palace as the nation – or at least those with a stake in it – offered thanks.

Hamilton was committed to Newgate, charged with 'firing at Her Majesty with intent to alarm, &'. He was tried on 14 June under the 1842 Act. Victoria told King Leopold: '*This* time it is quite clear that it was a wanton and wicked wish merely to *frighten*, which is very wrong and will be tried and punished as a misdemeanour.' Hamilton pleaded guilty – it was established that his pistol was not loaded – and was sentenced to seven years' transportation.

*   *   *

The following year saw the next attempt, and this time Victoria would suffer more than fright.

At 6.20 pm, on 27 June 1850, Victoria left Cambridge House after visiting her seriously ill uncle, Prince Adolphus, Duke of Cambridge. She stepped into her open carriage accompanied by three of her children, Albert, the Prince of Wales, Alice and Alfred, with an equerry and lady-in-waiting, Viscountess Jocelyn. A crowd had gathered outside the courtyard and as the carriage passed through the gate the spectators surged forward, surrounding it and knocking the equerry backwards. A tall, respectably dressed man stepped out from the throng. He took three paces and sharply struck the queen on the forehead with the brass knob of his small black cane. Her light bonnet was driven in by the force of the 'extremely violent' blow. The crowd rushed on the assailant, whose own face was bloodied by several furious punches. He was rescued by Sergeant James Silver of C Division and taken in custody to Vine Street station house. In a remarkable coincidence Silver was the same officer who had knocked the pistol out of Daniel McNaughton's hand as he attempted to fire a second shot into Edward Drummond. He recalled the latest incident: 'The crowd were very indignant, and it was with difficulty I could preserve him from their violence.'[11]

Victoria was stunned and possibly knocked unconscious for a few moments until roused by the tearful Lady Jocelyn. The queen got shakily to her feet and cried out to the angry crowd: 'I am not hurt.'

The Times reported: 'Her Majesty betrayed no feeling of alarm, and immediately after the occurrence drove up Piccadilly on her return to Buckingham Palace, the spectators cheering her loudly as she passed along – a mark of loyalty and affection which her complete self-preservation enabled her to acknowledge with her usual courtesy and condescension.' She was treated for her injuries – a black eye, severe bruising and a headache. Her doctor declared that it would have been much worse if the brow of her bonnet had not 'absorbed some of the force of the blow'. She carried the faint scar above her eyebrow for some years afterwards. Victoria was indignant. She wrote in her journal: 'For a man to strike *any woman* is most brutal and I, as well as everyone else, think this *far* worse than any attempt to shoot.'

The man questioned at Vine Street was unlike any of the previous assailants. He was 43-year-old Robert Pate, a retired lieutenant who had served for five years with the 10th Hussars, selling his commission in 1846 when the regiment was about to embark for India. His father was a wealthy property owner and corn merchant in Wisbech and had been High Sheriff of Cambridge a few years previously. Pate had been living for over two years in an elegant suite of third-floor apartments in Duke Street. Inquiries found that he was 'of regular habits and paid his bills with great punctuality'. He was 6 foot 2 inches tall, pale-skinned, fair-haired and balding, and dressed as a dandy. He wore a moustache, but 'has not a very military bearing'. Victoria had previously noticed his foppish appearance, whirling the same cane, on several outings to Hyde Park. Pate refused to speak, other than to admit that he had wielded the cane, adding in reference to several witnesses: 'Those men cannot prove whether I struck her head or her bonnet.' He offered no explanation for his action. Large quantities of papers were removed from his lodgings, but they gave no clue as to his motive.

At his trial on 11 July Pate's counsel offered a plea of insanity. Pate walked 'without the slightest discomposure', bowed slightly to the court, and spoke with a firm voice when pleading not guilty. Several witnesses to the attack gave evidence. One of them, Samuel Cowling, said: 'The blow fell partly on the bonnet and partly on Her Majesty's forehead. It was not a violent blow, but it was a hard blow. He did not strike with all his force, but it was a hard blow.'[12]

The defendant continued to offer no reason for what he regarded as a 'light tap'. Much was made of the pathetic nature of his weapon, 'no thicker than a goose-quill', only 26 inches long and weighing less than 3 oz. But Mr Cockburn QC, for Pate, relied heavily on his 'peculiar' state of mind. This he traced back to his army days. From the start Pate had been regarded as an eccentric, but as he discharged all his duties well and was generally well-regarded, no action was taken. In 1842, however, a fellow officer's hound bit his much-loved Newfoundland dog and three favourite horses. After they showed symptoms of rabies, all the animals were put down. He lay down with one of the horses and wept, clearly in some sort of emotional shock. Cockburn told the court: 'He became reserved and morose, and ceased to take any pleasure in his duties.' When he was sent to Dublin with a detachment of troopers, he went absent without leave and returned to his father, claiming that persons in Ireland were conspiring to kill him. He fancied that the regimental cook and mess-man intended to poison him. He told his colonel that bricks and stones in his stomach and bowels were giving him great pain, which no surgeon could relieve. A series of bizarre acts, after he bought himself out of the Hussars, culminated in the assault on the queen. That was 'the act of a madman ... motiveless and objectless', which only someone in the throes of lunacy could commit. Cockburn said that in other cases it could be argued that the culprit was acting out of desperation, or for fame, or even for what provisions prison could offer. None of those applied in Pate's case: 'He was a man fond of solitude, who had shrank from society, and it is not at all likely that he would seek a hideous notoriety by committing such an act. Besides, he was a man of education by his habits and associations from his very childhood, and he must have imbibed notions of loyalty repugnant to any act of violence towards his Sovereign.' Alternative motives connected to poverty or politics were equally absurd as Pate came from a wealthy family and held traditional, conservative views. The only explanation was that the offence was an act of momentary impulse, which Pate was unable to control.

Cockburn called witnesses from Pate's army days. Captain Frith, for a one-time close friend, said:

> I was very intimate with him, and remember hearing of the accident to his horses. His conduct was always that of a gentleman and an officer, and he was very much liked in the regiment. After the accident there was a great change in his manners and conduct. He frequently absented himself from mess and took long solitary walks. He also complained about the mess-man

and cook, and said they had conspired to poison him. I tried to convince him to the contrary, but could not do so. He also told me there were stones and bricks in his stomach. Sometimes he was very reserved and at others very wild and excited without any apparent cause, and I thought his mind was impaired by the loss of his dog and horses.

By coincidence Frith saw his former friend near Hyde Park Corner three hours before the attack. 'His manner was more excited than usual,' he recalled. 'He was in the habit of swinging his arms and stick, and on this day he did so more than usual and everyone turned back to look at him. I have met him at different times and he was always walking in the same remarkable way, but I had never seen him so excited as on this day.'

Pate's former commanding officer, Colonel John Vandeleur, testified: 'From the moment the prisoner joined the regiment I thought there was something strange in his conduct. His hair was cut very short, and I fancied his head had been shaved. He discharged his duties as an officer very well, and as to his being a gentleman there is no doubt about that. He was a person of mild demeanour and very much respected in the regiment.' After the slaughter of his animals Pate was repeatedly on the sick list. 'He was labouring under a delusion,' the colonel added.[13]

After leaving the army and paying off debts Pate had £1,200 left to live a quiet, gentlemanly life. He shunned his family home and when his father John visited him in London he was shocked and alarmed by his son's 'extraordinary' appearance. Pate's valet, Charles Dodman, detailed his extraordinary daily routine. He rose at 7 am and plunged his head into a basin of water. He then had a bath, into which he placed half a pint of whisky and camphor, shouting or singing all the time. He never mixed socially and kept his blinds drawn. Each afternoon, precisely when the chimes of St James's struck quarter past three, he would leave his apartments to take a ride in a cab. He would only pay in shillings turned head upwards, refusing to carry any other coins. His servant would have to provide small change for gate and bridge tolls. For 18 months the route was the same: over Putney Bridge to Putney Heath where he would leave the cab and disappear into the bushes for 10 minutes. His regular cab-driver, Edward Lee, said:

Sometimes he would tell me to gallop, and then he would pull me up and make me go at a foot pace. At Barnes Common he got out again and walked through all the furze bushes, and then went home by Hammersmith Bridge.

I always thought he was not right in the mind, and at winter time I was alarmed. In all weathers, rain, hail or snow, he would get out and walk through the bushes, and he did so when it was quite dark. When he came back to the cab he sometimes looked like he had walked through a pond.

The daily cab rides had ceased two years earlier – presumably because Pate could no longer afford the 9 shilling fare as his wealth dwindled – and he became even more reclusive. In 1949 his sister went to live with him, as his whole family were fearful for his health. She introduced him to a surgeon, James Starton, who had previously seen him in Kensington Gardens and judged him from his appearance to be insane. 'He was throwing his arms and hands around in a most extraordinary manner.' On another occasion Starton suggested that he study the classics for peace of mind, but Pate replied that 'no man in England can teach me anything'. Early in 1850 Pate's father referred him to Dr John Connolly of the Hanwell lunatic asylum, the same physician whose testimony saved Oxford's life. Connolly, however, felt that examination would irritate him and advised no action. After his arrest Connolly did examine him on a number of occasions and declared that he was of unsound mind. He told the court: 'It seemed to me that he has a very small share of mental power, and unfit for all the ordinary duties of life. In conversation he would undoubtedly know the difference between a right and a wrong action, but I should say that he would be subject to sudden impulses of passion.'

Many other witnesses gave similar testimony, Connolly's view had swung previous juries and even Prince Albert believed that Pate was 'manifestly deranged'. But Cockburn himself acknowledged that there was a growing reluctance to allow a royal assailant to 'escape' justice. In his summing up the Attorney General told the jury:

I would not deny that this gentleman has displayed great eccentricity, nor that his conduct on certain occasions has been extraordinary, but these circumstances are very far from justifying acquitting him upon the ground of insanity. Nothing more has been proved than that he was eccentric, and that he was very much affected by the loss of his dog and horses ...

Yet Pate, he argued, had bought himself out of the army, set himself up and was quite capable of managing his own affairs. The presiding judge, Baron Alderson, instructed the jury to be clear that an insanity plea could succeed only if there was evidence of a certain type of delusion which drove a defendant to commit a specific act. If, for example, a person had the delusion that another man was trying to kill him, and took counter-action, that could be a defence. But that did not cover a violent impulse which a defendant knew was wrong.

The jury took 3 hours and 45 minutes to find Pate guilty of assaulting the Queen. Baron Alderson told him:

> It is quite clear that you are a person of very eccentric habits and in some degree differing from other men, and it is probable that it has pleased God to visit you with some mental afflictions for which you are to be pitied. The offence that you have committed, however, is one of a very serious and important character. You have been found guilty of striking a woman which for a soldier is a very shocking thing; but when it is considered that the woman was your sovereign – that it was a lady entitled to the respect of the whole country by her virtues and her exalted position – that which in an ordinary case would be a very serious offence, under these circumstances becomes truly heinous.[14]

He sentenced Pate to seven years' transportation to Australia. The prisoner heard the judge in silence, turned and was taken to gaol without a murmur.

* * *

It was 22 years before Victoria again faced another would-be assassin, but they were not peaceful years.

Victoria bore Albert nine children and they enjoyed family life at Balmoral in Scotland and Osborne House on the Isle of Wight. But she hated pregnancy and childbirth, and complained that surely God could have found a better way. During her difficult pregnancies Albert increasingly took over the day-to-day political duties. He was acutely aware of the social problems which came with the industrialisation of Britain, and was sympathetic to the terrible working and housing conditions of the exploited, especially women and children. He battled with successive governments and dabbled, less successfully, in foreign affairs. According to the historian Joyce Marlow: 'Victoria herself cared greatly for the citizens of her expanding Empire *en masse*, but had little understanding of their mass problems, though she could always be touched by individual need.' The couple's popularity peaked with the opening of the Great Exhibition of 1851 in the new Crystal Palace. Victoria wrote: 'Albert's dearest name is immortalised with this *great* conception, *his* own, and my *own* dear country showed she was *worthy* of it.' By 1861 the stress had made Albert ill, but he continued working, amending despatches to Abraham Lincoln to keep Britain from military intervention in the American Civil War. He died on 14 December, aged 42, from typhus. A distraught Victoria wrote of her 'adored, precious, perfect & great husband, her dear Lord & Master, to whom this nation owed more than it can ever truly know'.

Victoria dressed herself, and her country, in black widow's weeds. Grief-stricken, she went into internal exile either at Balmoral or Osborne House, insisting that Albert's clothes and shaving equipment be laid out every morning as if he were still alive. As the months turned into years the popularity of the unseen queen plummeted. Her grieving, applauded at first, came to appear like self-indulgence. She neglected affairs of state to the consternation of her ministers, and 'To Let' notices were posted on the railings of Buckingham Palace. Her absence was a gift to the growing republican movement. A model family for the nation had become a chilly, remote, irrelevant institution. The queen's own manners in dealing with ministers and diplomats disintegrated. Rumours abounded that her Scottish ghillie, John Brown, was in fact her lover, and scurrilous verses were penned to 'Mrs Brown'. After a decade the queen began to emerge, but she was much changed. She was now stubborn, petulant and fat. William Gladstone told his wife that she weighed 11 stone 8 lb which was 'rather much for her height' – barely 5 feet. She was ruled by her own personal distractions. Even her devoted private secretary confided of 'the long-unchecked habit of self-indulgence that now makes it impossible for her, without some degree of nervous agitation, to give up, even for 10 minutes, the gratification of a single inclination, or even *whim*'. Her relationship with Gladstone was always cool and often hostile when she opposed his Liberal Reform agenda, although his great rival, the Conservative Benjamin Disraeli, enthused her with the romance of Empire. She had more difficulty understanding his concept of One Nation rather than a nation divided into the privileged and the poor. By the early 1870s the example of the Paris Commune resulted in a surge in republican fervour. The biggest shock she suffered after Albert's death came, however, when the Prince of Wales, like his father, was stricken by a near-fatal bout of typhoid fever. He recovered and, on 27 February 1872, she attended a service of thanksgiving at St Paul's Cathedral. She was back in the public eye. Two days later she was rewarded by another attempt on her life.

That day she took an afternoon drive, as she had done so often with Albert. With her in the open landau on this occasion were two of her sons, Princes Arthur and Leopold, her lady-in-waiting Lady Churchill and the kilted John Brown. They drove through Hyde Park and Regent's Park then returned, as always, down Constitution Hill. As a large crowd cheered, Brown stepped down at the palace's garden entrance to lower the steps of the landau to allow Lady Churchill to alight. A person whom Victoria at first thought was a footman appeared at her side. He was, she wrote in her journal that night, 'peering above the carriage door, with an uplifted hand and a strange voice'. A small pistol was spotted in his hand. In the ensuing commotion the 52-year-old queen panicked, clutched Lady Churchill and screamed: 'Save me!' Prince Arthur, aged 21, tried to jump out to reach the man and put himself between the stranger and his mother. But Brown had already seized the assailant and the pistol clattered to the ground. Victoria was badly shaken even though, unlike her sons, she had not seen the firearm.[15] She wrote that night: 'I was trembling very much and a sort of shiver ran through me.' The discovery of the pistol 'filled us with horror' and all 'were as white as sheets'.

The assailant, a 17-year-old Irishman named Arthur O'Connor, was the great-nephew of the great Chartist Leader Arthur O'Connor. He was described as 'weak-minded'. His unloaded pistol had a broken lock, a greasy rag stuffed into the barrel, and was of the type normally sold in curiosity shops. He protested that he did not intend to harm the queen, only to frighten her into signing a petition written on parchment, which he carried along with the pistol, for the release of Fenian prisoners. Undetected and smartly dressed with a black felt hat, O'Connor had scaled 10-foot railings to get into the garden gate courtyard while the police and attendants were busy keeping the entrance clear. A contemporary report read:

> As the Queen was preparing to alight a lad suddenly presented himself at the side of the carriage, holding a paper in one hand and a pistol in the other. He tried at first to attract the attention of Lady Churchill, mistaking her probably for the Queen, by whose side she sat, and then appeared to be about to address himself to Her Majesty, going around the back of the carriage ... The lad was immediately disarmed.[16]

The Times editorialised: 'We do not like to pronounce the lad mad – that word has been and is so much abused – but no sane creature could have embarked in such an enterprise as this miserable fellow conceived, and the sole effect of it is to make us all indignant that the Queen should have been exposed to outrage and insult ... by the prank of a half-witted boy.' The editorial continued: 'The ridiculous weapon with which the youth was armed was taken to the House of Commons, and the most cursory inspection was sufficient to convince everyone of the burlesque character of the attempt. Anything wilder or more irrational cannot well be conceived than this shop-boy's plan of over-awing the Crown ...'[17]

O'Connor was a clerk to the oil and colour manufacturers Livett and Franks and lived with his parents in Houndsditch. He was described as 'a lad of very mean aspect, poorly dressed ... He presented the appearance of an ordinary office lad.' He was searched and taken to King Street police station where he was seen by a doctor. Several MPs who tried to see him in his cell were rebuffed when the boy 'showed much aversion' to any visitor. That night a crowded meeting of working men in Southwark passed a motion registering their deep indignation of the 'dastardly attempt upon the life of the Queen' and offered their earnest prayers for her long-continued life and happiness.

O'Connor stood trial before Baron Cleasby at the Central Criminal Court on 11 April. He first entered a plea of guilty, but his counsel asked that it be withdrawn on the grounds that the prisoner was not in a fit state of mind to plead. The judge ruled that it would be better to try the question of whether or not the prisoner was in sound mind, and empanelled a jury. The prisoner's father, George O'Connor, employed by the Iron Steamboat Company, gave evidence. He said that his uncle, Feargus, had been confined to a lunatic asylum. 'Other members of our family have also been insane,' he continued:

> Arthur has always had bad health since he was six years old, and in 1866 he sustained a severe accident in Chancery Lane and was wounded on the head, and was insensible for some time. After this injury ... he became very irritable. He was always a studious and silent boy, and I never heard of him attending any political meetings, or that he had any political associates. I did not notice anything particular in his demeanour on the day the outrage occurred. I had previously heard that he was very restless at night, and he complained of his head, and in the morning he seemed fatigued and jaded.

Under cross-examination the elder O'Connor said that his son had worked hard – no employer ever complained about him – read Victor Hugo, Dumas, Thackeray and Dickens, and amused his younger siblings with story-telling. He said that he did not want his son to go to a lunatic asylum. Asked if he thought he was insane, George replied: 'Well, I should say, as he's standing there, he is not mad.' The prisoner's mother said that he was a quiet, gentle and studious lad, 'one of the best of boys'. Both parents regretted that his guilty plea had been withdrawn because the Broadmoor madhouse was worse to contemplate for him than a prison.[18]

Dr Tuke gave a long account of his interview with the prisoner. He described him as possessing a badly shaped head with a smaller than usual brain, but 'nevertheless very shrewd and intelligent, and conversed very clearly and rationally upon many subjects'. His conclusion was:

> The prisoner is a weak, delicate boy, both in mind and body, suffering from scrofula and a blow on the head, and that all these compound causes produced what I call exacerbation of insanity at or about the time when this act was committed. I consider it a very dangerous form of reasoning insanity, and I think that he would be very dangerous at large. He may be very much better at the present time, and may be very sorry for what he has done; but I do not think that he has recovered, and he is in my opinion liable at any time to a recurrence of his original condition.[19]

Despite the doctor's evidence, and luckily for O'Connor, the jury swiftly ruled that his mind was sound and that he was competent to plead guilty to an assault on the queen. Judge Cleasby told him that the law allowed him to impose seven years' penal servitude or three years' imprisonment, but he would take into account his youth, his clear regrets and sorrow, and the absurdity of the attempt itself. O'Connor was sentenced to one year's hard labour and 20 strokes of the birch. Victoria protested at the leniency of the judge's 'quirky' sentence, and told Gladstone that she was more afraid for her safety when assailants were not transported. Prince Arthur was presented with a gold pin for his bravery in shielding his mother, while John Brown received public thanks, a gold medal and a £25 annuity.[20]

The Duchess of Sutherland, Her Majesty's Mistress of the Robes, wrote to *The Times*: 'The Queen has always the idea that what has been attempted will be succeeded in some day; that she will be shot.'

Another ten years would go by before there was another incident – and this time the root cause would be poetry.

*   *   *

During that time, as Gladstone and Disraeli continued to play political leapfrog, Victoria enjoyed growing popularity. She had little understanding of or sympathy for the Irish Question which dominated the political agenda – her beloved Albert had been insulted by a Dublin crowd during their one joint visit – but she was fast turning into the grandmother of the nation. This was boom-time for the Empire and Victoria had a talent for plugging into popular patriotism. That royal fervour was one of the themes adopted by an unemployed Scottish clerk, Roderick Maclean, who fancied himself as a poet. He penned a poem dedicated to Queen Victoria and sent it to Buckingham Palace. It was returned by a lady-in-waiting, Lady Elizabeth Biddulph, along with a note stating that the queen 'never accepts manuscript poetry'. Maclean packed a pistol and 14 bullets.

Late afternoon on 2 March 1882 Victoria arrived at Windsor station in the royal train with her youngest daughter, Princess Beatrice, and the Dowager Duchess of Roxburgh. They disembarked and entered a closed carriage – it was a cold day – drawn by two greys waiting in the station yard. As the train began to pull out, she heard the cheering of a group of Eton schoolboys and what she first thought was a sharp burst from the steam engine. She was not alarmed until the ever-faithful John Brown pointed to someone being violently jostled by the crowd and said: 'That man fired at Your Majesty's carriage.' Beatrice 'saw the whole thing, the man take aim, and fire straight into the carriage', but had kept quiet to avoid upsetting her mother. The duchess had also seen what had happened but remained calm because she thought it was a schoolboy prank.[21]

The 'wretchedly-dressed' Maclean had fired once from 30 yards while standing in the road in plain view. The crowd made a general rush at him as, it appeared, he took aim for a second shot, and he was belaboured around the head by at least one schoolboy's umbrella. He was disarmed first by a local photographer, Henry Burnside, who snatched the pistols after the 'very sharp' report. He was then grabbed by Superintendent Hayes of Windsor Police before he could be harmed by the crowd. Hayes later testified: 'Upon hearing the report I sprang at him, caught him by the collar and neck ... I pushed the prisoner back against the rails. The prisoner said, "Don't hurt me; I will go quietly".' With the help of colleagues Hayes managed to haul him past jeering spectators to the local police station. On examining the attacker's medium-sized Colt revolver, Hayes found that two of the chambers were loaded with ball, two with blanks and two were empty. From the sound of the shot it seemed likely that only a blank had been fired. The site of the outrage was searched, but no marks or fragments of shot were found there.[22]

Hayes charged Maclean with shooting at the queen with intent to do her grievous bodily harm. Under initial questioning Maclean, 32 years old, slim and of medium height, said that he was famished with hunger. He had been staying in Windsor for a week after walking from Portsmouth. He was visited in his cell by a doctor, who swiftly pronounced him sane.

The royal routine was not interrupted and that night had a planned dinner at Windsor Castle. A telegram was sent from the queen to the Prince of Wales saying: 'In case exaggerated reports should reach you, I telegraph to say that as I drove from the station here a man shot at the carriage, but fortunately hit no-one. He was instantly arrested. I am not the worse.' The prince read it and went on with his planned visit to the Court Theatre production of *The Manager* to allay public anxiety. He was cheered by the audience. The following day Brown took Maclean's revolver to show the queen, who noted that it 'could be fired off in rapid succession'.

That day a more thorough search found a bullet embedded in the ground of the station yard, 15 yards from the queen's waiting room, and what looked like bullet marks were found on a truck which had been standing nearby. The bullet perfectly fitted the empty chambers in Maclean's pistol.[23]

* * *

None of the queen's previous assailants had a conventional background, but Maclean's was harder than most to establish.

Apart from the poetry rejection note, Maclean carried spare cartridges, a pocket book, a comb and a signed note which he wrote in the station waiting room the afternoon of the attack. It was unaddressed and read:

I should not have done this crime had you, as you should have done, paid the 10s per week instead of offering me the insulting small sum of 6s per week and expecting me to live on it. So you perceive the great good a little money would have done, had you not treated me as a fool, and set me more than ever against the bloated aristocrats, led by that old lady Mrs Vic., who is an accursed robber in all senses.

As news of the incident spread a firm of solicitors in Dover telegrammed the Mayor of Windsor saying that eight years before they defended a man called Roderick Maclean at Maidstone against the charge of attempting to derail a train. Maclean, despite his dishevelled appearance, seemed well educated, claimed to speak several languages, and vigorously cross-examined witnesses himself in the first judicial hearing. He seemed to know something of the law and quibbled on the legal questions of intent when charged.

It emerged that Maclean came from a family of poor but respectable small tradesmen. His father found it impossible to induce him to enter the trade or any other form of business. In 1866, aged 16, he received severe head injuries in a fall, 'which were the origins of the grave mischief from which he subsequently suffered'. In 1874 his parents obtained a medical certificate declaring him to be of unsound mind. He scribbled poetry to pass the time, tramped the country and developed a variety of obsessions. In June 1880 he was sent to the Bath and Somerset lunatic asylum at Weston-super-Mare, where he was declared a lunatic but, after a long spell of probation, was allowed to leave. He wandered from town to town, resting in the wards of workhouses. In February 1881 he was spotted by the Reverend Archibald Maclachlan at Newton Valence, staggering down a lane and apparently in great pain. Maclean fell to the ground as if in an epileptic fit, but then continued on his journey. By extraordinary coincidence the clergyman was a witness to the Windsor Station attack just over a year later. Maclean became convinced that the British public were conspiring to do him injury. He wrote to various authorities saying that unless a law to protect him was enacted, he would take someone's life. In a letter to an artist and family friend of 20 years, Maclean wrote: 'As the English people have continued to annoy me, so antagonistic towards me, making me raving mad, I can hardly contain myself. I mean, if they don't cease wearing blue, I will commit murder. Perhaps by the time you receive me I will be in prison.' His perambulations took him to Southsea, where he bought a revolver from a pawnbroker for 5s 9d, and then to mean lodgings at 24 Victoria Cottages, Windsor.

Maclean was tried for his life at Reading Assizes on 19 April. Unlike most of his predecessors, the authorities charged him with high treason. Victoria's popularity was at a peak, she was a 62-year-old grandmother and public indignation was ferocious. The two counts against him, as dictated to the court by Lord Chief Justice Lord Coleridge, were that he 'traitorously and maliciously made a direct attempt against the life of our said lady the Queen' and that he attempted to 'effect his most evil and wicked treason' by firing at Her Majesty. Such acts, Coleridge maintained, deserved the death penalty.

The Attorney General, prosecuting, told the jury that the crime was clearly premeditated and that the weapon used, although small, could have caused the queen serious injury or death. After hearing evidence from Superintendent Hayes of Maclean's arrest, several eye witnesses were called. One was Roger Errington, a cattle spice manufacturer from Sunderland, who said: 'I saw the Queen enter her carriage. As it moved off, I heard a cheer from a number of Eton boys. I then heard the report of a pistol, and saw a puff of smoke from the barrel of a pistol in the prisoner's hand.' The photographer James Burnside had been standing outside the station gate. He said: 'I heard the report of a pistol and turned around. I saw the figure of a man with a revolver in his hand, and my eye ran along the barrel to the front panel of Her Majesty's carriage, as if I was taking aim myself. I rushed forward and seized the prisoner's right hand with the revolver, pressing it down and taking it from him.' Francis Orchard, a royal servant for 16 years, saw Maclean standing within the barrier. 'He stepped from the crowd and I saw his hand extended in the direction of the carriage, six or seven inches above the panelling,' Orchard said. 'I saw the flash of the pistol, and then the crowd gathered round him, and I saw him no more.' Other witnesses attested to Maclean waiting at Windsor Station for the royal train, and to the discovery of the spent bullet.[24]

Montagu Williams, Maclean's defending counsel, did not contest the facts of the case, nor did he question a single prosecution witness, but concentrated on the defendant's state of mind. Pointing to the man in the dock, he said that 'few who looked upon him had any doubt that insanity had marked him for his own'. Evidence from the medical men who had treated Maclean since his mid-teens proved crucial. Despite close cross-examination from Lord Coleridge, Dr Charles Hitchins insisted that Maclean was 'incapable of moral restraint'. Even more important was the evidence of Henry Manning, medical superintendent of Laverstock asylum, who had examined Maclean twice after his arrest, and had concluded he was insane. In a report to the prisoner's family, read in court, Manning said that Maclean was suffering from three main delusions: the English people were determined to keep him in debased circumstances and to starve him; people mocked him by wearing blue, his own favoured colour for clothing; and he was gifted with supernatural powers expressed by the numerals 4, 14, 44, 440, and so on. Asked by the judge whether Maclean would have known he was doing wrong in attacking the queen, Manning replied: 'I should say that he knew it was wrong, but that he was impelled by a delusion to do it. I have frequently been told by patients who have afterwards recovered that they knew they were doing wrong at the time, but were wholly unable to resist the impulse. I mean an absolutely irresistible moral impulse, as strong as if it was physical.'[25] Six other medical witnesses were called by the defence.

Despite a certain scepticism from the bench displayed in the judge's summing up, the jury was convinced. After deliberating for less than 20 minutes they returned a verdict of 'not guilty, but insane'. Lord Coleridge ordered Maclean to be detained at Her Majesty's pleasure.

Victoria was again displeased, believing Maclean to be guilty and deserving the death penalty. On 23 April her private secretary, Sir Henry Ponsonby, wrote to Gladstone on her behalf suggesting an amendment to the law to make such verdicts more difficult to justify:

> Punishment deters not only sane men but also eccentric men, whose supposed involuntary acts are really produced by a diseased brain capable of being acted upon by external influences. Acknowledging that they would be protected by an acquittal on the grounds of insanity will encourage these men to commit desperate acts, while on the other hand a certainty that they will not escape punishment will terrify them into a peaceful attitude towards others.

But Victoria's anger quickly dissipated. In a letter to her eldest daughter, Princess Victoria, she wrote that she had been gladdened by 200 telegrams condemning the assassination attempt. 'The enthusiasm, loyalty, sympathy and affection shown to me is not to be described,'

she said, adding: 'It is worth being shot at – to see how much one
is loved.'

William McGonagall, a poet renowned for all the wrong reasons
and therefore possibly envied by Maclean, penned a new masterpiece.
It read, in part:

> God prosper long our noble Queen,
> And long may she reign!
> Maclean he tried to shoot her,
> But it was all in vain.
>
> For God He turned the ball aside
> Maclean aimed at her head;
> And he felt very angry
> Because he didn't shoot her dead.
>
> Maclean must be a madman,
> Which is obvious to be seen,
> Or else he wouldn't have tried to shoot,
> Our most beloved Queen.[26]

*   *   *

Lavish plans were laid to celebrate the queen's Golden Jubilee in 1887.
The faithful John Brown had died five years earlier and his place in her
affections had been taken by an Indian personal servant, known as the
Munshi. Victoria, proud of her Eastern Empire, immersed herself in all
things Indian as the pageantry was planned. Some of her civil servants
were, however, more concerned with all things Irish.

For almost two decades Irish-American groups had mounted an
intermittent terrorist campaign, targeting the House of Commons,
the Home Office and Scotland Yard. The most infamous raid cost
the lives of six people in Clerkenwell. Few were surprised when, a
few days before the Jubilee celebrations, the police revealed a plot to
blow up the queen, her family and most of the Cabinet at the event.
The police said it had been hatched in New York by the secret society
known as the Fenian Brotherhood, or Clan na Gael. It was immediately
dubbed the Jubilee Plot. Two Americans were arrested six months later
and sentenced to long terms of imprisonment. *The Times* published

evidence that the charismatic Irish Home Ruler Charles Stewart Parnell had condoned the planned outrage. The foul plot was nailed and the terrorist campaign neutered. Lord Salisbury's government was well satisfied: their rough counter-terrorism methods were vindicated, the republican movement at Westminster largely silenced and the political chances of Parnell badly undermined.

In fact, the Jubilee Plot was a sham orchestrated by the British secret services in one of their first recorded 'black ops'. The full story was only published in 2002 in Christy Campbell's book *Fenian Fire*. He revealed how British intelligence officers in Dublin, London and New York infiltrated the Brotherhood and encouraged violent attacks on British targets. The Foreign Office paid known republican sympathisers to lead the often bloody raids. The leader of the Jubilee Plot, Francis Millen, was one of those. His appointment had been personally sanctioned by Lord Salisbury. Millen had been recruited in Mexico City with the code name XXX. When the supposed plot was uncovered he was allowed to escape to New York, despite a massive police sweep publicly intended to net him.

The evidence published in *The Times* was later exposed as a forgery. Allies of Parnell offered Millen the massive sum of £10,000 to return to Britain and testify to the government's role in the affair. He agreed, but was found dead in New York.[27]

The murky plot provides a bizarre postscript to Victoria's brushes with would-be assassins. Her Diamond Jubilee in 1897 revelled in the British Empire at its zenith. The queen was now old and slow, although she continued to deal with state papers daily until the end of 1900. On 13 January 1901 she died peacefully at Osborne House, surrounded by her children and grandchildren.

8
The Wounding of the Duke of Edinburgh

'... and perished miserably'

Queen Victoria's fourth child, Alfred, Duke of Edinburgh, was enjoying the hospitality of a seaman's charity in New South Wales when he was shot in the back by a Fenian sympathiser. In the ensuing mêlée the would-be assassin aimed another shot as the prince lay on the ground. He missed, but hit another gentleman in the foot. They, and the assailant, became the latest casualties in the underground war for the freedom of Ireland.

The potentially lethal incident on 12 March 1868 showed that Britain's rulers could not escape the wave of political violence seen across much of the developing world.

*　　*　　*

Ireland had been drenched in blood since Henry II of England claimed sovereignty in the twelfth century. The wars of suppression and revolt cost hundreds of thousands of lives, leaving a dispossessed and rebellious peasantry, emotional trauma and simmering political discontent. The Irish were dehumanised in English eyes and in 1602 Lord Mountjoy, Lord Deputy of Ireland, likened the country to 'an overgrown garden that must be purged of weeds before it can be planted with good herbs'. In countless campaigns no prisoners were taken. During the English Civil War and its Puritan aftermath it is estimated that 618,000 Irish people died out of a population of 1.5 million, largely due to the famines caused by the scorched earth policies of occupying armies.

As the eighteenth century drew to a close the Society of United Irishmen was founded by Theobald Wolf Tone, an Irish patriot inspired by the American and French Revolutions. Its aim was to bring together Protestant and Catholic Irishmen of all classes in a crusade to sever the suffocating ties with England. In 1798 the United Irishmen, hoping for support from France, at the time England's enemy, rose up. The vicious war which ensued saw both Protestant and Catholics massacred, brief victories by some insurgents and cruel retribution. The French arrived too late and in too small numbers. The war, the costliest in Ireland for over a century, left 30,000 dead. A direct outcome was the 1800 Act of Union, which abolished the Irish Parliament and made Ireland an integral part of the United Kingdom rather than a puppet state exploited by English and Anglo-Irish landlords. The historian Lawrence James writes: 'Ireland was integrated into Britain as a wartime emergency measure, literally at gunpoint. It was an arrangement that satisfied neither the Irish nor the rest of Britain, which had to live with a dissatisfied and sullen partner.'[1]

Some penal laws were reformed, and in 1829 Daniel O'Connell secured entry to the Westminster Parliament for Catholics. He concentrated his efforts on a campaign to repeal, by constitutional means, the Act of Union and restore nationhood to Ireland once more. He failed largely because most Catholic supporters were too poor to stand as MPs under the stringent property qualifications. The vast majority of Ireland's growing population – over 8 million by 1841 – were landless tenants with few political rights and no social status, who scratched a living by cultivating potatoes on miserable scraps of land. The potato crop failed twice between 1846 and 1848, and over a million people starved to death. Millions more emigrated to America, Canada and Australia, halving Ireland's population. Absentee landlords, who thought everything of profits and little of their tenants, took the lion's share of the blame for the disaster, though not always fairly. But the sense of Irish nationhood remained strong, among those who stayed and those who left alike. The Young Ireland Movement, which included prominent Protestants, aimed to build on the ideals of the United Irishmen, and in 1848 attempted a revolution. It was a fiasco, easily put down with few casualties. However, in 1856 veterans of that revolt, many of whom had fled to America, founded the Fenians, also known as the Irish Republican Brotherhood. This was a secret society, bound by bloodcurdling oaths, and its aim was to achieve independence by armed revolution.

A short-lived invasion of Canada by Irish Brigade veterans of the American Civil War in 1866 and another attempted rising in Ireland in 1867 were botched embarrassments, and the Fenians went underground. Many were more comfortable there. The tradition of secret societies was buried deep in the peaty earth of Ireland and the psyche of its people. It was positively encouraged by the British Government's prosecution of seditious speaking, assembly and writing, and the suspension of habeas corpus following the 1848 uprising.[2] Fenians infiltrated England, and English police officers bought informers. It became a classic game of cat and mouse. Shortly after the failure of the Irish rising, which included an incredible plot to capture Chester Castle, steal the arms inside and dash to the ferry ports, news of a dramatic escape shocked the authorities and dazzled some sections of the populace. Two Fenian prisoners, Kelly and Deasy, were being taken from a Manchester court to the borough gaol when their barred van was surrounded by armed comrades. The van was locked from the inside and PC Brett who was accompanying the prisoners refused to give in. A shot was fired at the keyhole to smash the lock, and the bullet passed through killing Brett. Three of the assailants were executed after the prime minister, Lord Derby, rejected all appeals for mercy. He insisted that it was not a political offence, but simply murder, 'commonplace in everything save its peculiar atrocity'. They met their death with 'courage and composure', according to contemporary reports. Their deaths did not discourage Fenianism, but gave it a new impetus.[3]

On 12 December 1867 an attempt to free two Fenians held in the Clerkenwell House of Detention also ended in tragedy. A barrel of gunpowder hidden in a barrow was pushed against the gaol's perimeter wall, under the noses of detectives who had been warned of the rescue bid. The aim was to breach the wall of the exercise yard, but too much powder was used and 60 yards of the wall were blown in, while a terrace of small houses across the street were shattered. Six civilians died immediately, and another six succumbed later from horrendous wounds. A further 120 were injured. Some reports suggest that the blast, which could be heard and felt for miles, caused 40 premature

births in the district, with around half of the newborns dying.[4] Five
men and a woman were put on trial for the crime, but only one was
convicted and the evidence against him was tainted by the use of an
informer with much to gain from his testimony.

The cycle of outrage and execution aroused strong feelings not just
in Ireland and Britain, but also in Irish-settled outposts in America
and Australia. Not all those who were shocked and angered were
sworn Fenians. Among their sympathisers in Australia was Henry
James O'Farrell of Sydney, New South Wales. A Nationalist from
boyhood, he had trained to become a priest but turned to frontier
speculation. In those endeavours he failed, losing most of his savings
and growing increasingly embittered. He took to drinking and railing
against Britain as each boat brought mail and newspapers recounting
British persecution in his homeland. Quite when he decided to take
the assassin's way was never established. But early in 1868 he wrote
to Alexander Sullivan, editor of the Dublin nationalist publication *The
Nation*, informing him of his intention to shoot the Duke of Edinburgh
who was on a tour of Australia. O'Farrell said that he knew the act
would cost him his life – probably on the spot – but he felt justified
in taking extreme measures which would strike at the royal heart of
Britain. Sullivan though was in prison for alleged sedition, and the letter
was opened by his brother. He burnt it, knowing that if the writer was
serious, the crime would have been committed while the letter was in
transit on the high seas.

A few days later the Sullivans heard that the attempt had been made.
The prince was enjoying a picnic with fund-raisers for the Sailors'
Home at Clontarf, near Port Jackson, when he was shot. The Governor,
Sir William Manning, sprang at the attacker, who turned and levelled
his pistol at him. Manning stooped to avoid the shot and fell off
balance. O'Farrell pulled the trigger but the charge failed to detonate.
As Manning struggled to his feet O'Farrell took aim again but was
caught from behind by a coachbuilder, Vial, who pinioned his arms to
his side. O'Farrell managed to free his gun hand and took aim over his
shoulder at the Duke of Edinburgh who was lying prone on the ground.
A second shot was fired but went wide, hitting the foot of a bystander,
George Thorne.[5] The *Sydney Morning Herald* reported:

> The scene which followed almost defies description. No sooner had Mr Vial
> grasped the man who had fired the shots than several other gentlemen also

seized him, and had it not been for the closing in around them of the police and other persons, they would speedily have placed him beyond the reach of the law courts. The people shouted, 'Lynch him! Hang him! String him up!' and so on; and there was a general rush to get at him. Unfortunately for Mr Vial, some of the people mistook him for the Prince's dastardly assailant, and for a few seconds he was treated unmercifully. In the meantime the police, headed by Superintendent Orridge, got hold of the assassin, and they had the greatest difficulty in preventing the infuriated people from tearing him limb from limb.[6]

Prince Alfred was taken to his ship where the ball was easily removed two days later by naval surgeons. A week later he set sail for home. Thorne also made a speedy recovery.

The police struggled to get O'Farrell on board a ship in the harbour where it was assumed he would be relatively safe. By the time he reached the wharf all his clothing above the waist had been torn off, his eyes, face and body were bruised and bloody. He was unconscious when he was dragged aboard the *Paterson*. A number of sailors had a rope to hand and were ready to lynch him, but his life was saved by an officer. The assassination attempt inspired horror and consternation across the colony, tempered by prayers and thanksgivings offered in all the churches.[7] It also unleashed a witch-hunt.

After O'Farrell's initial examination the story spread that the prince had been the target of a Fenian conspiracy. O'Farrell had, it was claimed, been selected by drawing lots to execute the queen's son, and he had been sent from Ireland specifically for the task. The bid was intended to be made as soon as the royal visitor landed, but no opportunity had been found without endangering co-conspirators. The New South Wales Government offered a £1,000 reward for the capture of each accomplice. None was found and on 26 March O'Farrell was brought to trial before a special sitting of the Central Criminal Court at Darlinghurst.

The trial was adjourned for a few days due to the absence of any defence witnesses. O'Farrell was then returned to court to be found guilty of treason. He declined to give any reason for sparing his life and was executed in Darlinghurst gaol on 21 April.[8]

O'Farrell had left a written statement with the express instructions it should not be read until after his death. It was perused within hours of the trap door opening. In it O'Farrell denied that any other persons or organisations were involved. He also denied any connection with the Fenians, other than his sympathy with their aims and that he had contributed cash donations to their cause. T. D. Sullivan agreed:

> O'Farrell in this matter had neither confidants nor accomplices. Apparently he was no Fenian, but he was a Nationalist from his boyhood; and the accounts of prosecutions, imprisonments and executions, coming from home by every mail, weighed upon his mind. For some time previously he had not seemed to be 'all right'; he had lost money in speculation, he was falling into intemperate habits, and there had always been an eccentric strain in his character. He was well educated, having studied for some years with a view to taking Holy Orders, but he did not persevere in that intention. He took a wrong turn, and perished miserably.[9]

The Protestant population of New South Wales did not believe that, however. Life was made unpleasant for anyone known to have Irish Nationalist sympathies, and the search continued for alleged plotters. In Sydney charitable organisations collecting for the relief of the distressed Irish poor were listed as potential Fenian terrorists. O'Sullivan's younger brother, Richard, editor and part-proprietor of the *Sydney Freeman's Journal*, was threatened with violence, and friends acted as personal bodyguards when he walked through the city or took a cab home. In December 1868 the Legislative Assembly voted to set up an inquiry into the alleged existence of a 'conspiracy for purposes of treason and assassination'. The select committee reported in February 1869 that O'Farrell had acted alone and that there was no evidence of Fenians even meeting in the area, never mind taking action. Nor was there any evidence that Fenians abroad were plotting action in New South Wales. Nevertheless, in just seven hours the colony's Government passed a Coercion Act which shut down 'treasonable and seditious publications'. Faced with unacceptable restraints on his editorial policy, Richard O'Sullivan resigned as editor and emigrated to San Francisco, where he edited a weekly Irish organ, *The Monitor*. He died in 1880.

*   *   *

As O'Farrell was awaiting his fate a successful assassination rocked the Irish community on the other side of the world.

Thomas D'Arcy McGee was an Irish patriot, a renowned poet and a Canadian statesman who had once embraced Fenianism and who had enthusiastically supported the Young Ireland insurrection of 1848. But after his enforced emigration to Canada he modified his views, saw constitutional means as the way forward and threw himself into the advancement of his adopted country. For many Fenians, especially after the failed invasion of Canada, this was treason. He was not shy about expressing his change of heart. In one discourse he wrote: 'I am not at all ashamed of Young Ireland – why should I be? Politically we were a pack of fools, but we were honest in our folly.' About the American Fenians he said: 'They have deluded each other, and many of them are ready to betray each other ... for as sure as filth produces vermin it is the very nature of conspiracies such as this to breed informers and approvers.' He described them as 'Punch and Judy Jacobins', whose entire plan of action was to get their heads broken and then squeal for a doctor. He claimed that there was a class of demagogues who had done great mischief to the reputation of Irishmen. Such men, he said, were drink-sellers, lawyers and editors, always ready to give to the Church but rarely seen in church, never at a loss to propose a resolution or to savage the English.

Such outspoken comments from a one-time supporter was courting Fenian retribution. In April 1868 43-year-old McGee, who represented Montreal in the Ottawa legislature, left Parliament House after taking part in an adjournment debate. He was followed home by an Irish immigrant named Whelan, who shot him in the head as he was inserting his latchkey into the hall door. The bullet passed through his skull and lodged in a door panel. Whelan, who insisted he was acting alone, was tried, convicted and executed. A shocked Irish editor wrote: 'It was a local crime, planned and carried out by a small group of persons – possibly it was the design and work of one man.'

The murder gave rise to a heated debate, then and later, about whether the Fenians practised assassination against their own. In any underground organisation informers tend to be treated harshly, but some advocates insisted that murder was not common. John O'Leary, who was imprisoned from 1865 to 1874 then exiled until 1885 and who was long associated with Fenianism, wrote:

I cannot of course deny that during the long period of Fenianism there were some few cases of assassination, and that some few Fenians held (and hold) that the slaying of informers is justifiable; but I can most positively assert that up to the time of my arrest there was no case of assassination, nor, as far as I know, any project of assassination. At no time in my life have I held assassination of any kind justifiable, not even in its old Greek shape of tyrannicide, although many eminent men have held this last sort of killing no murder.

James Stephens, the founder of the Fenians, who was in exile until 1891, was opposed to the death penalty for either desertion or treachery among his followers. He personally forbade the assassination of Alexander Sullivan when that outspoken editor was at loggerheads with the Fenians. But Richard Piggott, writing in the 1880s, was of the opinion: 'That murders were committed by Fenians there is no doubt. At the same time I think there is all but positive certainty that none of them were sanctioned by the leaders of the movement.' One informer, Corydon, asserted that the Fenians had an assassination squad for dealing with men such as himself and over-zealous police detectives. Although this was never conclusively proved, one of the men he betrayed admitted as much. John Devoy wrote from New York in 1875:

> There were men killed for treason in the period referred to and there were propositions made to kill other men who were not killed; but those who suffered death were members of the Irish Republican Brotherhood who, beyond all reasonable doubt, gave information to the Government; and there was never a charge of treachery made, or a proposition to punish treachery, that was not fully known to certain men in the organisation.

9
The Phoenix Park Murders

'... not at the friendly stranger'

Lord Frederick Cavendish succeeded the draconian William Forster as secretary to the Lord Lieutenant of Ireland. His task, under the Liberal prime minister William Ewart Gladstone was to reverse years of repression and offer reforms to the long-oppressed people of Ireland. He had no great confidence in his abilities, telling a fellow peer: 'I had no tact, no real knowledge of Ireland, no powers of speaking.'[1] Gladstone thought otherwise. Cavendish arrived in Dublin in the company of the equally new Viceroy, Earl Spencer, on Saturday, 6 May 1882, made his official entrance into the city and took his oath at Dublin Castle. He began work immediately on the official papers. At around 7 pm he left the Vice-Regal Lodge for his own residence in the company of the Permanent Under-Secretary, Thomas Henry Burke, and together they walked through Phoenix Park.

A well-dressed man stood up in a carriage and waved a handkerchief. It was the signal for at least four assassins to strike. They surrounded Cavendish and Burke and stabbed them repeatedly with long surgeon's knives as one tried to shield the other. A boy named Jacob was bird-nesting some distance away and saw a group of men who appeared to be wrestling. He thought they were 'roughs' and did not pay them much attention until two of the men fell to the ground and the others jumped into a cab and drove off. The lad had witnessed the nineteenth century's first genuine political assassination – rather than those driven by madness – of a major British politician.

* * *

5. Front page of the *Illustrated London News* after the Phoenix Park Murders

After Fenian plots – real, botched or imagined – the focus had shifted to political activity in pursuit of land reform on behalf of the remaining tenant farmers and, ultimately, Home Rule. The campaign for land reform was begun in earnest by the former Fenian Michael Davitt, who founded the Land League in 1879. It swiftly turned into a mass movement and was strongly supported at Westminster by Irish MPs, of whom the undisputed leader was Charles Stewart Parnell. A spate of reprisals against landlords and rent collectors persuaded the Protestant Establishment that the Land League was merely a front for the Fenians. But Parnell, once elected president of the League, deployed his considerable organisational skills. The Catholic Church, at first suspicious of his motive, became his active ally. Public opinion swung towards Parnell as evictions increased, and the Government could not ignore the clamour for reform. William Edward Forster was made Chief Secretary for Ireland, and in 1880 the Government introduced a bill to offer compensation to evicted tenants. Its rejection in the House of Lords stoked the embers of land agitation. League operations spread and Parnell made what the authorities considered a highly inflammatory speech:

> When a man takes a farm from which another has been evicted, you must shun him on the roadside when you meet him, you must shun him in the streets of the town, you must shun him at the shop-counter, you must shun him in the fair and in the market-place, and even in the house of worship, by leaving him severely alone, by putting him into a moral Coventry, by isolating him from the rest of his kind as if he was a leper of old – you must show him your detestation of the crime he has committed; and you may depend on it, if the population of a county of Ireland carry out this doctrine, that there will be no man so full of avarice, so lost to shame, as to dare the public opinion of all right-thinking men within the county, and to transgress your unwritten code of laws.[2]

The Irish followed his advice and stepped up more extreme forms of intimidation. One of the first targets was the estate agent Captain Charles Boycott, and his name was adopted for an effective form of protest. The landed and their agents were attacked, riots erupted and throughout the autumn of 1880 the government of Ireland was paralysed. (The total number of agrarian crimes rose from 301 in 1878 to 863 in 1879, to 2,590 in 1880, and to 4,439 in 1881.) Parnell labelled the Irish Chief Secretary 'Buckshot' Forster because he had authorised the use of buckshot by soldiers suppressing riots.

In October the Government struck back, arresting Parnell's secretary, T. M. Healy, on the charge of justifying murder. The following month Parnell and four other Land Leaguers were arrested, but at their trial in early January 1881 the jury could not reach a verdict and the defendants walked free. Forster demanded a rigorous new bill to protect persons and property in the tumultuous land under his charge. That bill suspended habeas corpus, while another gave the police wide powers to search for arms. Parnell and his followers used every procedural device to block both bills. 'The Government wants war, and they shall have it,' he said. The new Coercion Acts were pushed through after a marathon 42-hour debate. Parnell and 26 followers at Westminster were suspended for the rest of the day's sitting during one especially heated parliamentary debate. Gladstone aimed to balance the draconian legislation with a bill to recognise tenants' rights and to set up a tribunal to fix fair rents, but this was not enough to halt the civil unrest sweeping across Ireland. Furthermore, Parnell's partial support for the new Land Act caused dissent within the Land League ranks and enraged the revolutionary wing of the movement. His efforts to persuade them that he had not sold out ironically enraged Gladstone and his ministers, including Forster. In October Parnell was arrested at Morrison's Hotel, Dublin and charged with inciting others to intimidate. Within days several of his colleagues were also rounded up, while others fled overseas. The Land League was declared an illegal organisation, and more steps were taken to suppress dissent.

Pressure grew on Gladstone to reach an accommodation with Parnell, and a deal was struck using the Irish MP Captain O'Shea as the go-between. The pacts that ensued, known as the Kilmainham Treaty, included steps to write off rent arrears, improve justice and wind up secret societies. Parnell and his colleagues were released on 2 May 1882. Forster, complaining bitterly at what he saw as the Government's appeasement of law-breakers, resigned, as did the Lord Lieutenant, Earl Cowper. They were succeeded by Lord Frederick Cavendish and Earl Spencer.

Cavendish was born at Eastbourne on 30 November 1836, the second son of the seventh Duke of Devonshire. He graduated from Trinity College, Cambridge, in 1858 and served as a cornet in the

Duke of Lancashire's yeoman cavalry. From 1859 to 1864 he was private secretary to Lord Granville, during which time he travelled in the United States and Spain. In 1865 he became Liberal MP for the northern division of Yorkshire's West Riding. After serving as Gladstone's private secretary, he became a junior Lord of the Treasury

THE ILLUSTRATED LONDON NEWS, MAY 13, 1882.—453

THE LATE MR. T. H. BURKE, UNDER-SECRETARY FOR IRELAND,
MURDERED ON SATURDAY LAST.

6. The Irish Under-Secretary, T. H. Burke, murdered with Lord Cavendish (*Illustrated London News*)

and was Financial Secretary from April 1880. He remained in that post as he took up the Irish appointment. The *Annual Register* described him as 'an industrious administrator who seldom spoke in the House except on subjects of which he had official cognisance or special experience, but he took an interest in educational questions, and on every side he was highly esteemed for his urbanity and devotion to business'.

Burke's origins were less elevated but he had fine connections. He was born in Knocknagur, Galway, on 29 May 1829. His mother was the sister of Cardinal Wiseman and was also related to the descendants of Sir Ulick Burke of Glinsk, on whom a baronetcy had been conferred by Charles I. After an eclectic education in Belgium, Germany and Trinity College, Dublin, Burke became a supernumerary clerk at Dublin Castle in 1847 thanks to the patronage of the Irish Under-Secretary, Sir Thomas Redington. His talents were swiftly recognised, and he was soon placed on the permanent civil service list. He served in the various departments of the Chief Secretary's office, including a stint in the London office, and was permanent secretary to three Chief Secretaries, including Sir Robert Peel. In May 1869 he was appointed Under-Secretary for Ireland, a post he filled diligently until his death. He was a Catholic, a bachelor and heir-presumptive to his cousin, Sir John Lionel Burke.

Rumours circulated for some time that Burke wished to resign, but he could not get a pension without a special arrangement with the Treasury. He spent most of his time in Dublin Castle, working until late seven days a week and taking no holidays. A later report said: 'He did not fear danger, knowing that he was but a piece of official machinery to perform the work cut out for him and having no voice in the councils of the Government and no hand in the guidance of their policy.'[3] He stuck to well-known routines, confident in the belief that no party would bear him animosity. He was deluding himself. Burke's name was attached to numerous detested proclamations. Strangers were his enemies.

Burke and Cavendish chatted amiably that May evening as they entered Phoenix Park and strolled in the fading light. It is unlikely that they noticed the gang until they were upon them. The rest was savage butchery as four men struck them repeatedly until both Burke and Cavendish were lying on the ground, gasping for breath through bubbles of blood. One attacker wiped his weapon on the grass. The assassins sped away in a cab drawn by a chestnut horse with a peculiar gait, leaving no trace but the gory bodies behind them. A number of people were within a few hundred yards of the incident, but none heard or saw the attack, apart from the young bird-nester and a Royal Dragoons officer, Captain Greatrex. Both believed they were watching drunken horseplay. The officer was close to the assailants when they tumbled into the getaway vehicle. Greatrex remarked casually to them, 'That was rough work', to which one of them replied, 'Rough, indeed.' Two men riding tricycles found Lord Cavendish lying across the main carriageway, with Burke a few feet away on the pathway. Both were in large pools of blood. Cavendish twitched in his death throes. Burke gave one last breath as blood oozed from his neck. The cyclists, now joined by Greatrex, called the police who carried the bodies to Steven's Hospital.[4] Burke was recognised at once, while Cavendish, newly arrived in the city, was identified by a medallion and telegrams in his pockets. Robbery was swiftly ruled out as there was a £5 note and several sovereigns in Cavendish's pockets. An initial examination found that Cavendish had been stabbed several times in the chest, with one deep wound penetrating his right lung. Burke had been stabbed several times around the heart, and his throat was slashed almost completely across. His clothes were badly torn and wounds to his hands suggested he had put up a fierce defensive struggle.

'The suddenness and magnitude of the crime for a moment seemed to paralyse all efforts to track its perpetrators,' according to one contemporary report. 'It was many hours before the news of the catastrophe reached the Cabinet – some time, indeed, before the identity of the victims was established in Dublin – and it was then too late to expect to catch the murderers red-handed.'[5]

The public heard nothing until the following day, but by the end of that Sunday the news had spread across the nation. In Dublin that night tar-barrels burned and the authorities feared a riot. The bells of St Patrick's Cathedral tolled a single muffled chime. A dispatch sent from the city before midnight read:

> The excitement produced by the news of the Phoenix Park tragedy has not been equalled here in the lifetime of the present generation. At first the news was received with a feeling of incredulity, succeeded, however, by one of horror, shame, and indignation among every class in the community to

the very humblest. The feeling, in fact, is one of immense and universal execration at the deed.

In London news of the murders caused consternation in gentlemen's clubs and the roughest ale-houses, in theatres and churches alike. Newspaper offices were besieged by crowds anxious to get their hands on the latest editions. The capital's Irish population quickly announced their abomination of the crime, and their strongly worded declarations did much to prevent a backlash. So too did prayers offered to the families of the victims in Roman Catholic churches. Flags were flown at half-mast above municipal buildings. Messages of grief and horror were sent by public meetings in Manchester, Liverpool, Eastbourne and Glasgow. Similar messages came from Londonderry, Dungarvan, Limerick, Waterford, Belfast, Newry and other parts of Ireland. The impact of the slayings was truly sensational.[6]

A Cabinet council was hastily convened as some clamoured for vengeance through repressive measures. *The Times* reported speculation that the assassins were not members of any political organisation in Ireland, but that the crime was an 'exotic' one. The editorial cautioned against repression.[7] But it swiftly became clear that the Kilmainham Treaty, designed to address legitimate grievances and offer goodwill to the Irish poor, had died with Cavendish and Burke. That first Cabinet session, however, was more concerned with the ministerial reshuffle required by Cavendish's murder. The Admiralty Secretary, G. O. Trevelyan, accepted the Irish Secretaryship, while Colonial Office minister L. H. Courtney was appointed Financial Secretary. The knock-on effect saw eight further appointments.[8]

On the morning of that murderous day Parnell, newly released from gaol, went to Portland Prison to pick up fellow Land League detainee Michael Davitt and talked of the new 'treaty' with the Government. On hearing the news of the killings they held a hurried meeting with John Dillon in Westminster Palace Hotel. The three men agreed to issue a statement to the Irish people denouncing the crime. The address was speedily written, printed and posted on the Sunday. Its closing passage said:

> We appeal to you to show by every manner of expression that almost universal feeling of horror which this assassination has excited. No people feels so intense a detestation of its atrocity, or as deep a sympathy for those whose hearts must be seared by it, as the nation upon whose prospects

and reviving hopes it may entail consequences more ruinous than have fallen to the lot of unhappy Ireland during the present generation. We feel that no act has ever been perpetrated in our country during the exciting struggle for social and political rights, of the past 50 years, that has so stained the name of hospitable Ireland as this cowardly and unprovoked assassination of a friendly stranger, and that until the murderers of Lord Frederick Cavendish and Mr Burke are brought to justice, this stain will sully our country's name.[9]

Parliament met briefly the following day so that party leaders could pay tribute. Gladstone bore generous testimony to the value of both Cavendish and Burke, saying that the loss of the civil servant and of the minister was as irreparable to the country as it was to their friends and families. Parnell said that he spoke for himself, his party and for every true Irishman in expressing his horror at the crime. He knew that the Government would take steps to repress such outrages, but said that ministers should understand that the murderers were men who absolutely detested the cause of Home Rule. In fact, he insisted, the crime had been committed to discredit the cause and to act as a deadly blow against his party and its so far publicly unspecified pact with the Government.

In Dublin the coroner addressed 17 jurors: 'Words are inadequate to express the horror, indignation and shame with which I feel overwhelmed in proceeding to discharge one of my duties on this day of rest.' He praised Burke's 'courteous, gentle and unassuming manner' and said that the murders of such 'a most inoffensive and unobtrusive official', together with a young Chief Secretary who had been just six hours in the country, would bring disgrace on the Irish nation. *The Times* reported the post-mortem held in the Lord Secretary's Lodge:

The scene was one indescribably horrible. On a table near the window nearest the conservatory lay the body of poor Mr Burke, stark and ghastly, his finely-chiselled face, which ever had the stamp of dignity upon it, scarcely recognisable through the blood which filled his mouth, while his neck and chest bore gashes which looked as if inflicted by a butcher's knife. On a table at the other end of this room was stretched the body of Lord Frederick Cavendish, presenting an appalling spectacle, and the room, which recently had been full of life and gaiety, was now become a shambles, the sight being rendered more hideous by contrast with the associations of the place. The mirrors on the walls and the furniture which remained still in the room were suggestive of refinement, luxury and social enjoyment, while the two mangled corpses, surrounded by a group of medical operatives, with coats off, aprons on and saws in their hands red with the blood of the victims, presented a sight which even those familiar with the terrors of the battlefield could not look upon without emotion.[10]

The examiners found that Cavendish had eight gaping wounds. A gash in his right armpit had severed an artery and would alone have caused death. Other deep cuts were found between his ribs, in his side and his back, while his left arm was slashed to the bone as he raised it to protect himself. Burke had eleven wounds, including three to his fingers, three to his chest and a gash across his throat, 3½ inches deep, which had severed his jugular vein. A stab to his back, drawn downwards, pierced his breast, gutting him. It was this which the doctors believed had actually killed him, although the other wounds would most certainly have proved fatal too. *The Times* reported: 'The murderers were determined to make their bloody work complete, and they must have done it with amazing rapidity. The deadly wounds were given from behind with furious violence, and the other wounds indicated an insatiable blood-thirstiness, as any of the principal ones would have served the full purpose of the assassins.'[11]

The following day the prominent Home Ruler, Alexander Sullivan, called on Cavendish's widow, Lucy Caroline, a maid of honour to the Queen, and left his card indicating his sorrow at her loss. Her brother replied on her behalf:

She was deeply touched, and I hope that your example may be followed by others of the Irish leaders. She knows that no-one who knew her husband, either in public or private life, bore any feeling of enmity towards him, and she believes that those who murdered him did not know who he was. She clings to the hope that even this catastrophe, by awakening men's consciences to the guilt and horror of such desperate crimes, may tend in some measure to the opening of brighter days for your country.[12]

Cavendish's funeral took place at Chatsworth House on 11 May and his remains were buried in nearby Edensor churchyard. The Duke of Devonshire and Gladstone led the procession to the grave, followed by 300 MPs and more than 30,000 mourners and onlookers. It was akin to a state funeral. A window to Cavendish's memory was later placed in St Margaret's Church, Westminster, at the expense of MPs. Burke was interred in Glasnevin cemetery, and Viceroy Spencer erected a memorial window to him in the Dominican Church, Dublin.

On the evening of Cavendish's funeral MPs returned to Westminster and Parliament opened at 9 pm to legislate in response to the murders. Sir William Harcourt, moving the bill, said that the act of the preceding Saturday was not an isolated event; rather, it was the inevitable outcome of the secret societies and combinations which spread their influence throughout Ireland and prevented the people from expressing their real feelings. Foremost among evidence of the terrorism was the intimidation of juries.[13] As a result the Government had no option but to set up special tribunals, with no juries, to try certain categories of crime. Whenever the Lord Lieutenant decided that an impartial trial could not be had for treason, murder, attempted killing, aggravated violence and attacks on dwellings, he would be empowered to appoint a special commission of three judges of the superior courts. Their verdicts would have to be unanimous, and there would be an appeal procedure. The bill also proposed that in proclaimed districts the police would have full power to search, by day or night, for the 'apparatus of crime' – daggers, masks, threatening letters, and so on – and to arrest persons prowling the streets by night and unable to give an account of themselves. It also proposed to revise the Alien Act to give power to arrest strangers and to remove those who might be thought a threat to public safety. Incitements to crime, membership of a secret society, aggravated assaults against the police and process-servers and intimidation would be 'summarily punished'. Rabble-rousing newspapers would be closed down and forfeits taken for their good behaviour when they were allowed to publish. The Lord Lieutenant would have the powers to deal specifically with unlawful assemblies. Among the more minor clauses were powers to carry on inquiries after a criminal had escaped, to compel witnesses to attend and to appoint additional police. Barely noticed at the time, these clauses would prove crucial to apprehending the murderers.

Not surprisingly, the Prevention of Crime Bill was bitterly contested. Parnell spoke of the even temper with which the British public had greeted the murders, but regretted that the framers of the bill did not share that composure. The crime gave the Government no warrant to place the lives and liberties of the Irish people at the mercy of such judges as the notoriously harsh Chief Justice May. He predicted that it would lead to 'one hundredfold more disaster' than the coercive policy of Forster, which had failed. Another Home Ruler said that the assassinations had occurred at the end of Forster's two-year administration of Ireland and warned that such repressive measures would be followed by a similar stain. The bill would carry out the object of those who had committed the murders, he said. For the Government, George Goschen said, to loud cheers, that responsibility with governing Ireland lay with the Executive, not with MPs 'steeped to the lips in treason'. Leave to introduce the bill was given by 327 votes to 22.

In the interval between the second and first readings, Forster told his constituents in Bradford:

> The Government has a most serious task to perform, mainly connected with Ireland, with which I have had so much to do. They have to prevent crime, to prevent murder, to relieve Ireland of the terrorism which overshadows it, and they have to do this without giving way to passion, without giving way to injustice, without forgetting the condition of the Irish people, and without forgetting that there may still be something owing to the Irish people in completion of the great measure which was lately passed. They have to do all this, and for that a strong Government is required.[14]

The bill suffered further opposition from an unlikely quarter: the Irish bench expressed unwillingness to carry out the duties mapped out for them, while the Tories and Radicals alike viewed with grave suspicion the proposed powers to suppress newspapers and disperse public meetings. Even pro-Liberal journals scented danger in the proposals to deprive men accused of such vague charges as intimidation the right to trial by jury. Taken together the measures could wreck the trend towards conciliation with Land Leaguers and others who wanted reform. Gladstone passionately agreed that 'conciliation means justice ... but justice means justice for all, and includes the use of force for the punishment of evildoers'. He insisted that the bill was not provoked by the Dublin assassinations, but that 'dreadful occurrence' made it impossible to delay it any further. Its main basis was not the slaughter of persons of rank and station, but the widespread misery inflicted on a large body of people for the exercise of their legal rights and the discharge of their legal obligations. The bill was finally carried by 383 votes to 45.[15] Any hope of reconciliation between Gladstone and Parnell was gone, and with it any move towards devolution, far less independence. Miles Hudson puts it succinctly: 'The Phoenix Park murders delayed rather than hastened Home Rule for Ireland and indeed might have prevented the eventual achievement of a united Ireland.'[16]

During this period the search for the murderers drew a blank. Rumours that three assassins had been recruited in America were impossible to substantiate. But repressive legislation quickly bore the fruit of sinister dissent. In the next two months a cache of 400 rifles, 25 cases of revolvers, several kegs of powder and about 100,000 rounds of ammunition were uncovered in a Clerkenwell stable, far exceeding any discovered since the outbreak of Fenianism. In Ireland the agent to the Marquess of Clanricarde and his servant were shot dead, and a Belfast man was killed with a scythe. In November a number of Fenians attacked detectives who were watching them. One constable was shot dead and an assailant severely wounded. Nationalists complained bitterly at the hanging for murder of five men, particularly Sylvester Poff, who many believed was completely innocent. Tensions rose over the administration of justice imposed by Westminster.

The generosity of Lady Cavendish's sentiments in hope for good out of her husband's slaughter were not matched by events. The Home Ruler, journalist and future Mayor of Dublin, Timothy Sullivan, wrote:

> The immediate effect of the Phoenix Park outrage was to darken the political skies, and blot the vision of peace and friendship that a moment before had looked so fair. Social and party strife went on no less fiercely than before. The landlords and the loyalist party were in fighting temper; evictions were carried out in increased numbers, and under circumstances of great cruelty a spirit of vengeance was evoked amongst the unfortunate victims of oppression and wrong, which led to the commission of deplorable crimes; these were followed in turn by the pains and penalties of the law, and so the vicious circle was completed.[17]

*   *   *

On 13 January 1883 the people of Dublin were rocked by a mysterious police raid on a number of houses and the arrest of 17 people. They were mainly labourers and unemployed men, but one, James Carey, was a prosperous tradesman who had recently been elected a town councillor. Many considered him a prospective Mayor of Dublin. Carey, aged 38, was the son of a Kildare bricklayer who had continued his father's trade for 18 years, working for a Dublin builder. He then set up a business of his own, obtained several large contracts and became the city building trade's leading spokesman while thriving in his Denzille Street yard. He made more money subletting a large number of tenement houses, which he rented from his former employee and sublet to the poor. His arrest shocked the city because, in the words of one commentator, 'everyone believed in his piety and public spirit; there was hardly a society of the popular or religious kind of which he did not become a member'. He was elected a town councillor, not on political grounds, but, as he said, 'solely for the good of the working men of the city'.

Two days later two more men were seized. All the arrests were made under the new Act, which allowed Dublin Castle police to examine witnesses without bringing any specific charges against them. Bail was refused and all the prisoners were charged with a catch-all conspiracy to murder certain government officials and other persons. The arrests caused astonishment on both sides of the Irish Sea. The disaffected Irish believed that the authorities had made another needless blunder by arresting inoffensive men and putting them to needless and irrelevant examination. The refusal of bail caused particular indignation. Others in authority feared that the Castle had acted too hastily and without the level of proof needed for successful prosecutions. *The Times* was more positive: 'there is at length a probability of securing the clue to a series of atrocious crimes, perpetrated with a cold-blooded deliberation and remorseless purpose not easily paralleled'.

Doubts were largely removed on 20 January when the prisoners were brought before the court. One of them, a labourer and old-time Fenian called Robert Farrell, turned informer. His evidence shocked everyone, even knee-jerk conspiracy theorists. Farrell revealed the existence of a secret cabal within the larger Fenian organisation, the Irish Invincibles, whose main motivation was the assassination of government officials and ministers. Each member knew only the colleague who swore him in and another he introduced himself. Their chief purpose was to assassinate William Forster during his tenure as Chief Secretary prior to Cavendish's appointment. Farrell described 'with great coolness and elaborate minuteness of detail' a series of plots to take Forster's life. Each had failed because of the bungling of prearranged signals or a miscalculation of the time at which his carriage would pass certain points. Moreover James Carey, it was revealed, had joined the Fenians in 1861, later became treasurer of the Irish Republican Brotherhood, was involved in courts martial that led to assaults and executions of suspected informers, and in 1881 took an oath as a leader of the

Invincibles when that organisation established its headquarters in Dublin. Knives were found in Carey's house, 'deadly looking weapons, such as are used by surgeons for amputations'.[18]

On 3 February the inquiry turned to the Phoenix Park murders. The medical men who had examined the two corpses testified that the knives found corresponded with the wounds. A chair-maker and his wife, who lived by the park's strawberry beds, identified the shoemaker Edward O'Brien and Joseph Brady, a stone-cutter, as men they had seen in the vicinity of the attack. Other witnesses described a cab seen speeding from the park after the outrage. A week later the cab-driver, Michael Kavanagh, also turned informer. He testified that he had driven Brady, Tim Kelly, Patrick Delaney and one other he could not identify to Phoenix Park. There Carey waved his white handkerchief to signal the attack. Kavanagh said that he saw the murders committed, then his passengers got back in the cab and he drove them away. This evidence was damning, but Carey throughout maintained an air of cool effrontery. He had protested the loudest when first arrested, but then remained aloof from his fellow prisoners. His social status kept him apart, although his temper snapped on one occasion when he punched the prison governor. On the first day of examination he smoked a cigar as he left the prison van and was dressed flamboyantly, particularly in comparison to the coarse working clothes of his co-prisoners.[19]

But the biggest surprise of a sensational inquiry came on 17 February when Carey himself turned informer. His jailors broke his bravado by revealing that several of his colleagues had already been persuaded to expose the full conspiracy and condemn him to the gallows. If he agreed to give evidence admitting to the murders and identifying others in court, his life would be spared and his future provided for. He agreed, although his friends later claimed that he could have revealed a lot more about the leadership of the Invincibles.[20] T. D. Sullivan wrote: 'It has often been said for unfortunate Carey by persons of some knowledge of those matters that he could have done "more harm" had he been so disposed, and that in fact he kept back from the authorities much that they would have been glad to learn. And the statement is probably true.'[21]

All the same, Carey revealed a lot from the witness stand of his Fenian membership since 1862 and his role as treasurer of the Irish Republican Brotherhood. 'We tried several persons by court martial,' he said. 'Up to 1879 we tried informers only. During that time we never tried or arranged the death of any but informers or traitors to ourselves.' By his own testimony Carey was the worst of the assassins. He admitted luring the others into the conspiracy, plotting the murder of Forster, arranging the Phoenix Park assassinations, supplying the weapons and giving the signal for the deed to be done. He said that the head of the Invincibles was a mystery man known only as 'Number One'. The society was constructed to ensure that the Invincibles, numbering never more than 250 across Ireland, Scotland and England, were recruited from among the most loyal Fenians. Their first targets were to be Forster and Earl Cowper, but local leaders could choose their own victims for assassination. He was given 50 sovereigns, two Winchester rifles and a box of knives to wage war on the 'tyrants'. Carey asked for a short break and as he passed the dock the prisoners hissed at him. One exclaimed: 'You have done all you can, you perjured scoundrel!' Carey glanced back and said: 'Ah! You were all trying to forestall me.'[22]

To public astonishment, on his return to the court, Carey revealed that it was Burke, not Cavendish, who was the intended victim. Burke, the conscientious civil servant, had been far too successful in helping to identify and track down Fenian secret societies, and Number One gave the order that he should die. The assailants had not recognised Cavendish, who died simply because he was there and because he tried to shield Burke. A contemporary report stated that it was understandable that Cavendish was at first assumed to be the prime target:

> The Government had recalled a thoroughly unsuccessful and unpopular Chief Secretary, and were sending in his place a young man of ability, of unprejudiced sympathy with the work entrusted to him ... It seemed almost certain that his murder was the deliberate answer of the secret societies to any attempt on the part of England to hold out the hand of fellowship to Ireland. It is gratifying, as far as anything in the hideous tragedy can be gratifying, to find that this theory was erroneous. The evidence of the chief criminal made it clear that ... the assassination was entirely aimed at Mr Burke, a man who was well known to be one of the most dangerous enemies the secret societies had in all the range of Castle authority. He was believed to have all the threads of their workings in his hands; it was at him that the blow was levelled, not at the friendly stranger.[23]

Carey's evidence, in which he identified all his co-conspirators and the actual killers, virtually closed the inquiry, and the subsequent trials through April were each a foregone conclusion. Joe Brady and three others – the builder Daniel Curley, Michael Fagan, a blacksmith, and Caffrey, a van driver – were sentenced to death. Two juries could not agree on the guilt of Tim Kelly, a popular and good-natured lad of just 20 and a chorister in a Dublin Catholic church. The third attempt by the prosecution succeeded. All five were hanged. On the eve of his execution Kelly sang the haunting ballad 'The Memory of the Past'. Delaney, who had taken part in the stabbing, pleaded guilty and had his death sentence commuted to penal servitude, the same fate that awaited two more minor conspirators. The other prisoners received varying prison sentences.

Carey tried to implicate members of the Land League, but no real connection could be shown to the Invincibles. He named the wife of a secretary to the English branch of the Land League of smuggling assassination weapons to Dublin, but withdrew when confronted with her. Some members were arrested, but were soon released for lack of evidence; others fled to America before Carey could implicate them in his plots.

The identity of the mysterious 'Number One' who allegedly headed the Invincibles and bankrolled the murders was never established. But *The Times*' Dublin correspondent quoted 'most trustworthy sources' suggesting he was an Irish-American who had lived for long periods in France and Germany. He was also styled 'The General' and had access to almost limitless funds from the United States. He was 5 feet 10 inches tall, aged about 50, full of face, with a long fair moustache but otherwise clean shaven. He was of military bearing and walked with a slight limp due to a leg injury sustained in the Franco-Prussian War. He, like many Fenians, had served in the Irish Brigade during the American Civil War. It seems certain that he had returned across the Atlantic before the trials.[24]

Carey remained for some time in Kilmainham Prison for his own protection. Nationalist anger at his betrayal was so great that few would have bet on him lasting more than an hour on the streets of Dublin. From his cell he wrote repeated letters to the town council, of which he was still a member, boasting that he would soon resume his seat among them. He was furious with the Castle authorities for refusing to pay him any reward and tried to rebuff their efforts to smuggle him out of the country. No one outside the prison knew exactly when and how he was removed, but there was speculation that he would be successfully hidden under an assumed name in a distant Crown colony.

Early that summer Carey was in fact put on board the *Kinfauns Castle* bound for the Cape of Good Hope, under the name of James Power. On the journey he became friendly with a fellow passenger, a bricklayer and Fenian sympathiser called Patrick O'Donnell, and the two men spent many happy hours chatting in the bar. The vessel arrived in Cape Town on 27 July and the passengers disembarked. While staying in a hotel O'Donnell was shown a newspaper containing a portrait of James Carey, the notorious informer. He recognised him immediately as his new friend 'Mr Power' and said, in such an offhand way that it did not attract any attention at the time, 'I'll shoot him.' He followed Carey on board the *Melrose* for the short onward voyage from Cape Town to Natal and on 29 July, 12 miles off Cape Vaccas, the pair were in the refreshment salon together. O'Donnell drew a revolver and fired three shots into Carey, killing him almost instantly.

O'Donnell was brought back to London and tried for ordinary murder, with no mention made in court of the Fenian connection. He was executed at Newgate on 17 December without having said a word about his motives in planning the revenge killing, or naming any accomplices, if indeed there were any.[25]

*   *   *

Forster maintained his attacks on Parnell, accusing him of condoning terrorism. 'It is not that he himself directly planned or perpetrated outrages or murders,' Forster asserted, 'but that he either connived at them or, warned by facts and statements, he determined to remain in ignorance.' Parnell dismissed that as a lie.

Parnell threw himself into the constitutional campaign for Home Rule and the general election of 1885 saw 86 Nationalists returned to Westminster. This was the height of Parnell's powers and convinced Gladstone that Home Rule was inevitable. But poor health and the scandal of Parnell's affair with Mrs Kitty O'Shea saw his influence dwindle and the hopes of many crumble with it. Another damaging episode came when *The Times* published letters in 1887 purporting to show that Parnell had embraced terrorism and was tacitly involved in the so-called Jubilee Plot to murder Queen Victoria (see chapter 7). The key evidence was a letter signed Parnell in which he expressed regret at having to condemn the Phoenix Park murders. The Government refused Parnell's demand for a select committee investigation into the authenticity of the letters and instead established a special commission to look into the charges they contained. This proved a mistake. *The Times* letters were forged by Richard Pigott, who broke under cross-examination. The reputation of *The Times* was severely damaged, and no link between Nationalism and terrorism was found. However, Parnell was a largely broken man, his party split by the acrimony which greeted Mrs O'Shea's lurid divorce proceedings. Parnell married Kitty in June 1891 and died in Brighton in October of that year, exhausted by a by-election campaign.[26]

The Fenians were spent as an effective force, betrayed by informers and politically irrelevant once the constitutional case for Home Rule got up steam. Outrages under the banner Clan-na-Gael continued, including a dynamite explosion in Glasgow and an 1885 bid to blow up the Houses of Parliament. But further assassinations were left to subsequent generations.

10

The Cairo Gang and the Pass of the Flowers

'His place will be taken by weaker men'

Lloyd George was driven to despair by Britain's failure in the autumn of 1920 to subdue a ragged band of Irish Republican Volunteers. Barely 3,000 of them, poorly armed but with widespread support from the civilian population, were running rings around 50,000 troops stationed in Ireland, 15,000 police and several thousand of the feared and despised Black and Tans and the even more ferocious Auxiliaries. The Volunteers were invisible, many continuing their jobs by day while raiding by night. They struck in roadside ambushes and at police stations and army barracks. Informers were slain and the police and security services paralysed. In what became known as the Black and Tan War the British employed terror tactics against entire communities, but their sanctioned acts of murder, arson, looting and torture simply stiffened the resolve of their opponents while provoking contempt and disgust elsewhere.

Masterminding the guerrilla war was the charismatic Michael Collins, a superb tactician who had built up an impressive intelligence network while cycling, impervious to any danger, around Dublin. All conventional efforts to track him down came to nothing. Lloyd George gave directions that the elimination of Collins by any means must be given top priority. The authorities decided that the best way was to hire a group of assassins, headed by Colonel Sir Arthur Winter, from the most elite ranks of British Intelligence serving in the Middle East where their ruthlessness had become a byword in subduing opposition in the newly mandated territory of Palestine.

This hit-squad of 16 men began arriving, one at a time or in pairs, in early September. They posed as commercial travellers and took rooms in several lodging houses, or booked into hotels. They became known as the Cairo Gang, partly because they had been recruited in that Egyptian city and partly because they became regulars at the Café Cairo in Dublin, a bar also frequented by Collins' Volunteers, military intelligence and the secret service. The Cairo Gang's orders were clear: kill Collins and dismantle his intelligence organisation. The assassin had become a tool of the state. Or so it was conceived.

*   *   *

Michael Collins was born on 16 October 1890 at Woodfield Farm near Clonakilty, Co. Cork. He was the eighth child of an elderly Irish Nationalist and a wife half his age. He grew up in a close and loving environment, doted upon by his parents and siblings. Politics was a major topic of conversation around the hearth, especially once the bright hopes of Home Rule were dashed by Parnell's fall. Michael, aged seven, was at his father's bedside when he died. According to the boy, his father's last words were: 'I shall not see Ireland free, but in my children's time it will come, please God.'

Home Rule was strongly resisted by most Protestants, particularly those in the majority in the northern counties. The Industrial Revolution had brought them increasing prosperity and power, which they were determined not to relinquish. Belfast was the leading centre of industry and union workers had little sympathy for the southern 'bog-trotters'. They knew that if Home Rule was granted they would become a minority in a largely Roman Catholic self-governing Ireland. When a third Home Rule bill was passed in the Commons in 1912 Sir Edward Carson, supported by the British Conservative and Unionist Party, set up a provisional government. He obtained arms from Germany and created a military organisation, the Ulster Volunteer Force, to resist Home Rule.

The Irish Volunteers was set up the following year to counter the UVF and the seeds of armed revolution and civil war began to sprout green shoots. At Westminster the Government was unwilling to challenge Carson and his Unionists head on. When the Home Rule bill was finally enacted in 1914 a provision enabled Carson's provisional government to opt out for a certain period. The provisions of the Act were in any case suspended at the outbreak of the First World War. Many members of the Irish Volunteers, on the advice of Irish Parliamentary Party leader, John Redmond, joined the British army to fight the Germans. But a large section of Volunteers followed Padraic Pearse and James Connolly, leader of the trade union Citizen Army, into an armed rising. Among them was 25-year-old Michael Collins.

Collins had spent the previous nine years working in London as a Post Office clerk. There he became active in Sinn Fein debates, Gaelic athletics and the hard-drinking pub scene. In 1907 he secretly joined the Irish Republican Brotherhood. Within a year he was made a section master and by 1914 was treasurer of the Brotherhood's London and South England district. Political activity consumed him and he failed the civil service examination, which would have enabled him to become a Customs and Excise officer. He quit the Post Office and joined a London stockbroker firm as head of messengers. Shortly before the outbreak of war he became a clerk at the Board of Trade in Whitehall. On the day war was declared he was in Liverpool playing for London against Scotland in the British Hurling Championship final. Angered by the neutering of the Home Rule bill, Collins helped form a London company of the Irish Volunteers which he drilled by night after his working day in Whitehall. Collins was restless and considered joining his brother Patrick in Chicago. Instead, he returned to Ireland in January 1916 to avoid conscription. He had another enemy to fight.

Collins was deeply involved in planning the Easter Rising, including an ill-fated attempt to land German arms and ammunition on the Kerry coast. On Easter Monday, 26 April he was one of 1,000 Volunteers who took out their hidden weapons and took on the British Army. The first casualty was an unarmed policeman at Dublin Castle, but the rebels failed to realise that the military headquarters were virtually undefended as the occupants were enjoying a day at the races. Instead they seized a number of prominent public buildings around the city as Pearse proclaimed the Irish Republic a sovereign state. The Rising's leaders occupied the General Post Office, while other groups grabbed the Four Courts – Ireland's judicial headquarters – St Stephen's Green and Bolland's Flour Mills. In Mount Street a dozen Volunteers led by the young carpenter Michael Malone held off 2,000 Sherwood Foresters newly arrived in the city. For six bloody days the Volunteers stood their ground against the combined might of the British Army, police and security forces. At the height of the Rising there were 30,000 soldiers in the city, while the rebels were pounded by field guns and a warship which sailed up the Liffey.

Volunteer Staff Captain Collins was in the thick of the fighting in and around the GPO and was credited with resourcefulness, courage, efficiency and good humour under fire. He later wrote:

> Although I was never actually scared in the GPO I was – and others also – witless enough to do the most stupid things. As the flames and the heat increased so apparently did the shelling. Machine-gunfire made escape more and more impossible. Not that we wished to escape. No man wished to budge. In that building, the defiance of our men, and the gallantry, reached unimaginable proportions.[1]

Their courage was never in doubt, but in military and political terms the Easter Rising was a fiasco. By the time the rebels capitulated 64 of their number were dead and over 200 wounded. The Crown forces lost 134 dead and 381 wounded. The biggest losers by far were the civilian population. Caught in the merciless bombardments which devastated the city and cut down in crossfire, at least 220 civilians were killed and around 600 injured. The Fenians took much of the blame, and many spectators jeered the defeated Volunteers as they were marched into captivity. That mood changed the following month when the British Government turned valuable captives into martyrs. Fifteen ringleaders were shot by firing squad in a series of executions spread over more than a week. James Connolly, wounded in the GPO, was tied to a stretcher to be shot after falling from his chair. John MacBride, who had fought with the Boers, refused a blindfold, telling the priest: 'It's not the first time I looked down their guns, Father.'

Collins was one of 500 prisoners initially taken via the Holyhead ferry to the military gaol at Stafford. It was a grim place, but Collins was a model prisoner both there and later at Frongoch Gaol in Wales. Surrounded by like-minded comrades, prison life was seen by many as akin to attending a Republican university. The threat of hunger strikes and the political outcry of detaining so many men without trial saw the prisoners released and returned to Ireland by the end of the year. Collins was one of the last, arriving in Dublin on Christmas Day.

The growing support for Sinn Fein, the Irish independence party, was made clear in the 1918 general election when it gained 73 of the 105 parliamentary seats. The Sinn Fein members met in Dublin in January 1919 and issued a declaration confirming the Republic proclaimed in 1916. They constituted themselves as the Dáil, or national parliament, and set up a provisional government under the presidency of a former maths teacher, Eamon de Valera. Collins, now established as a fierce orator who commanded intense loyalty, was its finance minister. The British Government refused to acknowledge the Dáil and stepped up repressive measures. The Volunteers re-formed themselves into the Irish Republican Army. They engaged in a relentless guerrilla war against the British 'occupation' and its genius, both in terms of strategy and propaganda, was Michael Collins.

Collins built up a remarkable intelligence-gathering network, organised prison break-outs and orchestrated hit-and-run raids. The first casualties were two constables escorting gelignite to a Tipperary quarry. Although such killings were not authorised by the Dáil, Collins said after the raid: 'The sooner the fighting is forced and a general state of disorder created ... the better it would be for the country.'[2] After 15 months, 20 police officers were dead at the hands of the IRA. Lloyd George and his Coalition Government covertly sanctioned a shoot-to-kill policy and the assassination of known terrorists. One atrocity begat another. The Government authorised the creation of two special forces, which swiftly became notorious. The Black and Tans – so called because of their deliberately mismatched uniforms – were brutal veterans of trench warfare and the prison yard. Their task was not to track down the IRA, but to exact vicious reprisals on civilians for terrorist acts committed by others. They were free to murder, burn and loot, and did so with drunken gusto. They were followed by a bigger, generally better-educated force known as the Auxiliaries, recruited from the officer class of the armed forces. They were more refined but just as brutal as their coarser comrades.

Collins created what became a classic guerrilla structure made up of small active service units supported by safe houses, suppliers and intelligence-gatherers fed by informers, who included several men who had infiltrated Dublin Castle's G-Division. More men and women in military installations around the country also supplied information, although arguably the most important assets were the eyes and ears of ordinary people going about their relatively normal lives.

British Intelligence based in Dublin Castle repeatedly tried to infiltrate Collins' network and the growing IRA, but informers who took their pay were usually found with a bullet in the head. In December 1919 Collins embarked on a strategy to eliminate the government men. His principal target was the Lord Lieutenant of Ireland, Viscount French, previously commander of British forces on the Western Front. Collins heard that he was due to leave his Co. Roscommon country estate on the 19th and return to Dublin by train, with an armed cavalcade taking him the last two miles. But the ambush was hastily organised and French's train reached Ashtown station a few minutes early, taking them by surprise. Three volunteers were in the process of wheeling a cart onto the road as a barricade when a constable ordered them to clear the way. The officer was blown off his feet by a lobbed grenade, but otherwise unharmed. French was in the leading car which, alerted by the explosion, sped off towards the city. The Volunteers, assuming it only contained bodyguards, let it through and focused their fire on the second vehicle, wounding the driver, Detective Sergeant Halley.[3] One of the ambushers, Martin Savage, was wounded and was hauled away by his comrades.

In March 1920 Thomas MacCurtain, the Sinn Fein mayor of Cork, was murdered by counter-terror forces in reprisal for the killing of a local policeman. Collins' men fought a pitched battle with soldiers as they rescued an IRA man from a prison train in Limerick. Two soldiers died. In September 1920 a soldier was killed and four wounded as they attended a church parade. Their comrades went on a rampage burning and smashing shops. Some days later a popular head constable was killed by the IRA in Balbriggan. The Tans were unleashed and for 36 hours they burned and looted the town, firing indiscriminately. Two local men were bayoneted to death.[4]

Tit-for-tat killings continued. Collins and his commanders moved steadily towards the tactics of assassination as a military tactic. After failed attempts on the life of the commander of the hated Essex battalion in West Cork, Major Percival, and a member of the local judiciary, a local IRA commander, Tom Barry, wrote: 'The death of Percival and this Judge would have far exceeded in real value to our armed fight the deaths of 50 soldiers or Black and Tans. Percival was a leading instrument in the plan for our destruction, while the Judge was an important prop to British power.'[5]

Collins authorised the slaying of a district inspector on 31 October following the death of a hunger striker. The following day an 18-year-old medical student, Kevin Barry, was hanged. The day after that a constable was shot dead. Just before midnight on 11 November lorries full of around 100 Black and Tans burnt down the small town of Granard. On the way back the Tans, by now roaring drunk, were ambushed by 20 Volunteers who killed around 20 and wounded many more.[6] It was a remarkable success, but the Tans could kill with impunity. By then coroner's courts had returned 22 verdicts of wilful murder involving Crown forces. Lloyd George justified the policy at a banquet: 'We have murder by the throat ... when the Government was ready we struck the terrorists and the terrorists are now complaining of terror.'

By then the Cairo Gang had struck, although their existence would not be acknowledged until later. A Limerick fund-raiser and loan organiser, John Lynch, was shot in his bed at the Royal Exchange Hotel, Dublin. It is possible that he was mistaken for Liam Lynch, leader of the Cork IRA. Dublin Castle announced that he had been resisting arrest, but one of Collins' police informers reported: 'There is not the slightest doubt that there was no intention whatever to arrest Mr Lynch.' On 11 October the Cairo Gang raided the home of Professor Carolan where they found two dangerous IRA gunmen, Dan Breen and Sean Treacy, in bed. They shot their way out, killing two of the undercover men. Breen was badly injured as he crashed through a conservatory roof in the escape, but was sheltered in a nearby house and later recovered. Treacy escaped unharmed. Carolan was put against a wall and shot in the head but lingered long enough to relate the story. Treacy felt obliged to attend the professor's funeral but was recognised. In the ensuing gunfight Treacy and one of the Gang were killed.

From such incidents and his intelligence-gatherers Collins realised that a murder squad was operating outside the brief of the Tans, the police and the army, with its own chain of command and intelligence structure. A police sympathiser supplied Collins with the names and addresses of every Secret Service man in the Gang, while his spy in Dublin Castle confirmed their remit. Top of the list were Colonel Aimes and Major Bennett, followed by the other members of their Gang, two Irish collaborators – Mahon and Peel – and Major MacLean, the Castle's chief intelligence officer. The Republican's Army Council authorised their synchronised slaughter on the morning of Sunday, 21 November, when the city would be full of spectators for a football match.

That Saturday Vaughan's Hotel was raided by the Auxiliaries who arrested Conor Clune, a young Gaelic scholar with no connection to the Volunteers, who happened to be in the wrong place at the wrong time. He was sent to the infamous interrogation rooms in the Castle. Later that night Captain J. L. Hardy, the liaison officer between Dublin Castle and Scotland Yard and a notorious torturer, had better luck with a raid elsewhere which netted two genuine plotters, Dick McKee and Peadar Clancy. They joined the innocent Clune and all three were subjected to hours of terrible torture. Collins was unaware that two of his men had been captured – they did not reveal the plot – and the eradication of the Cairo Gang went ahead more or less as planned.

Collins had already infiltrated a man into the Gang's main lodging house as hall porter, and he had provided duplicate room keys. The morning was cold and bright when, shortly before 9 am, groups of Volunteers from the Dublin Brigade descended on eight separate locations across the city. The hall porter in the lodging house, and servants in other establishments and hotels, unlocked the front doors to allow the Volunteers to enter. It was cold-blooded murder. Most of the 19 officers killed within the next few minutes were shot in their beds, often alongside their wives or mistresses. One woman threw herself across her lover but was pulled from their bed and the man shot. Another woman miscarried minutes after seeing her husband killed where he lay. An elderly major was shot scrambling out of his window while his wife screamed in terror. Another officer managed to reach the back garden in his pyjamas, but was cut down. One Volunteer, enraged by missing a colleague of Captain Hardy, thrashed the officer's mistress with his sword scabbard. But generally great care was taken not to harm the women.

A few officers were dragged from their rooms, lined up and shot. Charles Dalton recorded: 'Knowing their fate I felt great pity for them. It was plain they knew it too. As I crossed the threshold the volley was fired. The sights and sounds of that morning were to be with me for many days and nights.' Later Dalton prayed for the dead in church. A Captain Baggelly was killed by Volunteers who included the future Irish prime minister Sean Lemass. In another incident an officer's servant escaped and fired at the assailants with a .22 pistol, but few of the dead got within reach of their weapons. Most of the hit squads got clean away, but those raiding houses in Mount Street and Pembroke Road ran into patrols of Auxiliaries. After running battles they too escaped, dragging their wounded with them.

A young officer of the Royal Army Medical Corps was shot dead by mistake in the Gresham Hotel, and almost half the Cairo Gang escaped the massacre by not being where they were expected to be. But the surprise and scale of the slaughter inspired panic in the British intelligence machine and officers and their wives fled to the security of Dublin Castle.

Collins received reports of the successful outcome of the raids 'white and defiant with an expression of pleasure', but his mood turned sombre. He sent word to the Gaelic Athletic Association urging them to cancel the planned football match between Dublin and Tipperary. He was told that was impossible because of the huge crowds already converging on Croke Park. When he heard of the capture of McKee and Clancy he said: 'Good God! We're finished now. It's all up.'[7]

That afternoon lorries full of Auxiliaries and soldiers drove to Croke Park and surrounded the ground. The Auxiliaries opened fire on the packed crowd with rifles and machine guns. Thirteen spectators and the Tipperary goalkeeper were killed instantly and hundreds more were wounded or trampled in the ensuing panic. Later, Auxiliaries and police officers rounded up a group of civilians near Trinity College and ordered them to run. Seven were shot in the back and two died, one of them a 10-year-old boy. In the Castle McKee, Clancy and Clune, badly beaten, were shot by their drunken Auxiliary guards 'while trying to escape'. When their bodies were loaded into a truck the officer in charge pulped their faces with his torch. When reclaimed by relatives, they were found to have sword and bayonet puncture wounds although, unusually, their genitals were intact. By the end of the year the informer who had betrayed McKee and Clancy was shot in the chest and head and left in a ditch.

The day became known as 'Bloody Sunday'. It was certainly the bloodiest day of the conflict since the Easter Rising. The death toll including the 19 British officers, the football match victims, the prisoners killed and the man and boy shot in the back – in all 37. The *Irish Independent* wrote: 'Dublin has just passed through a weekend the like of which it has not experienced since 1916.'[8] The British Government simply listed the officers killed and claimed the killings were motiveless, saying only that several victims were involved in preparing courts martial. Chief Secretary of Ireland Sir Hamar Greenwood claimed that the football match slaughter was justified. He insisted that the army had been trying to apprehend Tipperary units of the IRA and were fired on from the crowd. 'There is no doubt,' he said, 'that some of the most desperate criminals in Ireland were amongst the spectators. The responsibility for the loss of innocent lives must rest with those men, and not with the police or military who were forced to fire in self-defence.' His statement convinced very few. In London *The Times* expressed horror that 'an army already perilously ill-disciplined and a police force avowedly beyond control have defiled by heinous acts the reputation of England'.[9]

There were no honours for the Cairo Gang, the remnants of whom either fled or were absorbed into other units. Winston Churchill said that the murdered men were 'careless fellows'. Lloyd George said in a message to intermediaries opening secret talks with Sinn Fein: 'Tragic as the events in Dublin were, they were of no importance. These men were soldiers, and took a soldier's risk.'[10]

An assassination squad had itself been assassinated.

*   *   *

Many Sinn Fein leaders went into hiding, but Collins was imbued with a recklessness which saw him cycling through Dublin's streets and narrowly escaping capture time after time. In November there were 1,000 arrests, but Collins was not among them. The excesses of the Tans and the Auxiliaries continued while the army conducted 'official' reprisals, destroying houses believed to have sheltered terrorists. Martial law was declared in December in the eight most troublesome counties. The British Cabinet, however, balked at army commander General Sir Nevil Macready's proposals to send firing squads to all corners of Ireland.

Martial law succeeded only in boosting IRA recruitment: by 1921 it was 5,000 strong, with another 4,500 interned. The army cordoned off towns and villages, imposed curfews, sent armoured convoys into bandit country, levied more reprisals against civilians and co-opted the RAF to mount air patrols. All such tactics met with limited success, but the IRA under the command of Collins and others managed to absorb the damage. They launched a whirlwind of ambush and targeted slaughter, boosted by a consignment of Thompson machine-guns supplied by American allies.

Among the most active was the West Cork Brigade. Its flying column commander, Tom Barry, described a typical attack, at Crossbarry on 19 March 1921, on a British army convoy: 'I flattened against the ditch as the leading lorry came on, but suddenly it halted and the soldiers started shouting, for unfortunately, despite the strictest orders, a Volunteer had shown himself at a raised barn door. The British started to scramble from their lorries but the order to fire was given and C's Section opened up at them.' Three other sections also blazed away at the soldiers on the road below as a Volunteer played Irish martial tunes on his bagpipes.

> Volley after volley was fired, mostly at ranges from five to 10 yards at those British and they broke and scattered, leaving their dead, a fair amount of arms, and their lorries behind them. The survivors had scrambled over the southern ditch of the road and were running panic-stricken towards the south. Three of our Sections were ordered out on to the road to follow them up. Using rapid fire they chased the enemy who lost many men.[11]

In June the British Cabinet agreed that it was a war of attrition which they could not win, especially as the clock was ticking and the 1914 Home Rule Act was due to take effect, creating separate Parliaments in Belfast and Dublin. Lloyd George invited Sinn Fein's leader, Eamon de Valera, to join negotiations under a general truce. A flurry of IRA activity left 20 people dead in the last 36 hours before the truce took effect. De Valera, well aware that any solution would be hugely unpopular in some quarters, cynically left the negotiations to Collins and Sinn Fein's founder, Arthur Griffith.

The two veteran fighters talked peace in London, Collins with a £10,000 British bounty on his head. After a Downing Street meeting, members of the British administration had wildly differing views of Collins. One civil servant, Andy Cope, who had facilitated the peace talks, reported that 'Michael Collins is showing frankness and considerable reasonableness', but Army commander General Nevil Macready found him 'a great disappointment, flippantly trying to get out of corners by poor jokes in bad taste'. Whatever the differences in personalities, Collins, the rest of the negotiating team and the

British Government agreed in October on the creation of a 26-county independent Irish Free State rather than a Republic. Ulster would have a separate identity, subject to a commission to define its borders. It was unstated, but tacitly understood by Collins and Griffith, that Ulster eventually would be swallowed up as demographics would, in the long term, result in a Catholic majority. The alternative, Lloyd George threatened, would be all-out war. Collins accepted despite deep reservations: 'I may have signed my actual death warrant.' War Office papers, kept secret until 1993, showed that failure to agree a treaty would have led to a massive escalation of British occupying forces, the internment of 20,000 and the death penalty for possession of arms.

The treaty which took effect on 4 January 1922 was popular in Ireland, as shown by elections, in which 72 per cent voted in favour. But Sinn Fein was divided. De Valera was implacably opposed, as were many of Collins' friends and lieutenants, who again took up their guns and rejoined the IRA. The new country was sliding towards civil war.

That conflict was given a kick-start on 22 June, six days after the Irish electorate overwhelmingly endorsed the treaty. Sir Henry Wilson, an Ulster Unionist MP, field marshal and recently retired Chief of the Imperial General Staff, unveiled a plaque in London's Liverpool Street Station to railwaymen killed in the First World War before going to his own death.

Wilson was a renowned veteran of Britain's colonial wars and represented that era's finest. He had signed up with the Royal Irish Regiment as a youngster, switched to the Rifle Brigade, was wounded in Burma and served in the Light Brigade in the Boer War. He had received a DSO with five clasps, the Grand Cross of the Legion of Honour and the Grand Cross of the Russian White Eagle. During the Great War he served in the War Cabinet where he was, openly at least, an ally of General Haig. He was intelligent, opinionated, ambitious and immersed in politics. Duff Cooper wrote: 'Faced with the problem of how to be loyal to Lloyd George and Haig at the same time, [Wilson] solved it by being loyal to neither.'[12] That was probably an unduly harsh judgement.

Dressed in his full military regalia the 61-year-old Wilson stepped out of a taxi outside his Eaton Place house. Two plainly dressed men stepped out from behind a hedge, drew concealed revolvers and fired

CHARGED WITH THE MURDER OF
SIR HENRY WILSON : JAMES CONNOLLY

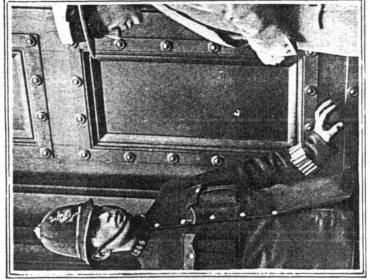

SHOWING A BULLET-HOLE THROUGH THE DOOR ; THE ENTRANCE
TO SIR HENRY WILSON'S HOUSE, WHERE HE WAS MURDERED.

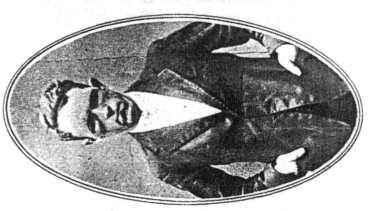

CHARGED WITH THE MURDER OF
SIR HENRY WILSON : JOHN O'BRIEN

7. James Connolly and John O'Hara, convicted of murdering Sir Henry Wilson on 22 June 1922 (*Illustrated London News*)

twice into his body at close range as he mounted the steps to his front door. As the old soldier tried to draw his ceremonial sword they fired seven more bullets into him. Wilson, though a hard-line Unionist, had previously complained about Black and Tan murder squads, telling Churchill that such a policy was 'suicidal'. The two assassins, Western Front veterans Reginald Dunne and Joseph O'Sullivan, who had lost a leg at Ypres, were surrounded by an angry mob, badly beaten and captured. In the violent confusion a constable was shot and wounded. Dunne might have got away but delayed his flight to help his disabled colleague.[13] Both were hanged in Wandsworth Prison in August, while a crowd waiting outside the gaol sang 'Wrap the Green Flag Round Me, Boys'. But Arthur Griffith, the first president of the Irish Free State, condemned the murder, saying: 'It is a principle of civilised government that the assassination of a political opponent cannot be justified or condoned.'

Historians have long argued over who ordered Wilson's assassination, but it seems likely that it was Collins, now leading the pro-Treaty faction. During the London peace talks Wilson had suspected that Collins was using them as a cover for clandestine operations in England. He believed his suspicions were confirmed when Irish Volunteers raided the Combermere Barracks in Windsor. (In fact, the raid was organised by Collins' rival, Cathal Brugha.) Wilson made much of the raid, enraging Collins and causing him much embarrassment. Taylor wrote: 'Perhaps the order was given before the treaty, and Collins had forgotten to countermand it; perhaps it was given in the belief that Wilson was organising Unionist forces in Ulster to resist Sinn Fein.' The latter is more likely. Wilson had indeed been appointed military adviser to the Craig administration in the North and wrote: 'Owing to the action of Mr Lloyd George and his Government, the 26 counties of south and west Ireland are reduced to a welter of chaos and murder, difficult to believe, impossible to describe. A further consequence of the course pursued is seen by the state of unrest, suspicion and lawlessness that has spread over the frontier into the six counties of Ulster.'[14] He recommended the replacement of the old, discredited police force with the Royal Ulster Constabulary backed by the militia B Specials. The Specials in particular were conniving at anti-Catholic pogroms in Belfast. In March a group of Specials had broken into the home of the MacMahon family and lined up the father, four sons and a lodger. Four were killed but one brother survived wounds to his head and chest. Wilson was put forward as a possible leader of a breakaway, 'diehard' Unionist Party committed to keeping Ulster Orange. In May Collins had said to a confederate: 'We'll kill a member of that bunch.'

Whoever was to blame, Wilson's murder was met with such a furious reaction in England that the Government informed Dublin that British troops would be sent back to deal with republican terrorists unless the Free State took action. Lloyd George, presented with the murder weapon and incriminating papers found on the killers, said: 'The ambiguous position of the Irish Republican Army can no longer be ignored by the British Government.' The coalition administration had little choice because Conservative and Unionist fury risked bringing down the Government. But the unfortunate fact remains that the Irish civil war began on British orders.

Collins, now Commander-in-Chief of Free State forces, saw as his first target the Four Courts which, since April, had been occupied by an IRA battalion. Using field guns supplied by the British, he attacked on 28 June. After a successful two-day assault 65 were dead, 270 wounded and more than 60 buildings were destroyed. The leader of the Four Courts rebels, Rory O'Connor, surrendered and was later executed. He would not be the last. Churchill personally congratulated Collins, saying: 'Now all is changed. Ireland will be mistress in her own house and we over here are in a position to safeguard your Treaty right and further your legitimate interests effectually.' Such messages reinforced the anti-Treaty rebels in their belief that Collins was Churchill's stooge. Harry Boland, who had fought alongside Collins and was considered a friend, wrote to an American supporter: 'England has again waged war on us, this time she has employed Irishmen to do her dirty work ... the black and tans have given way to the green and tans. Hamar Greenwood is outdone by Mick Collins.'

*   *   *

The Irish civil war lasted 16 months and was fought with ferocity on both sides as old comrades became bitter enemies. Around 540 Free State troops were killed and losses on the Republican side have been estimated at over 3,000 dead and in excess of 12,000 prisoners held in detention. Old scores and feuds were settled under the cloak

of patriotism, families were divided, atrocities rivalling those of the
Black and Tans were committed on civilians and unarmed foes. New
hatreds replaced the old. The Catholic bishops condemned the anti-
treaty dissidents saying: 'They have wrecked Ireland from end to end,
burning and destroying. They have caused more damage to Ireland
in three months than could be laid to the charge of British rule in so
many decades.' The IRA historian Tim Pat Coogan admitted: 'Terrible
things were done. Men were chained to mined barricades and blown
to pieces, interrogations were conducted with the aid of a hammer and
men went mad or were found to be castrated.'

As Collins won the military war, the decommissioning of IRA
weaponry became, then as 80 years later in the North, an obstacle to
the peace process. Collins, like so many others, was waging war on
former comrades. One of them, Harry Boland, a Republican officer
forced into the hills, wrote: 'I am certain we cannot be defeated even
if Collins and his British Guns succeed in garrisoning every town in
Ireland. Can you imagine me on the run from Mick Collins?' A few
days later Boland received a letter from Collins himself. 'Harry – it
has come to this,' he wrote. 'Of all things it has come to this. It is in
my power to arrest you and destroy you. This I cannot do.' Two days
later Boland and another man were arrested by Nationalist troops
while getting ready for bed in the Grand Hotel, Skerries. Boland was
shot dead 'while attempting to escape'.[15]

In July 1922 County Cork was the last stronghold of Republican
guerrillas. Collins rejected advice to negotiate and swept through the
county, taking Cork and subduing the surrounding districts despite his
increasingly poor health: overwork and stress had given him severe
bouts of dyspepsia. George Bernard Shaw, who met him in Dublin at
a funeral, reported that 'his nerves were in rage and he kept slapping
his revolver all the time he was talking'. To another guest Collins said:
'Do you think I shall live through this? Not likely!'

He returned to Cork, his home county, to promote a peace treaty
against the advice of his lieutenants. Although the county was
vehemently anti-treaty, he was convinced that no man there would
raise a hand against him. Collins was due to marry his fiancée, Kitty
Kiernan, on Tuesday, 22 August, but postponed the wedding until after
the peace treaty he was sure was just around the corner was agreed.
Just after 6 am that morning he set off for a tour of West Cork to

open negotiations with prominent Republicans. The IRA promised him safe conduct and even outlined details of mined roads and bridges. Nevertheless Collins travelled with an armed escort. Two Crossley tenders carrying 24 soldiers led the cavalcade, followed by Collins' Leyland-Thomas open touring-car, behind which was a Rolls-Royce Whippet armoured car. Ahead of the vehicles a motorcycle scout, breaching every security rule, alerted cottages along the route that 'the Commander-in-Chief is coming'.

They first drove to Macroom, where Collins visited a captured IRA leader, Florrie O'Donoghue. He told the prisoner: 'I've been all over this bloody country and no one has said a bloody word to me.' He added: 'No one can stop me.' Collins' car overheated twice, forcing unscheduled stops for water. At about 9 am they reached the crossroads to Beal na mBlath (the Pass of the Flowers) but the lead driver was unsure of the route they were meant to be taking. Directions were asked for at Denny Long's pub and Long pointed them down the Bandon Road. Unknown to Collins' party Long was a look-out for a meeting of top-level Republicans at a nearby farmhouse. He reported the cavalcade and the Republicans, reasoning that Collins would eventually return along the same route, decided to set an ambush. According to some sources the real target were Dublin IRA men believed to be in Collins' convoy who had aroused the enmity of the local IRA, although this may have been an excuse dreamt up later. Under the command of Tom Hales they blocked the road with a brewer's dray, set mines on the road and placed snipers on high ground and in bushes behind a stream. De Valera watched the preparations. He is reported to have said: 'It would be bad if anything bad happened to Collins. His place will be taken by weaker men.'

Collins reached Bandon and went on to Clonakilty where the town came out to greet their local hero. After lunch at Walsh's Eldon Hotel in Skibbereen they toured the district, Collins standing in his staff car and soaking up general adulation. In Rosscarberry six of Collins' escort were locked up after a fight with local soldiers over a stolen bottle of whiskey. The tour was in danger of turning into a pub crawl, although Collins who was suffering stomach cramps stayed relatively sober. The schedule was in disarray, however, and a planned visit to Crookstown was cancelled. They returned to Bandon and left at around 8 pm to head down the Pass of the Flowers. Collins had been warned several times of a planned ambush, which was common knowledge in the area, but he merely shrugged: 'Yerra, sure they'll never attack me.'

The ambushers, meanwhile, had grown tired of waiting and most had gone to Long's pub for a pint or two before returning home. Six men stuck it out but decided that the mines should be deactivated so that local farmers could use the road the next morning. Hales removed the fuse from one and was carrying the other when the Commander-in-Chief's cavalcade came around the corner. He dived over a hedge, thinking only of escape, as his comrades opened a ripple of small arms fire.

The cavalcade halted in front of the dray cart and Emmet Dalton shouted: 'Drive like hell.' But Collins picked up his rifle and ordered the driver to stop, saying: 'Jump out and we'll fight them.' In this he was breaking one of the prime rules of guerrilla warfare – stopping in unfamiliar territory to tackle an unseen enemy with no idea of its strength or position. But it fitted his frame of mind. Private Jim Wolfe, a member of his escort, said afterwards that Collins had a 'boyish view' of actual soldiering. He had the men and the weaponry and he would 'show them'.

He first took cover in front of his touring car, unsure where the main threat was coming from. Immediately the windscreen was shattered and Collins rushed to the other side. Jock McPeak, the Scots machine-gunner in the armoured car, slowly raked the hillside with his Vickers. His first bursts were long and wasteful of ammunition, but McPeak claimed later that his intention was to let the attackers know that there was a machine gun and had better keep their heads down. By the time he started his second belt he was firing short bursts of two or three rounds. During a lull in the fighting, 'I opened the hatch to get some cool air into the turret, which was stifling. I had no sooner opened it when a bullet struck the lug which fastens the cover from the inside and sheered it off.' The machine gun jammed at a crucial moment thanks to the inexpert handling of a staff officer feeding the ammunition belt into the gun. The armoured car moved slowly up and down the road, but stopped when it risked becoming bogged down in the soft earth of the verge. The rest of the party took up positions, firing at the ambushers.

The men in Long's, alerted by the fusillades, emerged from the pub and began firing at the column from the hill-top, although they were too far away to do much damage. They were joined by an IRA flying column which, retreating from Nationalist soldiers in Kerry, had appeared on the scene by chance. Although some of the attacking reinforcements carried Thompson guns, they were too far away to be used effectively. The ground was rugged and dotted with bushes, making it hard for either side to pick out easy targets. Equally, many of the soldiers in the convoy were inexperienced. Much fern and shrubbery was mown down in the ragged battle, but no men.

During the mêlée Collins had remained behind the side of his car, exchanging fire with the original ambushers. When those six men ran off, Collins leapt to his feet and, waving his rifle, cried to his men; 'Come on boys! There they are, running up the road.' He loped 50 yards to get a better view and was seen standing upright in the middle of the road, taking aim.

As the light faded a former British Army marksman, Sonny O'Neill, paused to send one last bullet from his Lee Enfield rifle to the lone figure in the road before scrambling away to safety. No one can know whether that was the fatal shot, but with the engagement virtually over and no serious casualties on either side, Collins' men heard an anguished cry. Collins was lying in the road, blood pouring from a wound behind his right ear.[16] Sean O'Connell was one of the first to reach him and later wrote: 'With a dreadful fear clutching our hearts we found our beloved Chief and friend lying motionless firmly gripping his rifle.'

Collins was dragged into the armoured car where his wound was dressed. He never regained consciousness. He was taken first to Long's pub where some rudimentary first aid was tried, helped by several IRA men who had not taken part in the ambush. Collins was loaded into his car and taken to a local curate to receive the last rites. It has never been satisfactorily explained why the party did not return immediately to Bandon where medical help was available. They did not and the result was tragic farce. The motorcade again lost its way, almost drove over a precipice and then got stuck in a muddy field. Collins' corpse had to be manhandled for several hundred yards across the mire, its carriers covered in his blood and brain tissue.[17]

Collins was not yet 32 when he died. Guilt was expressed by members on both sides of the ambush. McPeak said: 'I suppose every man in a way, felt more or less responsible that the Commander-in-Chief should have been killed while the rest of us escaped without a scratch – except the motor-cycle outrider Lieutenant Smith.' The IRA denied for decades that Collins had been deliberately targeted and assassinated. Tom Barry described it as a 'canard'. He spoke to several of the ambushers a week after the attack and always insisted that the column had been lying in wait for several days to attack Free State troops who regularly patrolled the road, and was ordered to withdraw. 'The main body of the column had retired over a mile and the small rearguard over a quarter of a mile from the ambush position, when a Free State convoy approached,' he wrote. 'The main column was out of sight and range, but the small rearguard turned and opened fire from nearly 500 yards range at the passing convoy, which immediately stopped. The Free State party dismounted and lying on the road returned the fire, but the rearguard after firing less than a dozen rounds hurried on after the main body. One of those long range shots had killed Michael Collins ...'[18]

Soldiers wept openly when Collins' body finally reached Cork. An order issued to all military units declared:

> Stand calmly by your posts. Bend bravely and undaunted to your work. Let no cruel act of reprisal blemish your bright honour. Every dark hour that Michael Collins met since 1916 seemed to steel that bright strength of his and temper his gay bravery. You are left each inheritors of that strength and of that bravery. To each of you falls his unfinished work.

*   *   *

Michael Collins was returned to Dublin on board the steamship *Classic* which had been diverted from her normal run to chug up the Liffey as the bells of St Colman's Cathedral tolled and green-uniformed troops stood to attention. Along the shore crowds wept and knelt in prayer. Thousands filed past as the body lay in state in the City Hall. On Monday, 28 August 1922 hundreds of thousands attended the state funeral. The coffin, draped in the Irish tricolour, was mounted on a gun-carriage drawn by six black horses. In a touch which Collins would have appreciated, the cortège stopped briefly beside Nelson's Pillar so that the flower-sellers could place their wreath on the coffin. General Richard Mulcahy, delivering the funeral oration, suggested that the people should emulate the strength of their fallen leader. He said: 'Men and women of Ireland, we are all mariners on the deep, bound for a port still seen only through storm and spray, sailing still on a sea full of dangers and hardships, and bitter toil. But the Great Sleeper lies smiling in the stern of the boat, and we shall be filled with the spirit which will walk bravely upon the waters.'[19]

Tributes came from friends and former enemies. Kevin O'Higgins said: 'His death was the quenching of our shining lamp.' George Bernard Shaw, in a letter to Collins' sister Hannie, wrote: 'Don't let them make you miserable about it: how could a born soldier die better than at the victorious end of a good fight, falling to the shot of another Irishman – a damn fool, but all the same an Irishman who thought he was fighting for Ireland.' Lloyd George said: 'His engaging personality won friendships even among those who met him first as foes, and to all who met him the news of his death comes as a personal sorrow.' Sir Nevil Macready, Commander-in-Chief of British Forces in Ireland, wrote: 'I deeply regret that he should not have been spared to see a prosperous and peaceful Ireland the accomplishment of his work.'

Winston Churchill later wrote:

> The presentiment of death had been strong upon him for some days, and he only narrowly escaped several murderous traps ... His funeral was dignified by the solemn ritual of the Roman Catholic Church and every manifestation of public sorrow. Then silence. But his work was done. Successor to a sinister inheritance, reared among fierce conditions and moving through ferocious times, he supplied those qualities of action and personality without which the foundation of Irish nationhood would not have been re-established.

The civil war did not die with Collins and the bloodshed continued. The Irish Government concurred with the military's policy of summary execution of Republican prisoners, while a further 77 were legally executed. Republican hard man Liam Lynch issued a directive that every officer of the Free State army above the rank of lieutenant was to be shot. But Lynch was killed in a skirmish in the Knockealdown Mountains and his death effectively killed the Republican determination to continue. A month later, on 24 May 1924, his successor, Frank Aiken, ordered a ceasefire.

The breach between South and North widened and in 1925 the Boundary Commission revealed that, despite promises given to Collins, not an acre of Northern Ireland would be ceded to the Irish Free State. That almost triggered another civil war and laid the foundations for an ongoing grievance which was to erupt into the Troubles a generation later.

Collins' biographer James Mackay argues convincingly that much of the mayhem would not have happened if the Big Fellow had not been assassinated:

> Seldom in the history of any country has a single unlucky bullet so utterly altered the course of events. Indeed, it would be no exaggeration to say that Ireland suffers the consequences to this day. Had Michael lived, it is highly probable that he would have brought the civil war to a speedy conclusion and succeeded in healing the breach with the North, leading to the removal of partition which few British politicians, from Lloyd George and Churchill downwards, regarded as anything other than a purely temporary measure.[20]

Other historians are less certain, among them Miles Hudson:

> The assassination of Michael Collins, although a shattering blow for many Irish people at the time, did not in fact alter the general situation. Even without him, the Irish Free State Government won the civil war against the Volunteers and it must be most unlikely that Collins, if he had lived, would have been able to prevent the eventual return to power of de Valera as the political pendulum swung in his direction.

He conceded, however, that his death created a glamour which has never faded: 'What remains is the vision of the brave, devil-may-care, highly charismatic and effective figure of Michael Collins, young, attractive and with compelling leadership qualities, a romantic icon still for very many Irish men and women.'[21]

Collins lies in Glasnevin cemetery in a plot reserved for members of the Irish armed forces slain on active service from the civil war to current UN peace-keeping operations.

11
The Attempt on Edward VIII

'how disrespectful, a revolver ...'

Mrs Alice Lawrence stood among the throng on Constitution Hill, patiently waiting for a glimpse of the new king in his state carriage. Edward VIII, returning by horseback to Buckingham Palace after a colours ceremony in Hyde Park, was still enjoying the full flush of his early popularity. Before becoming king just a few months earlier, he had been regarded as a Prince Charming, urging that 'something must be done' about poverty and the plight of the working class, declaiming against cant and hypocrisy, and eager to modernise the monarchy. He was adored by those who were allowed to know nothing of the weakness, petulance and selfishness in his character which would lead to the Abdication Crisis later that year. Mrs Lawrence, like all but one around her, craned her neck towards Wellington Arch, eager for a sign that the royal parade was on its way.

The exception, she noted out of the corner of her eye, was a short, stocky man in his mid-thirties she had earlier seen talking to a tall, well-dressed man with a moustache and wearing a tall hat. The image had registered because the shorter man's clothing – a well-worn and crumpled brown suit – contrasted markedly with the gentleman's attire. At 12.25 the sound of distant cheering signalled that the king had left Hyde Park and was only a few minutes away. The man in the brown suit turned to look repeatedly behind him at the railings of Green Park. He tapped his thigh with a newspaper held in his right hand.

Five minutes later the military band leading the parade passed through the Arch, followed closely by the king, gorgeously dressed in scarlet tunic and bearskin, on horseback. The ripple of applause turned into a wave of cheering.

When the king was level with Mrs Lawrence the man in brown to her immediate left let his newspaper drop, revealing a revolver in his fist. He levelled it at the king and Mrs Lawrence instinctively grabbed his arm and cried out. A few yards away Special Constable Anthony Dick spun round and struck the man on the arm. The gun spun across the road, landing harmlessly close to the hind leg of the king's horse. As the would-be assailant was bundled away anger swept through the crowd. One onlooker remarked: 'A revolver, how disrespectful.' Another shouted: 'You swine!'[1]

When Edward returned safely to the palace that afternoon, one of the first telegrams to reach him was from Adolf Hitler. It read: 'I have just received the news of the abominable attempt on the life of your Majesty, and send my heartfelt congratulations on your escape.'

The incident, on 16 July 1936, caused widespread alarm over royal protection. It was quickly agreed that in future police officers lining a royal route should always face the crowd, a practice which continues to the present day. It also spawned conspiracy theories which, as with most assassination plots, continue to thrive.

*   *   *

A press photographer captured the image of the man in brown being led away firmly by four constables gripping his arms. He was balding, podgy, his tie askew outside his waistcoat, with the appearance of respectability gone to seed. During the car journey to Hyde Park police station he gave his name as Patrick McMahon and told the officers that he had never meant to harm the monarch, but had 'only done it as a protest'. He was cautioned by Chief Inspector John Sands of Scotland Yard. In his clothing was found a picture postcard of the king and two rounds of revolver ammunition. The .36 calibre revolver retrieved from the scene was nickel-plated, loaded with five chambers and in good working order. The newspaper he had dropped bore the words 'May I love you' pencilled on the back page.[2]

After Sands' initial report the king was told later that night that Scotland Yard had 'unravelled the mystery'. McMahon was a 'frustrated Irish journalist who had convinced himself that the Secretary of State for Home Affairs had conspired to prevent him publishing a journal called the *Human Gazette*'. Sands apparently believed that this was not an assassination attempt, merely a device to publicise his perceived injustice.[3] Further investigations by Special Branch, and the behaviour of the prisoner, quickly threw that into doubt.

It emerged that McMahon had been born Jerome Banningan in Ireland in 1900 but was raised in Glasgow. He had dabbled in journalism and had spent three short terms in prison, the first two in Glasgow for embezzlement, the third in London for malicious libel against two policemen who, he had alleged, were taking bribes. He harboured deeply held resentments and was convinced that the state owed him restitution. Like several of Queen Victoria's attackers, he had left a paper trail of discontent. In a letter sent to the Home Secretary Sir John Simon, he claimed he was the victim of 'organised persecution' by 'your hirelings'. He added: 'I have been tormented for many months with unjust imprisonment. I demand justice.' Only hours before he aimed the revolver at the king he telephoned Simon's home, telling a receptionist that he had been forced to take the law into his own hands. The previous evening he had told a friend to scan the newspapers because 'something outrageous' was about to happen. Special Branch claimed that McMahon was a suspected Nazi sympathiser, and several witnesses came forward to confirm that they had seen him selling the Black Shirt newspaper in and around the Paddington area.[4]

At the Old Bailey in September McMahon made sensational claims. He said that the previous October he had been approached by an English intermediary who took him to meet representatives of a 'foreign power' – assumed to be Nazi Germany – outside their embassy. At a further meeting they focused on injustices in Ireland and suggested he might help the cause. Later, shortly after the death of George V, they urged him to join an attempt on the life of the new king, for which he would be paid £150. McMahon maintained that he had reported each meeting to MI5 and was acting as the security service's informant. He further claimed he had met an MI5 officer on the Monday before the supposed attack, who had told him to go through the motions so that the real plotters could be identified and picked up. The widespread view, expounded by *The Times*, was that McMahon's 'melodrama' was concocted to bolster his defence.

But McMahon's solicitor, Alfred Kerstein, approached the War Office and the Metropolitan Police and received reluctant confirmation from Chief Inspector Sands that McMahon had indeed corresponded with MI5. He refused to elaborate or reveal the name of the MI5 man who had met McMahon or give any details of what was said at that meeting. Kerstein appears to have identified him nevertheless and subpoenaed a 'Major K.C.' to appear at the trial. The officer ignored the subpoena. Further evidence of a German connection was also uncovered. The police insisted that the pencilled note referred to McMahon's wife Rose, who was sometimes called May. But a fellow tenant of McMahon's Westbourne Terrace address was a May Galley. She was a close friend of Austrian émigrés, one of whom two years later would be investigated in connection with Soviet spying at Woolwich Arsenal.

The judge and the court rejected McMahon's claims. Medical evidence was given stating that he was neither insane nor mentally defective, but was 'quite unreliable and habitually in a state of fantasy'. The authorities, however, felt they could not justify McMahon's initial two charges under the Treason Act. They could not prove intent to kill, or even that he had tried to pull the trigger. Sands said in a statement kept secret for 37 years: 'There can be no doubt he was seen to take the weapon from his pocket and, whatever his project, he was prevented from carrying it out effectively by those around him. No person heard the click of the trigger. We must stand by the evidence that either the revolver was knocked from McMahon's hand or thrown by him. Our view is in favour of the latter.' The two treason charges against him were dropped.[5]

McMahon was found guilty of producing a revolver near the person of the king with 'intent to alarm' and was sentenced to 12 months' hard labour. The judge concluded that he was someone who believed that notoriety would attract attention to his supposed grievances.

McMahon had barely begun his sentence when the king abdicated to marry the American divorcée Wallis Simpson. Later, he renewed his friendly acquaintance with Hitler and, to his grave, was accused of Nazi sympathies. McMahon served his time and faded into obscurity, refusing to speak about his real intentions that day. The secret, if there was one, died with him in 1970.

But the case continued to receive sporadic attention from conspiracy theorists. Who was the well-dressed man seen conversing with him minutes before the incident? Who was MI5's 'Major K.C.' who spoke to him a week earlier? If, as Scotland Yard admitted, McMahon had corresponded with the security services, what was the substance of that correspondence? And were the authorities, from the king downwards, suspiciously hasty in accepting that the attack was the work of a deranged loner? In the climate of 1936 any evidence of Nazi plotting against the life of the monarch would have been inconvenient. So too would evidence that MI5 was either encouraging a plot in order to swoop on the would-be assassin, or had been alerted but had taken no action.[6]

The release of Metropolitan Police files held at the Public Record Office in January 2003 added to the suspicions. An article published in the *Guardian* said:

> In the final analysis, if anyone was seeking to manipulate an impression-able malcontent with three minor convictions for fraud, whose story in the event of arrest is unlikely to be believed. Who better than George Andrew McMahon? Whether McMahon, the classic 'lone nut' assassin, ever had any intention of pulling the trigger may never be known. However, it now seems likely that the story he told the Old Bailey jury may have been the tip of a much larger iceberg.[7]

Nevertheless the released files do point to a more mundane answer. Sands inclined to the view that McMahon had thrown the revolver. The file shows that immediately after his arrest McMahon told him: 'I intended to shoot myself in front of the King, but I lost my head. I could easily have shot him, but I only threw it.'[8]

McMahon changed his story in court, possibly to gain maximum publicity for his grievances. The police kept the early statement under wraps while they considered charging him under the Treason Act. But it certainly seems plausible that a man consumed with resentments, a fantasist seething at not being taken seriously by the Home Office or the secret service, may have tried to commit suicide in the most spectacular fashion. And then bottled out.

12
British Assassinations Overseas

'How many children, how many parents?'

The creation, retention and eventual dismantling of the British Empire provided a fertile killing ground for assassins who used legitimate grievances, internal strife and tribal loyalties as a reason to target diplomats, civil servants, missionaries, traders and occasional military leaders.

In the nineteenth century Britain fought several punitive wars following attacks on their officials, usually with bloody outcomes. In 1897, for example, the acting British consul-general in Nigeria, J. R. Phillips, and his party were massacred while travelling to visit the King of Benin. An expedition under Rear Admiral Sir Harry Holdsworth Rawson was despatched upriver and men armed with Maxim machine guns left hundreds of natives dead at a cost of just 11 of their own. Such gunboat diplomacy continued well into the twentieth century, but the growth of nationalism within those vast areas of the globe painted imperial red saw an upsurge in the art of individual assassination. The global turmoil which followed the collapse of the Soviet Union and the break-up of the Balkans provided more opportunities for the assassin's craft. I have chosen three examples to illustrate all.

*　　*　　*

Egypt's importance to Britain was boosted by the opening of the Suez Canal in 1869 and the long decline of the Ottoman Empire. In 1882 political turmoil, the bankruptcy of the Egyptian administration and uncertainty over the Canal led the British to invade and secure victory at the bloody battle of Tel-el-Kebir. Egypt became a protectorate, with the British controlling much of the administration and the army. A nationalist movement was dormant for the first decade of the twentieth century, but within days of the armistice in 1918 the nationalist leader, Said Pasha Zagloul, tried to open talks on Egyptian independence. He was rebuffed and rioting broke out first in Cairo and Alexandria and then across the country. Zagloul and his lieutenants were deported to Malta, but that only deepened the crisis. Trains were derailed, telegraph lines cut, shops looted and street lamps torn down. Eight British soldiers who had been on leave seeing the sights at Luxor were taken off a train and murdered. In Cairo barricades were erected, homes burned and rifle fire was heard every night. The rioting was suppressed, but disturbances continued for the next five years. During the worst period of unrest between 1919 and 1922 there were 30 murders or attempted murders of British officials or soldiers by firearms and five more by bombs. Professor Robson of the Cairo Law School was shot in the back and killed as he walked home, possibly by some of his own students. Rioters were also cut down in cold blood by Egyptian police and troops under British command.

In February 1922 Egypt was declared an independent state, with the Sultan as king and a new constitution. But the British High Commissioner continued to advise the king and each ministry had a British adviser, while British judges sat on court benches alongside their Egyptian counterparts. The unrest continued and martial law, in force since 1914, remained until July 1923. Zagloul was allowed to return from exile in time for new elections and in January 1924 he was made prime minister. But further talks concerning a total British withdrawal collapsed and the country was in crisis once again.

At lunchtime on 19 November, Sir Lee Stack Pasha, *Sirdar* (commander-in-chief) of the Egyptian army and Governor-General of the Sudan, set off by car from the War Ministry in Cairo for home, sharing the back seat with his aide-de-camp, Captain Patrick Campbell. As the chauffeur, Fred Marsh, slowed down to pass a tram-line in the city centre, the car was surrounded by gunmen who blazed away with .32 pistols, hitting all three occupants. Marsh accelerated and the ambushers took chase, firing continuously, for 50 yards. They then shot their way through the crowd, hitting an Egyptian policeman. Before leaping into a waiting taxi the attackers threw a bomb, which did not explode, and got clean away. The following day Sir Lee died from shock and loss of blood from a cross-cut ('dum-dum') bullet.[1]

The police made house-to-house searches, found the escape taxi and arrested the usual suspects. Informants pointed to a secret society led by a lawyer and MP, Shafik Mansour, who had been questioned over previous political assassinations but released for lack of evidence. Again, no hard evidence could be found and the investigation ground to a halt. The authorities recruited an undercover spy called Helbawi who was serving a prison sentence connected to the attempted murder of a previous prime minister in 1914. Shafik's gang welcomed him and he reported that two members, the brothers Enayat, were most likely to crack under interrogation. The authorities told him to urge the Enayats to flee the country by train to Tripoli, so that they could be arrested in the desert where the chances of escape were minimal. On 31 January 1925 the brothers boarded the train at Alexandria. It was duly stopped, the men arrested and their carriage searched. Four automatic pistols and ammunition were uncovered in a basket of fruit. British forensic expert Sir Sydney Smith found that the markings on the dum-dum bullets and the cartridge cases matched those of the murder scene. Faced with such strong evidence, the younger 19-year-old brother confessed, followed by his 22-year-old sibling.

Their statements led to the arrest of six more gang members, including Shafik Mansour, who had a perfect alibi for the time of the crime – he was lunching with a government minister – and an engineer, Mahmoud Rachid. In the latter's home was found all the tools needed to convert the .32 ammunition to dum-dums and a bolt-hole for the murder weapons. Shafik strenuously denied heading the assassination conspiracy but, on hearing of the Enayat brothers' confessions, he began to act like a mad man, pacing his cell, tearing his clothes and making loud speeches as if on a public platform. Smith regarded it as 'no sign of madness as the poor devil had good reason to despair'. The doctor put him on a better diet and a few days later visited him in a more comfortable room. Smith, who was to become one of Britain's leading criminal forensic scientists, described Rachid's state:

> He was still sleeping badly and did not eat much, and he complained of headaches and many other pains. He answered questions sensibly but was in a dull, apathetic state. His memory for recent events was extremely bad,

and the whole of his mental faculties seemed dulled. He said that he had overheard that he was to be flogged, and he was afraid that he would die if this happened. He had also heard that the King had given orders that he was to be hanged, and this made him very agitated. I asked him if, as a lawyer, he believed such things could happen without a trial. He started crying – he always did when reminded of his status as a lawyer – and said he did not now believe what they had told him. Altogether he was extremely anxious and depressed, but the expectation that he would shortly be executed was not likely to have a soothing effect on him ... I felt rather sorry for him, but my sympathy was banished by the facts that he was responsible for the cold-blooded murder of several of my friends whose butchered bodies I had had to dissect.[2]

The trial was held at the end of March, six months after the assassination. Eight men, including the Enayats, Shafik and Rachid, were accused of murder or incitement to murder. The case rested on their confessions, some retracted, the evidence of informers and the forensics. Smith's expertise in what was only just becoming accepted as a new science proved critical. No one was capable of shaking his solid belief that the weapons found when the brothers were arrested and the equipment found in the engineer's home provided a perfect match to the bullets and cartridges found at the murder scene, including those extracted from the Sirdar's body.

On 7 June all eight defendants were pronounced guilty and sentenced to death. The Enayat brothers went berserk in the dock, one of them shouting: 'To death – my brother and I? Traitors! Liars!'[3] One convicted conspirator had his sentence commuted to life imprisonment, but the other seven, including the brothers and Shafik, were executed.

*   *   *

On 7 November 1944, as the war in Europe raged, Churchill stood in the Commons chamber and announced the death of his close friend Lord Moyne 'at the hands of foul assassins'.[4] His killers were not Nazis or their agents, but Jewish liberationists. Churchill said that the Jews had lost 'a well-informed friend'. His assassins thought otherwise.

A scion of the renowned brewing family, Walter Edward Guinness was born in Dublin on 29 March 1880, the third son of the Earl of Iveagh. Eton-educated, he volunteered in the Boer War and was wounded and mentioned in despatches. He was elected Conservative

MP for Bury St Edmunds in 1907. During the First World War he served with the Suffolk Yeomanry in Egypt and in the bloodbath of Gallipoli. In 1922 he was appointed Under-Secretary for War. Later, his ministerial career peaked when he was made Minister of Agriculture. After the defeat of the Conservatives, he retired from politics in 1931 and was created Baron Moyne. During the 1930s he served on various commissions and indulged his love of travel. After the outbreak of his third war, and the return to power of Churchill, he again took political office, and in 1941 became Secretary of State for the Colonies and Leader of the House of Lords. In August 1942 he was appointed deputy Minister of State in Cairo, and in January 1944 Minister Resident in the Middle East.

His main task was to address the Zionist Question. Jewish resistance to the British Mandate in Palestine began before the outbreak of the Second World War with the formation of Irgun, made up of extremists determined to create a separate Jewish state. But faced with the war against Nazism, Irgun chose to support the Allies to fight a common enemy. A splinter group led by Abraham Stern disagreed and continued a campaign of terrorist attacks and murders against British targets. Stern was killed in a shoot-out with Palestinian police early in 1942, but his death did not disrupt the campaign by his compatriots, who continued to be known as the Stern Gang. In 1944, with the forces of Nazi Germany in retreat, Irgun resumed its attacks on the British administration in Palestine. Under a new leader, the future Israeli prime minister Menachem Begin, it bombed immigration and tax offices and police stations. Such attacks, with Hitler not yet defeated, were condemned by the Jewish Agency and the Hagana (the Jewish Defence Force), the forerunner of the Israeli Army. The Stern Gang and elements of Irgun began looking for a high-profile target. They settled on Lord Moyne.

Much has been made, particularly by apologists, of the choice of Moyne as a target. Zionists even now claim that he was responsible for the *Struma* tragedy. It was claimed that in December 1941 Moyne forced the Turks to send a refugee ship, the *Struma*, back into the Black Sea after refusing a permit to allow the passengers to stop at Palestine en route to Mauritius, resulting in the loss of the ship and 426 men, 269 women and 70 children. In fact, Moyne was not stationed in the Middle East at the time. He was also blamed for the

1939 British White Paper on Palestine which did not envisage a Jewish homeland, even though he took no part in writing it. Neither was he an outspoken anti-Zionist, partly because of his sympathies for all the people of the region, and partly because he had been in Cairo as Minister Resident only for a matter of weeks, little enough time to offend anyone even in that fevered atmosphere. It was also claimed that when the German Final Solution architect, Adolf Eichmann, eager to rescue the wreckage of the Third Reich, sent his emissary Joel Brand to suggest that a million Hungarian Jews might be exchanged for trucks and equipment, Moyne replied: 'What would I do with a million Jews?' But Brand's testimony has been discredited, and at that stage of the war there was never any question of such bargaining, except in the over-excited imagination of frightened Nazis. Individual members of the Stern Gang, including those chosen to commit murder, may well have believed any or all of the above. But those who ordered the assassination knew better. The reason Moyne was targeted was simple: he was the highest-ranking British official within reach of the Stern Gang, a 'soft' target, and his death would send a clear message to the British Foreign Office, deemed to be pro-Arab, that Zionist terrorists were a force to be reckoned with.[5]

Moyne was living at 4–6 Hassan Sabry Street, an opulent villa in Cairo's garden suburb, whose former occupants had included General Sir Archibald Wavell. There were oak doors, fashionable white furniture and a sunken bathtub. On 6 November 1944 Moyne and his driver, Lance-Corporal Fuller, returned from a day's work – as they did at the same time every day – from his offices where he co-ordinated the region's war efforts. It was a quiet neighbourhood with a small police hut at the end of the road, often manned by a lone constable. Nearby were North Africa's premier polo and cricket fields. Hidden in the bushes outside the villa were two young men in their early twenties, Eliahou Bet-Zouri and Eliahou Al Hakim, members of the Stern Gang.

The men opened fire at close range as Moyne and his driver got out of the car. Neither stood a chance. The assassins cycled off towards a pre-arranged safe house. But at that moment a police constable from another district was passing on his motorcycle. He heard the shots and gave chase. He overtook the men at Fouad Al Awal bridge and, with help, subdued them.

Under immediate police interrogation both men confessed, but insisted they had been carrying out the orders of a Zionist organisation. They said that Moyne had to die to send a message to Britain: 'Stop interfering with Jewish immigration into Palestine ... or else.'[6] The Stern Gang, by then commanded by another future Israeli premier, Yitzhak Shamir, claimed responsibility in a statement which read:

> We accuse Lord Moyne and the Government he represents with murdering hundreds and thousands of our brethren; we accuse him of seizing our country and looting our possessions. We were forced to do justice and fight ...

The assassins were condemned by all sides. The pro-Israel newspaper *Ha'aretz* described the murders as 'one of the worse abominations since Zionism began'. World Zionism leader Chaim Weizmann, later to become Israel's first president, described the assassination as 'a far more severe shock and more numbing than that of my own son'. In a letter to Churchill, he wrote: 'I can hardly find words adequate to express the deep moral indignation and horror which I feel. I know that these feelings are shared by Jewry throughout the world.'[7] Ben Gurion, later Israel's first prime minister, described the assassins as traitors to the Jewish people. And the *Zionist Review* said: 'The dastardly acts of the Stern Gang are morally indefensible and politically crazy. Murder is alien to the high teachings of Judaism. Thou shalt not kill is one of the 10 Commandments.' Rabbis added their voices. Joseph Hertz, Chief Rabbi of the British Empire, said it was his 'solemn duty to give expression to the horror and sorrow of every Jew over the dastardly murder of a great public servant. The criminals are men crazed by the fiendish butcheries of kith and kin in the human slaughterhouse of Poland.'[8]

Crazed or not, Bet-Zouri and Al Hakim were sentenced to death and hanged. They were buried in a corner of the Jewish cemetery in Bassateen, near Cairo.

As the war against Germany drew to a close, both Irgun and the Stern Gang stepped up their operations against the British administration in Palestine. Police stations, RAF airfields and military arsenals were attacked in 1944–5. A British judge and six officers were kidnapped and released in exchange for Jewish detainees. In June 1946 the British High Commissioner Sir Allan Cunningham ordered *Operation Agatha*, sending 17,000 troops into Jerusalem in a bid to crush Irgun and its offshoots. Their response, on 22 July, was the bombing of the King David Hotel which housed the Secretariat of the British administration and its military headquarters. A party of up to 20 Jews dressed as Arab workmen unloaded milk churns filled with 225 kg of explosives. A gun battle erupted when an officer who had spotted them and a policeman were shot dead. The terrorists lit the fuse and escaped. The explosion tore apart the seven-storey building, trapping many people in the rubble. In the following days 91 bodies, including those of 15 Jews, were recovered. Irgun claimed to have given the British a warning message. That was denied by the survivors.

The terrorist outrage was condemned by the Jewish Agency and led to further military crackdowns. British courts began sentencing Irgun prisoners to death for terrorism, and that fate met the bombers of the British Officers club in Haifa in which over 30 were killed or injured. But the terror attacks continued, with bombs and machine-guns targeted on clubs and restaurants frequented by British military personnel and civil servants. In one of the most infamous incidents, two British sergeants were kidnapped and hanged from eucalyptus trees at Nathanya, their bodies booby-trapped.

But after years battered by global conflict, Britain was in no mood for a prolonged bloodbath. Full details of Jewish losses in the Holocaust pricked consciences in the UK and strengthened the hand of Jewish Americans who backed the partition of Palestine into Arab homelands and a new state of Israel. After much more bloodshed as Arabs fought the parcelling up of their lands, Ben Gurion proclaimed Israel's independence in Tel Aviv on 14 May 1948.

In the decades that followed, Moyne's assassins became folk heroes. Many of those who had publicly condemned them at the time now hailed them as part of the liberation struggle. Moyne's reputation was smeared. During an Egypt–Israel prisoner exchange in 1975, President Anwar Sadat released the two bodies. Israeli premier Yitzhak Rabin gave the two Eliahous a full military funeral and they were buried at Mount Harzl, an area reserved for the most renowned Israeli citizens.

*   *   *

On Thursday, 8 June 2000 Britain's 52-year-old defence attaché in Athens, Brigadier Stephen Saunders, was stuck in a traffic jam on his way to the British embassy. Two men on a motorcycle pulled up alongside his unmarked car and shot him four times in the chest. Saunders left behind his wife, Heather, and two daughters, Nicola, 16, and Catherine, 15.

Within hours the Greek 'November 17' guerrilla group claimed responsibility, saying the assassination had been carried out because of the officer's efforts in co-ordinating NATO's bombing of Yugoslavia. Their allegation was described by the Ministry of Defence as 'utter fantasy'. An official said that Saunders was with the UN observation mission to Iraq when the bombing of Serbian forces in Kosovo started.

Officers of Scotland Yard's anti-terrorism branch and Foreign Office investigators flew to Greece to help local police find the culprits. The Greek Government offered a reward and Foreign Minister George Papandreou promised to do 'everything possible to bring the perpetrators to justice'. There was massive pressure to do just that. The US State Department had previously described Greece as 'one of the weakest links' in the fight against terrorism, and there were international concerns about its ability to provide effective security for the 2004 Olympic Games. One Greek politician, who had himself survived an assassination attempt, said: 'Greece is the only country where it has been impossible to not only smoke out terrorism, but even to make a single substantial strike against it.'[9]

There was little doubt that 'November 17' was sympathetic to the Serbs because of their common hostility to Turkey and the ethnic Albanians in Kosovo. The group's 17-page statement also claimed responsibility for a series of rocket attacks the previous year on three foreign banks and the residence of the German ambassador, in which no one was killed.[10] The group's 25-year history was even bloodier. It was born as a Marxist-Leninist resistance to the military junta which ruled Greece from 1967 to 1975, and was named after the date in 1973 when a student uprising was crushed by army tanks which killed 20 youngsters at an Athens polytechnic. Its leader was a shadowy figure codenamed Lambros, who was believed to have fled the Greek junta and built up the beginnings of a terrorist network from other exiles living on or near student campuses in France. When they were ready they returned to Greece. The highly secretive group's first known attack was the murder of Richard Welch, America's CIA chief in Athens, in December 1975. He was shot while returning from a party. The .45

calibre pistol used became the group's weapon of choice. Welch was targeted because of the US's support for the junta, but the group was fiercely anti-Western up to and beyond the end of the Cold War. In 1994 they planned to blow up a British aircraft carrier using anti-tank mines, but the plot was fruitless.[11] The same year the group killed a former governor of the Greek state bank, after calling for a popular uprising against capitalism. Experts reckoned the group had no more than 25 active members, including members of the same families. Yet despite the group having admitted 21 killings, the Greek police were reportedly unable to identify a single member. That gave rise to claims that because the 2000 political establishment emerged from the original resistance to the Colonels, 'November 17' had influential friends. Few were surprised at the lack of progress of the investigation into Saunders' murder in the next two years. There were no arrests. Then, a blunder on the part of the terrorists gave the police their first lead.

On 29 June 2002 an icon painter, Savas Xiros, was seriously injured and captured when a bomb he was planting in Athens exploded prematurely. A gun discovered close by was found to have been stolen from a police officer during a 1984 'November 17' robbery. Xiros was interrogated and police discovered two arms dumps containing anti-tank missiles, handguns and automatic rifles. Forensics matched one .45 to that which had killed Saunders. Xiros's brother Vasilis was arrested and admitted to the murder of Saunders and to the killing in 1997 of Anglo-Greek businessman Constantinos Peratikos. Another brother, Christodoulos, was also arrested. Fingerprints found at the arms caches were found to belong to 58-year-old economist Alexandros Giotopoulos, a long-time 'November 17' suspect. Although his fingerprints had been on record since a minor conviction in 1970, police had never before had enough evidence to arrest him for terrorism. Greek special forces commandeered a fire-fighting helicopter and flew to the island of Lipsi. Giotopoulos was detained as he tried to escape by hydrofoil. Investigators claimed he matched the profile of Lambros.

More arrests followed, with investigators under pressure during the West's 'war on terror' which followed the September 11 suicide attacks on America by unrelated Islamic terrorists. In March 2003 Giotopoulos and 18 others were charged with murder, bombings and robbery. The 23 murder charges could not include that of Richard Welch because of the Greek judicial system's 20-year statute of limitations. Nevertheless, it took Greek prosecutors six hours to read out more than 2,000 charges. The chief prosecutor grew so hoarse that he had to hand over to a junior colleague. Giotopoulos pleaded not guilty to all charges, claiming that the accusations were an 'Anglo-American fabrication'. He added: 'I am here because the Americans want it. I come from a well-known left-wing family.'[12] Alleged top hitman Dimitris Koufodinas also denied the charges, saying: 'This is a trial of extreme measures.' Savas Xiros refused to enter a plea, claiming that evidence had been extracted from him under psychological pressure, the threat of deportation to the US and while he was on medication. 'I consider this court inappropriate and illegal,' he said.[13]

The trial lasted nine months. Giotopoulos was found guilty of planning the assassination of Brigadier Saunders. Koufodinas and the two brothers, Savas and Vasilis, were convicted of carrying it out. Koufodinas and Savas were both in their forties, but the younger brother was 31, suggesting he had grown up in a terrorist family. They were sentenced to life imprisonment. Koufodinas' wife, Angeliki Sotiropoulou, was acquitted of being an accomplice.

The Brigadier's wife, Heather, still grieving with her two daughters, said: 'Nobody really wins in this situation. But if they are taken off the streets for a while and given a piece of their own medicine, albeit in no comparison to what we have suffered, then that is perhaps justice.' She added: 'We will never get proper justice. They killed 23 people – but that is 23 widows, there's goodness knows how many children, how many parents. They will all carry this scar for the rest of their lives.'[14]

Mrs Saunders had taken out a civil action to ensure she could give evidence at the trial. She was awarded on OBE for her part in the campaign to find and convict her husband's killer. Within hours of his murder she had made an appeal for information outside the gates of the British Embassy, saying: 'I only hope that the people who carried out this cowardly act on an unarmed man on his way to work will realise the total devastation that they have caused. Not only have they killed my husband, but they have now destroyed me and my entire family.'

During the trial she said: 'It's not blood that I seek in revenge. I just want these people deprived of their freedoms and taken away from their family and loved ones as I, my two daughters and my mother-in-law were taken away from ours.'[15]

13
The Troubles to Airey Neave

'one of freedom's warriors'

Between 1968 and 2002 almost 3,650 people died violently in Northern Ireland and Britain as a result of military, paramilitary or sectarian activity; many more were crippled, maimed or left traumatised and bereaved. In many senses virtually all the deaths could be considered assassinations as they were casualties either of terrorism or of that era's narrow war on terror. They were killed to further opposing political aims, to settle scores, to finance terrorism or to fight it. By focusing on the assassination of well-known, overtly political figures I intend no disrespect to less vaunted victims and their families. There is, I hope, an understanding that the deaths of three-year-old Jonathan Ball or twelve-year-old Timothy Parry in Warrington, for example, or the numerous other children, women, men, soldiers, civilians, police officers and bystanders killed during the course of a war conveniently called The Troubles are inherently and humanely no less important than the deaths of Lord Mountbatten and Airey Neave.

*   *   *

The Six Counties of Northern Ireland remained a province of the United Kingdom, to the dismay of the largely Catholic Republican movement and the delight of the Protestant majority in the North. It was never a place of peace. Sectarian problems were exacerbated by militants on both sides and the ongoing activities of paramilitaries. By the 1960s the Catholic minority were seething about the injustices of their treatment, some imagined, mostly real. The Protestant and Orange stranglehold on political institutions and industry denied many Catholics votes, jobs and decent housing. A civil rights movement was born out of a newly vocal Catholic middle class who regarded Sinn Fein and the IRA as outdated and irrelevant. Protestants controlling Stormont and the other levers of power became increasingly nervous.

The flashpoint came in Londonderry on 5 October 1968, when television cameras captured RUC officers savagely attacking a peaceful civil rights march. There were 77 civilian casualties, including the Republican Labour MP for Belfast West, Gerry Fitt. He later recalled: 'A sergeant grabbed me and pulled my coat down over my shoulders to prevent me raising my arms. Two other policemen held me as I was batoned on the head. I could feel blood coursing down my neck and on to my shirt. As I fell to my knees I was roughly grabbed and thrown into a police van.'[1] The images of that bloody clash were broadcast around the world and unleashed fury in the Catholic community. The civil rights movement was given an enormous boost, but Stormont's premier, Terence O'Neill, initially refused to concede the key demand of one man, one vote. O'Neill was, however, prepared at least to seek a compromise, but any hope of that was shattered by the hard-line Home Affairs minister, William Craig. He declared at a Unionist rally: 'There is all this nonsense about civil rights, and behind it all there is our old traditional enemy exploiting the situation. The civil rights movement is bogus and is made up of ill-informed people who see in unrest a chance to renew the campaign of violence.' That Christmas O'Neill wrote privately: 'What a year! I fear 1969 will be worse. The one thing I cannot foresee is peace.'

He was right. In January another civil rights march was ambushed at Burntollet Bridge by Loyalists armed with stones and cudgels, whilst the police stood by and watched. More and more demonstrators filled local casualty departments. Hard-line Unionist MPs demanded O'Neill's resignation for failing to control events. Over 1,000 B Special police officers were mobilised to guard public utilities after several electricity and water installations were bombed. At the time the IRA were blamed, but later it was shown to be the work of the Protestant paramilitary Ulster Volunteer Force as part of their campaign to loosen O'Neill's shaky grip on power. O'Neill called an election, but the results were messy and inconclusive. One of his last acts before stepping down was to push one man, one vote through Stormont, but by then it was too late to stop civil and sectarian unrest turning into a more sinister beast.

O'Neill's successor was James Chichester-Clark, a distant relative. He possessed none of the talents necessary to prevent Northern Ireland sliding into even more violent mayhem. Petrol bombs became the weapon of choice on the streets as pitched battles were fought between Catholics and Protestants, Republicans and Unionists, the Orange Order and police. Protestant mobs charged police lines and smashed Catholic homes. In Belfast and Londonderry – known as Derry by the Republicans – barricades went up, houses were torched and traffic gridlocked by crowds surging in every direction. The Stormont administration had clearly lost control. Families on both sides of the Ulster divide began to pull ancient pistols and rifles from dusty caches. Eight people died in those early disturbances, four of them killed by the police, and 750 were injured, 150 of those with gunshot wounds. Reluctantly, Chichester-Clark asked the Labour Government headed by Harold Wilson to send in troops to restore order and, in particular, offer greater protection to Catholic communities than his own over-stretched and exhausted police forces could provide.

At first the arrival of the 2,500 troops was warmly welcomed by Catholics, who had seen 1,500 families driven from their homes. The IRA's failure to protect them from Protestant mobs was treated with contempt – the slogan 'IRA – I ran away' was painted on a wall in the Falls Road. The IRA itself split and a new force, the Provisionals, came into being specifically to protect Catholic enclaves. It quickly turned into a political killing machine. Protestant vigilante groups also morphed into paramilitary forces. There were killings, and a UVF member blew himself up while attempting to set a bomb, but in the early months the troops kept the peace and an eerie calm descended on the Province.

It didn't last. The army, so warmly welcomed at first, increasingly clashed with the Republicans and working-class Catholics, especially in Belfast. In July 1970 the army imposed a curfew and sealed off a large section of the Lower Falls Road district to conduct a house-to-house search for weapons. It was not a gentle operation and cordial relations with the populace were fatally poisoned. The following month a Catholic teenager was shot dead by troops during a riot in North Belfast.

At Westminster, the new Conservative prime minister, Edward Heath, appointed Reginald Maudling as Home Secretary. In that role he, not Stormont, had control of military operations. Maudling sparked a political storm when he spoke of the concept of 'an acceptable level of violence' in Northern Ireland. Internment without trial for suspected terrorists was introduced in August 1971. It further boosted IRA recruitment.

Sean O'Callaghan, the son of an IRA veteran, joined the Provos at the age of 17 that year, and later described those sent with him to a training camp in Kerry:

> The young recruits ... were by and large the type of ordinary young men you would find in any British or Irish city. They listened to the same music, wore similar fashionable clothes and often followed the same English soccer clubs. They all had their youth and their anger. They saw their primary duty as protecting their own areas: the Provisional IRA was born and forged in the white heat of sectarian warfare. The vast majority had no coherent political outlook. In fact, they mainly despised politics. A youthful fascination with guns and bombs, and a desire to get even with the Prods, was all the motivation they needed. Ill-educated and ill-equipped, they were vulnerable to republican propaganda. The hard leadership of the Provisionals, mainly older and embittered men who had waited all their lives for such an opportunity, plied them with guns and turned their hatred into a lifelong commitment to violence. They had been ground down by bigotry, starved of hope. In other cities they might have rioted and returned to normal life, but the IRA gave them a sense of purpose and a cause to kill and die for.[2]

Jackie McMullan, later gaoled for life for attempted murder, recalled:

> In my teens I was arrested maybe 20 times. Every male aged 13 to 65 would have been arrested, the vast majority for screening. And every single one of my friends joined the Fianna [the IRA youth wing]. We'd be scouting; you wouldn't have participated in firing guns or in ambushes. After school there were riots. The Brits, probably bored out of their skulls, used to drive down the Glen Road every day as schools were getting out.[3]

Street violence and organised terrorism escalated on all sides. Three off-duty soldiers were shot dead by the IRA at Ligoniel, but the Catholic casualties rose faster. After a man and a youth were shot dead in a Londonderry riot Sinn Fein's Maire Drumm told a Bogside meeting: 'The only way you can avenge these deaths is by being organised. I would personally prefer to see all the British army going back dead.' A UVF bomb killed 15 in McGurk's Bar in North Belfast. Then, in January 1972, 14 people were shot dead by paratroopers in what became known as Bloody Sunday. The rioting which followed spilled across the border and the British embassy in Dublin was burned down.

The Bloody Sunday outrage more than any other swung large swathes of the Catholics behind the massive retaliation of the IRA, both the Officials and the Provisionals. The Officials bombed the Aldershot military barracks. Northern Ireland minister John Taylor was seriously injured in a gun attack. Provisional IRA bombed the Abercorn Bar in Belfast city centre, killing two and injuring 130. Another IRA bomb in Donegal Street, Belfast, killed seven. The British Government insisted on taking more control of law and order powers. The Stormont Parliament resigned in protest, and direct rule from London was imposed.

The new Secretary of State, William Whitelaw, opened talks with the Republicans. The Official IRA called off its terrorist campaign, while the Provisionals agreed a ceasefire. In July Sinn Fein leaders, including Gerry Adams, went to London for talks, but these collapsed. The terrorist war was on again. The rest of that month saw unprecedented carnage: 22 IRA bombs in Belfast killed 11 and injured more than 60. Two children and two soldiers were among the dead in what became known as Bloody Friday. Another bomb killed eight in Claudy, Co. Londonderry. The bodies of three Protestants, one a member of the Territorial Army, were found shot dead in Belfast. So too was a member of the Ulster Defence Association. In most bomb attacks the casualties included Protestants and Catholics. The Army and the Protestant para-militaries fought back in an endless litany of bomb, bullet and tit-for-tat killings.

In 1972, the bloodiest year in a bloody decade, 321 paramilitaries and civilians were killed and 3,902 injured; these included 129 soldiers and police officers killed and 578 injured. There were 1,853 bombs and 10,630 shootings, six times the number of the previous year. Many British soldiers found the hatreds hard to handle without developing prejudices of their own. A corporal in the Scots Guards recalled: 'My overriding memory of 1972 is of seeing bodies being dragged out of a blown-up house and the people on one side of the road screaming and laughing at the people on the other side. That really affected the way

I felt. It always seemed it was Catholics versus the army. Although I know that wasn't actually the case, it did seem that way at the time.'

The constant danger was recalled by a sergeant in the Royal Green Jackets:

We had a guy killed and two others injured by a single shot through the back window of a Saracen. The round passed through the head of the first man, killing him outright, took out an eye and damaged the nose of the second bloke, and ended up in the third guy's ass. The gunman had lain down on a table in the back kitchen of a house they'd taken over, propped up the letter box with a pencil and fired through the whole length of the house into the back of the passing vehicle. It was either a very lucky shot, or the gunman was very good. The Belfast IRA had a guy we nick-named 'One-shot Willy' working for them at the time, and we always reckoned he might have done it.

The horror of a war in civvy street was brought home to a sergeant in the Royal Military Police during the Bloody Friday bombing blitz:

The Oxford bus station, that was dreadful. They planted a bomb in the bus station, and a little boy was killed. A little shoe, the bits and pieces, we had to put them into plastic bags; and we had to photograph the bodies in the morgue. That was the worst incident I've seen in Ulster. I saw Chinese blown up in the Korean War but you get immune to that. It felt different when you saw your own countrymen being killed that way. I mean, I classified it as my own country.

More ceasefires came and went. Conferences were held; more secret talks; and more schisms opened up in the political parties and paramilitary groupings. The Heath administration set up a power-sharing executive in the Province under Ulster Unionist leader Brian Faulkner, but it was marked by fisticuffs and Unionist disputes. The death toll mounted remorselessly. That did not change with the election of another Labour Government, again headed by Harold Wilson. His efforts to achieve a solution through the Sunningdale Agreement on a new Assembly with all parties represented was wrecked by Unionist leaders Ian Paisley and Harry West. After Faulkner quit the Ulster Unionist Party to form the more moderate Unionist Party of Northern Ireland, the Assembly voted to endorse a new power-sharing executive. That triggered a massive Protestant strike organised by the Ulster Workers Council, which crippled industry, commerce and day-to-day life. Three days into the strike 32 people were killed by Loyalist bombers in Dublin and Monaghan, the single highest casualty rate of the Troubles. North of the border Loyalist barricades were left in place by the army, which saw its role as combating terrorism, not curbing street protests. RUC officers who tried to clear the streets were attacked and their families intimidated. Secretary of State Merlyn Rees shared with army chiefs the belief that the strike could not be defeated by direct confrontation. Wilson's patience snapped and he made an ill-judged speech describing Unionists as 'people who spend their lives sponging off Westminster'. The executive collapsed and the strike was called off. The hard-line Unionists had won.

Frustrated, the Provisional IRA stepped up active service unit operations on mainland Britain. In October 1974 five were killed and 54 injured when IRA bombs exploded in a Guildford pub. The horror of that attack was topped the following month when 21 were killed and 182 hurt in an IRA blitz on two Birmingham city centre bars.

On 27 November 1975 Ross McWhirter, aged 50, a co-founder of the *Guinness Book of Records* who had vociferously condemned Republican violence, was shot dead by the IRA at his home in Enfield, in Essex. McWhirter, who also presented BBC's *Record Breakers*, was prominent in the ultra-right-wing Freedom Association and had offered a £50,000 award for information leading to the arrest of IRA bombers. His wife, Rosemary, arrived home and was confronted by two men holding pistols. She ran into the house when her husband opened the door and seconds later heard two shots. McWhirter was hit in the head and chest, and died soon after being admitted to a local hospital. His wife and two sons were put under 24-hour police guard.[4] Conservative Party leader Margaret Thatcher recalled in her memoirs: 'His death had a personal significance for me, quite apart from the loss of a personal friend; within days I was assigned a team of personal detectives who have been with me ever since.'[5]

The killers used the McWhirter family car to escape. Two weeks later three members of the IRA active service unit who had killed McWhirter and carried out dozens of other attacks in London were cornered by police and, after an exchange of shots, took refuge with two hostages in what became known as the Balcombe Street siege. After six days the men gave themselves up. They were charged with ten murders and 20 bombings and jailed for life in 1977. They were freed under the terms of the Good Friday Agreement in 1999.

Sean O'Callaghan, who by the age of 20 was an IRA Volunteer and had taken part in a mortar bomb attack in which a female member of the Ulster Defence Regiment had died, later gave an account of what it was like to be an assassin, and the planning involved. In August 1974 he was ordered to kill Special Branch Detective Inspector Peter Flanagan, a Catholic RUC officer stationed in Omagh, where his father had been a police sergeant. Flanagan was an IRA target because of allegations, later disproved, that he mistreated Republican prisoners. 'I was the only full-time active service operator in the area and consequently the job fell to me – it was as coincidental as that,' O'Callaghan wrote later.[6] An IRA intelligence man told him that Flanagan visited Broderick's pub at lunch-time almost every weekday, parking his car in George Street.

> I went to Omagh and stayed with republican sympathisers in a house not far from Broderick's. For four days I checked out Flanagan's movements. I was happy enough to see his car there but I still had to check that he was in the pub. Omagh was a heavily garrisoned town with a large security presence. I could not afford to rule out the possibility that Flanagan's apparently very relaxed attitude might be a plan to flush out an IRA unit. Equally I couldn't afford to run the risk of alerting Flanagan by staying too long in the bar or by allowing him to pick up my southern accent. On the day that I finally went into Broderick's, he was sitting on a bar stool at the furthest end of the door. I walked to the opposite end of the bar and quietly, in a passable Tyrone accent, ordered a half-pint of Guinness. I drank it fairly quickly and then left.

O'Callaghan picked a teenage IRA Volunteer from Belfast, Paul Norney, as his accomplice and he was sent a young woman, nicknamed Lulu, as a driver. The team was assembled and two brand-new snub-nose Magnum .357 revolvers were sent to a safe house. On 23 August, helped by local volunteers, the three drove to Broderick's. Lulu remained outside, keeping the getaway car's engine ticking over. Norney checked that the inspector was in the pub, giving O'Callaghan the thumbs up.

'I was first through the bar; Peter Flanagan was at the bar reading the *Irish Independent*,' O'Callaghan recalled.

> He understood what was happening and began to move from his stool: 'No, please no!' I steadied, took aim and fired. He was still moving, trying to escape. He stumbled to the door leading to the toilets and fell through it. I fired eight times in total. I remember looking at him as he lay face down on the floor of the toilet. I have no recollection of blood, or anything else, really, beyond the certain knowledge that he was dead. I knew that I had

to keep calm and that the most important thing was to stay in control. I reloaded the gun just in case. This also reinforced control and discipline, allowing me to think ahead. We left the toilet and walked through the pub. The other customers and the barman were stunned, in shock. One woman said something. I told her to be quiet: 'Just sit down, shut up and nothing will happen to you.' Most of the faces were frozen; the murder had taken only seconds and it looked as though no one had moved. The owner was still standing with an empty glass and a towel in his hands. We walked out of the pub.[7]

That night O'Callaghan was troubled:

One clear thought flashed through my mind, the memory of which has never left me: 'You're going to have to pay for this some day.' Then, the notion seemed ridiculous. As far as I was concerned I had done no wrong. I had not committed a crime, a sin. I had no reason to feel guilty. After all, I was fighting for a righteous cause. So why? I don't know. But there was no mistaking the doubt. I pushed that troublesome thought away. 'Get your act together, you halfwit,' I told myself. I could not comprehend how such a thought could have even entered my head. Perhaps already something about the nature of what I was doing was beginning to get through to me. It was the first and only time that I have killed someone deliberately, in cold blood, and maybe the enormity triggered some religious or moral response from childhood.[8]

In 1988 O'Callaghan gave himself up, and two years later was sentenced to 539 years for murder and his other terrorist crimes. He was released after just eight years and it emerged that long before he had turned informer on the IRA. He worked with the Unionist leader David Trimble to secure a peace agreement. He remains on the run from his former comrades.

The cycle of terror, talks, ceasefires, more ceasefires and more terror continued. Attitudes hardened and pragmatism was replaced by more murderous determination. A generation was now steeped in the scars, mindsets and language of a civil war with many more than two sides. Each death created a score of mourners with little inclination to forgive and forget. The IRA and the UVF refined their assassination techniques. Their targets were police officers and soldiers, squealers from within their own ranks, double agents, paramilitary opponents, prison warders and innocents who simply wandered across an invisible sectarian line drawn without chalk down the middle of some bleak road. The 'Shankill Butchers', Protestant thugs, slashed and tortured

19 people to death and terrorised many more. The IRA began to go after more senior military and political targets.

In July 1976 Christopher Ewart-Biggs was appointed British ambassador in Dublin. Ewart-Biggs was a hero of more conventional warfare, having lost his right eye in the 1942 Battle of El Alamein. He wore a monocle over the glass replacement. As British consul in Algiers in 1961, before the French withdrawal, he had lived under the constant threat of assassination by French colonialists. He was 54 when he arrived to take up his new post in Dublin. He told journalists: 'I have one prejudice acquired during the war – a very strong and distinct prejudice against violence for political ends.' For the first twelve days he took routine precautions, varying the route between his office and residence. But at one spot in the road at Sandymount he had to choose right or left. He chose right and just 150 yards from his home an IRA landmine exploded under his vehicle. Ewart-Biggs and 26-year-old civil servant Judith Cooke were killed. The driver, Brian O'Driscoll, and another passenger, Permanent Under-Secretary Brian Cubbon, the highest-ranking British civil servant serving in Northern Ireland, were injured.

The envoy's widow Jane Ewart-Biggs campaigned vigorously to improve British–Irish relations and established an annual literary prize in his honour. She died, a Labour peer, in 1992. The IRA admitted detonating the mine, but no one was ever charged with the murders. At a memorial service 25 years later the then British ambassador in Dublin said that the murderers 'were unable to bury the ideals of reconciliation on this island for which Christopher Ewart-Biggs stood'.[9]

Shortly after the assassination the British prime minister, James Callaghan, appointed Sir Richard Sykes, a senior Foreign Office official with special responsibility for security, to work with the Irish authorities investigating the murders. Sykes, a much-decorated war hero, was a Foreign Office high-flier and intelligence expert, having served in China, Cuba and embassies which acted as listening posts on the Soviet bloc. He had also been a close friend of the slain ambassador. Working with Dublin he devised what became known as the Sykes Plan. Its contents were highly confidential, but resulted in a shake-up of security measures to protect diplomats.

Callaghan next posted Sykes to Holland as ambassador. It was a sensitive posting because several Dutch groups sympathetic to the IRA were believed to be engaged in arms smuggling. The British embassy in The Hague monitored these groups and organised surveillance of suspected safe houses for IRA men. During Sykes' tenure the British security services scored a number of significant successes. The biggest coup was a British–Dutch operation, which intercepted a 2-ton shipment of second-hand Czech arms at Schiphol airport. The cases bore false labels and were destined for Dublin. Sykes' role in gathering and sifting intelligence was well known and, after 43 bombs were located in a shed adjacent to Belfast Docks, Northern Ireland Secretary Roy Mason was briefed that the IRA was planning top-level reprisals.

At 9 am on 22 March 1979, in a small courtyard at the ambassador's residence, 19-year-old footman Karel Straub held the door of the official limousine due to take Sykes to the embassy, a five-minute drive away. Two men, one dressed in a black suit, the other in brown, stepped out of the shadows and fired long-barrelled pistols. Sykes and Straub were both hit in the head. Sykes fell into the car and the gunmen shot him three more times before the chauffeur, Jack Wilson, could drive off. Straub fell to the pavement and was shot again where he lay. The assailants, whom witnesses described as being in their late thirties, disappeared into a maze of alleys and side-streets. A few hours later both Sykes and Straub died in hospital within a few minutes of each other. Sykes, the father of three, was 58.[10]

A police spokesman said that they could not rule out the involvement of the IRA or the German Baader-Meinhof terrorist group. Another mystery puzzled investigators: the fact that Sykes, an experienced security practitioner who had tightened protective measures for other diplomats, had taken little or no precautions regarding his own safety. He was in the habit of leaving his house at the same time every day and from the same open-ended courtyard. He did not have a bodyguard despite repeated security scares. Furthermore, his chauffeur-driven vehicle was clearly a diplomatic car. Roger Harvey, the British chargé d'affaires in The Hague, said that there was no reason to take special precautions in such a 'hospitable' country. That was belied by the very reasons Sykes was chosen for the posting.

Later that month the Callaghan Government lost a vote of confidence and an election was called. The campaign had not quite kicked off when the IRA launched its biggest attack so far – this time on the House of Commons.

*   *   *

Just before 3 o'clock on the afternoon of Friday, 30 March 1979, MPs engaged in the last Commons debate heard a muffled blast. To journalists winding down at the end of the week in the press bar overlooking New Palace Yard, it was more like a sharp crack accompanied by a rattling of glasses. Looking down on the cobbles the up ramp from the underground car park was obscured, but above it a lazy wisp of blue smoke was rising. Reporters and staff who had experienced war and trouble zones recognised an explosion; others were uncertain and there was an eerie calm, a pause before all hell broke loose. The bombers had breached the haphazard security of the Palace of Westminster. There was just one casualty.

Airey Neave, the son of an eminent entomologist, was born in Knightsbridge in 1916. While still a schoolboy at Eton he learnt German during a visit to that country in 1933, the year Hitler came to power, and won a prize for an essay forecasting that Europe was heading for war. Shortly before the outbreak of war he halted his legal training and volunteered for service. In the May 1940 battle of Calais he was awarded the Military Cross. Wounded, he was captured and imprisoned in Poland. He escaped, was recaptured, interrogated by the Nazis and sent to the infamous, 'escape-proof' fortress of Colditz. After one failed attempt, he took part in a bold and meticulously planned escape in January 1942 while guards were diverted by a camp pantomime, entitled 'Ballet Nonsense'. He returned to London via Switzerland, Vichy France and Gibraltar, the first British serviceman to make a 'home run'. Neave returned with well-observed and valuable intelligence information and was soon serving in MI9, the secret service which planned escape routes for Allied airmen and helped organise resistance against the Nazis. During the war he was called to the Bar and in 1945 joined the British War Crimes Executive to collect evidence against prominent Nazis. Despite natural grievances against his former captors he performed that role with tact and patience, according to fellow officer-lawyers. From 1949 to 1951 he commanded the Territorial Army intelligence school, which later became 23 SAS regiment. He was a successful author of war memoirs and garlanded with decorations.

After two failed attempts to enter Westminster, he became MP for Abingdon in a 1953 by-election. He focused on defence, science and aviation policy and, while no star speaker, began to rise up the lower rungs of ministerial ambition. That ambition was stalled, however, while Edward Heath remained Conservative leader. Their mutual antipathy was based not only on politics: when Neave suffered a heart attack in 1959 Heath, then Chief Whip, told him his career was finished. As a backbencher he successfully urged compensation for British concentration camp victims and state pensions for the elderly excluded from the 1948 National Insurance scheme. He also called for the televising of Parliament, campaigned on behalf of refugees and warned against Soviet expansion. But he was appalled by what he saw as the slow demolition of his vision of what Britain should be under both Wilson and Heath. In 1974 Neave approached several potential candidates to challenge Heath as Conservative leader, but one by one they withdrew until Margaret Thatcher was the only one with a chance left and Neave, despite not being what would later be described as a Thatcherite, exercised all his tactical skills to get her elected. In 1975 his conspiratorial efforts succeeded and she became leader, ousting a sulky Heath. Neave ran her private office and was appointed shadow Northern Ireland Secretary of State. He worked with Whitelaw to prevent her taking the party too far to the right.[11]

The Northern Ireland portfolio was, he had told Thatcher earlier, the only one he wanted. He was strongly committed to the Union and his extensive intelligence background gave him an insight into terrorism and the measures he deemed necessary to combat it. He visited the Province frequently, spoke warmly of the sufferings of ordinary families but demanded the toughest action against the IRA and other paramilitaries, calling for 'concerted action on these mindless barbarians'. The IRA, he said, were 'not glorious Republicans but bloody murderers' and he advocated capital punishment for terrorist killers. He insisted that there was no difference between the IRA and its political wing, Sinn Fein, and believed that terrorism could be defeated if no compromise was offered. He opposed power-sharing, considered 'full integration' of Ulster into the UK and demanded an end to the release of internees. Thatcher left the Opposition portfolio firmly in Neave's hands. Although instinctively a Unionist – she insisted that any Conservative *had* to be a Unionist too – she had other interests. She trusted Neave implicitly to articulate that and to oppose any 'solution' which led to the sort of power-sharing which the Heath administration had attempted in the early 1970s.[12]

Moderate in many other areas, Neave was a hard-line Ulster man's dream ... and a target for the IRA.

Neave knew that well enough, but took few precautions. His parliamentary agent said that he knew his life was at risk, but reckoned it came with the territory. Neave told a journalist: 'If they come for me, the one thing we can be sure of is that they will not face me. They're not soldier enough for that.' Years earlier the writer Rebecca West noted: 'It is, I think, against his principles to care much about danger.'

As a shadow minister he was well briefed on terrorist threats, and there is strong evidence that he never severed his intelligence links. According to some sources, he had regular contacts with MI6. A 1987 investigation revealed that Neave used those contacts in a 'dirty tricks' campaign to discredit Wilson and the Labour Party, planting snippets in friendly newspapers suggesting they were stooges of the Soviets. Neave was, as several pointed out before and since, an instinctive plotter. According to Peter Wright's banned book *Spycatcher*, he was himself questioned over connections with far-right organisations and cabals determined to overthrow the Wilson administration. Neave came out of that gentle grilling having convinced Wright that he was 'loyal to the Crown and to British democracy'.[13] But Colin Wallace, a disgruntled former army information man, echoed many of Neave's own concerns when he wrote: 'The intelligence community saw the Irish situation as the front line of the left's threat to the UK, and of a great conspiracy by the Communist bloc to undermine the whole of the UK.'[14] That intelligence community clearly looked forward to the day when Neave, one of their own, was in power.

Neave's last speech in Parliament was on 16 March 1979 during a debate on police interrogation procedures. He praised the 'dedication and courage' of the RUC. But if he had ever become Secretary of State he would perhaps have done his utmost to root out brutality and torture of suspects by the security services. He told Gerry Fitt: 'I was interrogated by the Nazis and, Gerry, it leaves its mark on you.'

Callaghan's minority Government, meanwhile, stumbled on against the background of bomb blasts and pistol shots. The key issues, however, had more to do with domestic strife. Thatcher, aided by Neave, prepared for a third vote of no confidence in almost three years. On 28 March she won by 311 votes to 310. All but two of the Ulster Unionists voted with the Tories, thanks to Neave's diligence and diplomacy, while

Independent Republican MP Frank Maguire arrived at Westminster 'to abstain in person'. That night in the Opposition whips' office Neave sipped champagne, a broad grin creasing his face as he received plaudits for masterminding Thatcher's greatest political coup since she snatched the leadership. The following day, after an audience with the Queen, Callaghan announced a general election for 2 May.

The Irish National Liberation Army, a breakaway organisation with few big 'successes' under its belt, received reports from 'political sources' that Neave was planning a right-wing backlash in the event of a Tory victory. It is debatable when they started plotting a specific operation, but some time in March INLA Volunteers travelled to London after looking up Neave's Westminster Gardens flat address in the latest edition of *Who's Who*. They picked up explosives smuggled in the previous year from Palestine suppliers. They also obtained a mercury tilt-switch. The explosives, the switch, a detonator and the electric circuitry needed to link them were the components of a car bomb of the sort used twice before in the Province. The mercury switch could easily be obtained from radio spares. When attached to a vehicle moving up an incline the mercury would trigger an electric current to the detonator.

The 1 lb bomb was attached with magnets to the underside of Neave's Vauxhall Cavalier. It remains unknown whether that was done outside Neave's flat a few hundred yards from the Commons or in the underground car park itself. Security at Westminster was certainly lax, but experts have asked why the bombers would have taken such a risk when the car was regularly parked outside.

Most MPs had already returned to their constituencies to prepare for the coming election, but around a dozen were in the Chamber debating the Credit Union Bill. Enoch Powell was on his feet when Neave walked down the stone steps to the underground car park. It was a matter of moments to get in the car, start the engine and drive two floors to the ramp which emerges onto the cobbled New Palace Yard directly facing Big Ben.

The bomb exploded half-way up that final ramp, funnelling the blast in the confined space and sending glass and metal fragments through the windows of the offices adjoining the base of the clock tower. The car doors, windscreen and bonnet were blown out and the roof punched upward. A future Northern Ireland minister, Chris

8. The assassination of Airey Neave (PA Photos)

Patten, was in Margaret Thatcher's office in her absence. He exclaimed: 'That was a bomb!'

A number of parliamentary journalists quickly arrived on the scene and gazed down a few feet into the shattered car. I was one of them. The driver – it was some time before anyone identified him as Neave – was hunched slightly over the steering wheel, his black suit charred by the blast. His right leg was blown off below the knee, his left one still partially attached. I saw his face as a white mask, the muscles relaxed so that his skin seemed like bread dough; David Healy of the Press Association saw it as a mask of blood; the *Belfast Telegraph*'s Des McCartan referred to 'blackened, bleeding features amid the tangled wreckage'. So much for the accuracy of eye-witnesses. The police seemed frozen until one officer shouted: 'Clear the area. He's alive.'

A doctor and a nurse attended, as fire-fighters tried to free Neave from the wreckage. Ambulance man Brian Craggs struggled to give him oxygen, saying later: 'He was still breathing ... He never regained consciousness.' Craggs told reporters:

> The car was in a real mess, all the panels were twisted and the windows were shattered. I didn't recognise him. He was in a terrible mess. The whole of his front, including his face, was badly charred. We couldn't open the doors of the car so I climbed on the bonnet and through the hole where the windscreen had been. Then I crouched in the passenger seat. I saw then that the bottom of the car had been blown out. Anyway the poor chap had lost his right leg below the knee and his left leg was only held on by a flap of skin. Surprisingly, there wasn't too much blood around, but I think a lot had gone through the bottom of the car.[15]

Finally, Neave's inert body was freed and he was taken to the nearby Westminster Hospital. He died on the operating table eight minutes after arriving there. His wife, Diana, reached the hospital a short while later.

Mrs Thatcher was driving to the BBC studios in Portland Place to record an election broadcast when an aide told her that a bomb had gone off in the Commons underground car park. When she arrived the identity of the victim was confirmed. She later recalled: 'There was no way I could bring myself to broadcast after that ... I felt only stunned. The full grief would come later. With it came also anger that this man – my friend – who had shrugged off so much danger in his life should be murdered by someone worse than a common criminal.'[16] Outside her Flood Street home Thatcher told reporters: 'Some devils got him and they must never, never, never be allowed to triumph. They must never prevail.'[17]

Initially, reporters and politicians assumed that the assassination was the work of the Provisional IRA, and early suggestions that it was INLA were treated with derision because of the splinter group's poor track record. But INLA's claim of responsibility was accompanied by forensic information which only the bombers could have known. INLA described it as 'the operation of the decade'. A spokesman boasted: 'We blew him up inside the impregnable Palace of Westminster.' In a longer statement INLA said: 'Airey Neave was specially selected for assassination. He was well known for his rabid militarist calls for more repression against the Irish people and for the strengthening of the SAS murder gang, a group which has no qualms about murdering Irish people.'

Thatcher composed her tribute to the man who, more than any other, had made her leader:

> We do not expect these things to happen in this country, but somehow they have happened here ... The assassination of Airey Neave has left his friends and colleagues as stunned and grief-stricken as his family. He was one of freedom's warriors. Courageous, staunch, true, he lived for his beliefs and now he has died for them. A gentle, brave and unassuming man, he was a very loyal and dear friend. He had a wonderful family who supported him in everything he did. Now there is a gap in our lives which can never be filled. We cannot allow those who murdered him to escape.

That last sentiment was echoed by Callaghan, who added: 'I am shocked and appalled by this cowardly murder. This abhorrent act has robbed our country of a distinguished public figure and a very brave man.'[18] The SDLP's Gerry Fitt said: 'Those responsible for his death may have killed a friend rather than an enemy.' Neave had previously told him that anyone caught mistreating prisoners 'would meet the full fury of his wrath because he, as a prisoner of war, had suffered interrogation at the hands of the Gestapo'. Fitt added: 'I will never forget his words as he said "Gerry, it leaves its mark on you".'

One of Neave's successors, Lord Mayhew, said in a later tribute:

> To some it might seem odd that a man whom they had every reason to regard as a man of action, and a very private, even mysterious, person, should have chosen to enter Parliament. But Airey had seen totalitarianism in action. He believed that the only basis for political authority over people was their

consent, freely expressed, in Parliament. Freedom was a quiet passion with Airey, someone whose style was quiet but whose will was steel. Freedom under the law was the banner beneath which Airey marched to the end.

Neave's biographer, Paul Routledge, focused on his shadowy aspects:

> He was a spook who knew, and acted on, his beliefs and loyalties. He was not alone in this self-assurance. It is the stock in trade of the spy. Although he was not an orthodox MI6 officer, he remained close to the security services all his life. He may have been an elected politician in a democracy, but he shared misgivings about the world around him that were expressed most clearly by George Kennedy Young who talked of the spy as 'the main guardian of intellectual integrity' in a world threatened by lawlessness, disregard of international contract, cruelty and corruption.[19]

Enoch Powell's instant reaction reeked of bile. The Tory-turned-Unionist said: 'I am sure Airey Neave would have liked nothing better than to share the same end as so many of his innocent fellow citizens for whom the House of Commons is responsible.'[20]

Neave was 63 when he died. He left a widow and three children. Diana Neave had spoken to him just an hour before his death. He had told her he was going to his tailor's before returning home, after which they would drive to the country. She had heard the explosion from their flat but did not realise what it was until a friend and Conservative adviser told her that her husband had been taken to Westminster Hospital. She responded to his slaying with remarkable courage: two days after the murder she was sorting mail in Conservative Central Office as a volunteer election worker, convinced that her husband would have wanted her to help Thatcher secure victory. She said: 'I only want to be worthy of Airey.' She was later made a life peer and died after a long illness in 1992.

Nobody was ever charged with Neave's murder, but the spotlight was put on INLA, no longer seen as a joke in security and terrorist circles. It had been formed in 1974 by one of the Official IRA's former leaders, Seamus Costello, and financed and armed by a series of robberies. The organisation grew out of the Irish Republican Socialist Party which saw the Troubles as a direct extension of working-class struggle against 'British imperialist interference in Ireland' and developed contacts with foreign terrorist groups and states. It notched up at least 12 victims, including policemen and soldiers, but many of its operations were botched. Both the Official and Provisional IRA were not best pleased when INLA began to poach members, particularly from the Divis Flats on Belfast's Falls Road. In 1977 Costello was assassinated by the Provos, and the organisation almost collapsed without him. But its international links resulted in the successful smuggling of Soviet and Chinese grenades and a steady stream of arms from the Eastern bloc, mainly through intermediaries in the Palestine Liberation Organisation. INLA began to boast that whereas the Provos had five men for every gun, they had five guns for every man. But an INLA plot to assassinate Sir Robin Haydon, the British ambassador to Ireland, failed, as did several attacks on army targets. They were desperate for a 'spectacular' and Airey Neave was chosen as the target, allegedly by Ronnie Bunting, INLA's director of intelligence and adjutant of its Belfast brigade. Bunting was the son of a former army officer who worked in the medical records department of the Royal Victoria Hospital, Belfast. It seems likely that he chose Neave as much for his secret service connections as for his outspoken defence of Unionism.[21] Neave was determined to shake up the intelligence and security services and weed out careerists who created their own fiefdoms, so making them more efficient and thereby a more dangerous foe. He was also planning to make Sir Christopher Sykes head of MI6, although no direct connection between The Hague and Westminster assassinations has ever been found.

The unit responsible for the actual killing was never identified. There were several hoaxes, numerous conspiracy theories implicating MI6 and the CIA, and countless false trails. The truth seems to be the more mundane, but classic, tactic of the successful terrorist assassin. A masked INLA source told Routledge that the bombers had simply melted back into civilian obscurity. The security forces never came close to capturing them. The source said: 'They came out of professional lives they were in and went back, and no consequent change of activity or time lapse would suggest anything.'[22]

Thatcher echoed Neave as she entered Downing Street on 4 May, saying: 'There is now work to be done.' She appointed Humphrey Atkins as Secretary of State for Northern Ireland. They both continued, to some extent, Neave's twin-track approach of greater political integration of Ulster and military defeat of the IRA. Thatcher was frustrated by the failure to catch Neave's killers, and some Nationalists remain convinced that she authorised covert counter-assassination operations by the security services. But within a few months Neave's murder would be overshadowed by another 'spectacular'.

14
The Murder of Lord Mountbatten

'Look after the children'

THE success of INLA in killing a high-profile politician within the precincts of Westminster embarrassed the Provisional IRA's army council and spurred them into escalating their own campaign of targeted assassination. Former Northern Ireland Secretary Roy Mason later said: 'After Neave's death the Provos felt they had been made to look incompetent. Apart from their own cause, they were whipped into a new frenzied aim of neutralising the success of INLA.'[1]

Between April and the beginning of August 1979 the Provisional IRA went largely for 'soft' targets: two British soldiers standing outside the Andersonstown joint RUC and Army base in Belfast; two more gunned down in Ballymurphy; a prison officer shot as he left his sister's wedding in a church in Clogher, Tyrone; a female prison officer shot dead and three colleagues wounded by grenades outside Armagh women's gaol; a policeman and a soldier, both working undercover, killed at Lisnaskea, Fermanagh; an off-duty RUC man and a civilian murdered in Armagh. These were up-close and personal assassinations. But over the same period IRA bomb-makers continued to perfect their grisly art. Four RUC men died when a 1,000 lb bomb, the largest used by the IRA up to then, was detonated at Bessbrook, Armagh. Two RUC men were killed by a landmine at Cullabille, near Crossmaglen. And on 2 August two soldiers died by landmine in Armagh. Their deaths took the army total to 301 since 1969.[2] All these deaths were tragedies for the victims' families, friends and compatriots, but in the bloody fabric of recent history they appear relatively anonymous. Not so the man whom was being targeted for a hit designed to strike close to the heart of the establishment and the heart of the royal family.

* * *

Lord Louis Mountbatten, a 79-year-old Second World War hero who had played a key role in the granting of independence to India, was a patriarchal figure who had steered Elizabeth II and the Duke of Edinburgh through much of the queen's reign and who had acted as a mentor to the younger royals, especially Prince Charles.

Born Prince Louis of Battenberg, he had close family ties with the British royal family. He came first in his year at the Royal Naval College, Devonport, and saw action as a teenager in the First World War. During the 1920s and 1930s he was seen as a playboy naval officer with impeccable connections, delighting in fast cars, speedboats and polo. In 1939 he took command of the new destroyer HMS *Kelly*, but in May 1941, in a hopeless operation off Crete, the ship was sunk by dive bombers and torpedoes. Over half her crew were lost and Mountbatten only survived by swimming under the ship as she turned turtle. Many men were machine-gunned in the water. The *Kelly* became the basis of Noel Coward's wartime film *In Which We Serve*. Churchill put Mountbatten in charge of combined operations and he took much of the blame for the costly débâcle at Dieppe. Mountbatten was meticulous in the early planning of D-Day and claimed personal credit for selecting the Normandy landing beaches. But before the invasion of Nazi-occupied Europe he was made Supreme Allied Commander in South East Asia and accepted the formal Japanese surrender in Singapore. In 1946 he was named Viceroy of India and supervised the run-up to that country's independence and the partition into separate Muslim and Hindu states. In 1959 he was Britain's Chief of Defence Staff and opposed the stockpiling of nuclear weaponry.

In 1979 Mountbatten's political career was long past and at no time during his long service had he been involved in Northern Ireland. He told one reporter that he had no interests in the politics of Ireland or anywhere else. 'I am a man plumb in the middle,' he said. 'I loathe all manifestations of extremism, and I believe we should strive, above all else, for the dignity and human rights of mankind, regardless of race, colour and creed.'[3] However, on occasion he expressed trenchant and, to some, surprising views. In one of his last speeches, made at Strasbourg in March 1979, he passionately advocated arms control, saying: 'As a military man who has given half a century of active service I say in all sincerity that the nuclear arms race has no military purpose. Wars cannot be fought with nuclear weapons. Their existence only adds to our perils because of the illusions which they have generated.'[4] He urged modernisation of the British monarchy to ensure its survival, to the chagrin of those courtiers who regarded him as an interfering busybody. One biographer wrote:

> Mountbatten derived particular pleasure from his friendship with the Prince of Wales, who treated him as an honorary grandfather and attached great value to his counsel. Mountbatten always urged the prince to sow his wild oats and then marry and stick to a pure girl of good family; the advice was admirable in principle but proved impossible to apply in practice. It is conceivable that, if Mountbatten had lived and retained sufficient vigour, he might have played a father confessor role in the lives of both the Prince and Princess of Wales and helped to make their marriage less disastrous.[5]

His unique position so close to the throne – past, present and future – made him a legitimate target in the eyes of his murderers. A cousin to the queen, a mentor to the heir to the throne, a key adviser on the constitutional future of the monarchy and the United Kingdom – here was the victim the Provos needed to show that they, rather than INLA, were the real force to be reckoned with. He was also an easy target. For 35 years Mountbatten and his family had spent a month each summer at his castle, Classiebawn, overlooking the Irish fishing village of Mullaghmore and Galway Bay, just 12 miles south of the border with Northern Ireland. He was regarded with puzzled affection by the locals as he strode around the village in faded corduroys, fished for shrimp and occasionally took local children for short rides in his three-cylinder engined, 27-foot fishing boat *Shadow V*. Local police kept watch on the turreted castle and four armed Irish Special Branch personal security officers were on rotation when he was staying there. Mountbatten himself insisted that security should be as light and as unobtrusive as possible. When asked if he feared an IRA attack he replied with swagger: 'What would they want with an old man like me?' His vessel, moored at the public dock with ten or more other private vessels, was completely unguarded. In retrospect, given the proximity of the border, a known nearby refuge for Provos and the tenth anniversary of

British troops being deployed in Ulster, the police should have ignored his wishes. For some time there had been good intelligence that the IRA was considering targeting a royal and that spring, according to some intelligence sources, it had been known that Mountbatten's name was on an IRA hit list. So the laxity of security remains puzzling. The journalist Christopher Hudson wrote: 'Mountbatten was a war hero. Nobody wanted to put him in the position of showing the white flag to the IRA.'[6] Some time before dawn on 27 August an IRA bomber, or bombers, slipped through the shallows to plant their deadly package of at least 50 lb of plastic explosives on *Shadow V*.

Mountbatten arrived at the dock at 11.30 that Bank Holiday morning for a day's cruising with his daughter, 55-year-old Lady Patricia Brabourne, her husband Lord Brabourne, their twin sons Timothy and Nicholas, aged 14, and the twins' 82-year-old paternal grandmother, the Dowager Lady Brabourne. The craft could have been more packed with family members: two other children stayed behind to swot for exams and two young cousins also remained at home to watch a Laurel and Hardy film on television. Neither of the two armed protection officers with the party went on board. One had been violently seasick on a previous trip, and they took the view that the boat would remain in both visual and radio contact. Paul Maxwell, a 15-year-old Enniskillen pupil who had won the prize holiday job as boat boy, cast off and the bright green, clinker-built vessel slowly cleared the harbour's stone walls. It hugged the shore for a few hundred yards and then stopped so that Mountbatten's lobster pots could be inspected. Mountbatten was at the helm, the two women seated in the stern and Timothy was sitting on the cabin's roof. Mountbatten kept the engine revving as the boys reached for the lobster pots. Lord Brabourne turned to them and said: 'You are having fun today, aren't you.' It was a bright, sunny, windless day and the scene was the epitome of tranquillity.

A massive explosion shattered that peace at 11.39 am. The boat disintegrated and all seven on board were thrown into the water. Patricia later recalled an impression of a white ball of light erupting under her father's feet, then rolling over and over in the sea. She pinched her nose, as her father had done when he survived the wartime sinking of HMS *Kelly*, and she promised herself she would tell him that when she surfaced. Nicholas Brabourne and Paul Maxwell died instantly. Mountbatten's legs were almost completely blown off but he was still breathing when local fishermen, who had raced to the rescue, pulled him out of the water. He died a few moments later. Timothy was knocked unconscious by the blast but came to in the water and doggy-paddled through a floating tangle of wooden debris, clothes and bodies. He remembered inhaling water, diesel oil and his own blood. Lord Brabourne could only remember feeling cold and then finding himself lying in a dinghy on top of his wife, whose face was covered in blood. Alongside them was his mother who, as always, barely had a silver hair out of place.[7]

Two holidaying Belfast doctors set up an aid station on the dock, using doors for stretchers and ripping sheeting for bandages to staunch the injureds' blood flow. Lord and Lady Brabourne's legs were broken and their skin shredded by splinters. The Dowager had a shattered arm. She repeated in a whisper: 'Don't bother about me. I'm all right. Look after the children.' Ambulances rushed the survivors to Sligo General Hospital. Timothy and Patricia were operated on first as they were considered the most likely to die. Both were then put in the same intensive care unit. Doctors saved Lord Brabourne's legs. The Dowager Lady Brabourne died the following morning from shock and internal injuries.

Two hours before the detonation two Republicans had been detained at a routine checkpoint 70 miles away on suspicion of driving a stolen car. Police checks found they had possible connections with the IRA. They had the perfect alibi for the time of the explosion, leading to increased speculation that the bomb was triggered by a timing device. Two girls who had been living in a caravan in Mullaghmore that August were suspected of being IRA 'spotters' reporting on Mountbatten's movements to an active service unit in the seaside resort of Bundoran across the border. They were questioned for two days but refused to say a word or even acknowledge their interrogators. They were released.

A few hours after the blast a statement was issued by the Provisionals in Belfast: 'This operation is one of the discriminate ways we can bring to the attention of the British people the continuing occupation of our country.' Mountbatten had been 'executed' to show the British ruling class and its 'working-class slaves' that the war would continue until it 'tore out their sentimental, imperialist heart'. The statement added:

> The death of Mountbatten and the tributes paid to him will be seen in sharp contrast to the apathy of the British Government and the English people

to the deaths of over three hundred British soldiers and the deaths of Irish men, women and children at the hands of their forces.[8]

The assassination sent shock waves of grief and anger through the UK, the Republic of Ireland and the Commonwealth, most particularly India where a week of mourning was declared. Margaret Thatcher said: 'His life ran like a golden thread of inspiration and service to this country throughout this century.'

But the day's bloodshed was far from over. Later that afternoon a three-vehicle convoy of 2nd Battalion Paratroopers just inside the Ulster border near Warrenpoint was hit by a 700 lb bomb packed in milk churns hidden in a trailer-load of hay. One three-ton lorry was hurled across the road, spewing out bodies, limbs, injured soldiers and non-human wreckage. Survivors radioed for help and a contingent of the Queen's Own Highlanders with their commanding officer, Lieutenant Colonel David Blair, arrived by helicopter. Within moments of landing a second bomb was detonated in a nearby gatehouse, killing Blair and other rescuers. Blair was so close to the second bomb that his body vaporised. The final death toll was 18, the largest lost to the British Army in a single incident and the highest death rate suffered by the Paratroopers since Arnhem in 1944. Belfast reporter Ed Curran said:

> It was like a scene from some fictional war film. Everywhere in the debris was blood and human flesh. Overhead the late afternoon sky was obscured by dense smoke rising from the wreckage. The soldiers who had survived staggered around and some opened fire across the Lough at two young men whom they apparently took to be the bombers. The tragedy was now complete. The two were merely gawking at what had happened. One was shot in the arm, the other was killed.[9]

The Paras' commander, Colonel Jim Burke, said: 'We are very angry but we are not going to overreact because we pride ourselves in being professionals in every respect.' Thatcher flew to Belfast where she made a point of walking through a shopping centre, ostensibly to listen to public reaction to both outrages. Later she was flown by helicopter to the army's heavily fortified Crossmaglen base, the most frequently attacked outpost in the Province. (She returned to Northern Ireland on Christmas Eve, where a Paratrooper kissed her under the mistletoe.) Her gesture of defiance was clear. An IRA statement responded: 'The Iron Maiden's declaration of war is nothing but the bankrupt rattling of an empty tin.'

The following week the bodies of Lord Mountbatten, his grandson and the Dowager Lady Brabourne were flown to his Hampshire estate, Broadlands, before his state funeral in Westminster Abbey. Mountbatten was buried in Romsey Abbey on 5 September after a service which he had planned in minute detail a decade earlier, right down to the lunches to be served to mourners on the train from Waterloo. Philip Ziegler wrote:

> Mountbatten was a giant of a man and his weaknesses were appropriately gigantic. His vanity was monstrous, his ambition unbridled ... But such frailties were far outweighed by his qualities. His energy was prodigious, as was his moral and physical courage. He was endlessly resilient in the face of disaster. His flexibility of mind was extraordinary, as was his tolerance – he accepted all comers for what they were, not measured against some scale of predetermined values. He had style and panache and commanded the loyal devotion of all who served him.[10]

Timothy lost an eye in the explosion and was partially deafened. After two weeks in Sligo he and his parents were also flown home. Patricia recalled that when she had been told of the death of her other son, Nicholas, she could not cry proper tears for him because of the 120 stitches in her face and around her eyes.

Paul Maxwell, the 15-year-old boat boy from a less exalted family, lay overnight in Enniskillen Cathedral before a private funeral. His father, who had witnessed the explosion from a distance, said: 'He was a better Irishman than those who did this foul deed.'

Timothy returned to school and refused counselling until he was 30 despite the constant sound of the explosion inside his head. Although he had cried long and hard after hearing of his twin's death, he said years later: 'I had a sense that his legacy lived on in me and I was going to survive for both of us. I was not going to live only half a life in the shadows.' He married a teacher in 1998.

His mother felt guilty that she had barely mourned her father because 'the death of our twin dwarfed the pain'. But she too could see little point in bitterness. She refers to the physical damage still visible on her features as her 'IRA face-lift'.

At Mountbatten's memorial service in December Prince Charles slammed 'the kind of sub-human extremist that blows people up when he feels like it'. However, when he first returned to Northern Ireland after the tragedy he spoke not just of sorrow, but also of peace and reconciliation.

Investigations found that the bomb had been detonated from a cliff top using the controls of a model aircraft. The man who pressed the button was never charged or even questioned. Intelligence sources point to a Libyan-trained senior Provo who was later imprisoned for 20 years for involvement in a planned mainland bombing campaign intended to disrupt the 1987 general election.

The Garda mounted one of its biggest ever investigations, and charged the two men stopped at the checkpoint two hours before the explosion. Francis McGirl, a 24-year-old gravedigger, was believed to be a highly effective and experienced bomb-maker. Traces of green paint such as that used on *Shadow V* and traces of nitro-glycerine were found on his clothes. He was acquitted due to lack of evidence to place him at Mullaghmore. When he died in 1985 IRA wreaths were placed by his grave.

Thomas McMahon, a 31-year-old carpenter arrested with McGirl, was convicted. He was released in August 1998 as part of the Good Friday peace accord.

One of the men who detonated the Warrenpoint bombs, Brendan Burns, was killed in February 1988 when a bomb he was constructing exploded in his hands.[11] The other, at the time of writing, still lives in the area. Twenty-five years after the Warrenpoint attack the daughter of Colonel Blair, Alexandra, wrote:

> In a sense the absence of justice never mattered to my family. We knew that neither justice nor revenge would bring our father back. Instead, we were looked after by the tight-knit community of the Queen's Own Highlanders. Nobody could have wished for a closer family and without them we would not have survived ...
>
> There is no memorial at Warrenpoint for fear that it would be defaced. A harmony of a sort reigns in the area now, and with that lies the hope that one day both sides will talk openly and make a permanent peace.[12]

*   *   *

The double atrocities of 27 August had two main effects which operated both to the advantage and the disadvantage of the terrorists. Whether they cancelled each other out remains debatable.

First, the 'success' in killing a senior royal and the undoubtedly 'classic' terrorist operation at Warrenpoint showed that the IRA was back in the driving seat of UK–Irish terrorism. The *Republican News*, in its round-up of 1979, reported: 'Last year was one of the resounding Republican successes when the IRA's cellular re-organisation was operationally vindicated, particularly through the devastating use of remote-controlled bombs.'[13] Credit for that change of tactics was given to Gerry Adams.

But second, Thatcher did not respond in the way that the IRA's commanders expected. Given the ongoing operation to kill or capture the killers of Airey Neave, there were also turf wars between the British Army and the RUC over who should spearhead security operations against the newly rejuvenated IRA. Thatcher appointed Sir Maurice Oldfield, former head of the Secret Intelligence Service, to co-ordinate inter-service intelligence operations. What she did not do was embark on a knee-jerk reaction which might have satisfied her natural supporters but which, her political antennae detected, would have led to a repeat of the uncontrollable mayhem of the mid-1970s. Ed Moloney wrote:

> Despite the provocation, the incident did not tempt Thatcher into the sort of precipitate response the IRA had hoped for. The IRA, under Adams as under any of its leaders, operated on the principle that the more Britain resorted to crude repression, the greater degree of sympathy and support, passive and active, the organisation could count on from nationalists. The classic example of that was the one-sided internment operation of 1973, which had boosted IRA ranks enormously. For years afterwards the IRA lived in hope that the British would repeat that mistake. But Thatcher disappointed them.[14]

15
The Brighton Bomb

'we only have to be lucky once ...'

On 14 September 1984 a man with a slight Norfolk twang booked into Brighton's Grand Hotel under the name Roy Walsh. He left three days later, having left a bomb behind a bathroom panel. It was timed to go off 24 days later.

As the clock ticked towards the appointed time in the early hours of 12 October, Margaret Thatcher was in her room revising her speech for the closing day of the Conservative Party conference. She recalled: 'By about 2.40 am the speech was finished. So while the speech-writers themselves, who had been joined for a time by Norman Tebbit, went to bed, my long-suffering staff typed in what I was fairly confident would be the final changes to the text and prepared the autocue tape.'[1] Most MPs, party workers, aides, delegates and journalists returned wearily to their rooms, either in the Grand itself or in the numerous hotels and bed-and-breakfasts nearby. The Grand's pillared foyer bar was empty but for a handful of night owls having a last drink.

At 2.54 am the bomb exploded, blasting a gaping hole through the hotel's ornate, wedding cake façade. Masonry crashed through the ceilings of the rooms below the blast area. Floors collapsed like a house of cards. Debris decapitated parking meters on the promenade outside. There was silence as the dust settled, then a few screams and the sound of approaching sirens. Reporters having a nightcap in a nearby hotel with an all-night bar stumbled out to an incomprehensible scene. No one knew who had died, but the scale of the blast suggested that the Iron Lady and her entire Cabinet could be among the victims.

As alcohol evaporated in the bloodstreams of the hacks, it seemed that the IRA had succeeded in their long-cherished aim.

*　　*　　*

The attack on the prime minister had been intended to be the bloodiest 'spectacular' to date and stand as a monument to a new set of IRA 'martyrs'.

In December 1980 a two-month hunger strike in the Maze Prison's notorious H-blocks was called off with one prisoner critically ill and no concessions given to demands that special category status be restored to convicted terrorists, which had previously given them a certain degree of autonomy behind its grim walls. But in March 1981 the hunger strike was resumed, with IRA prison leader Bobby Sands the first inmate to refuse food. From his bed Sands stood for Parliament and in April won the Fermanagh-South Tyrone by-election. In May, after 66 days fasting, he died and many thousands attended his funeral in Belfast. Three more hunger-strikers died, then another six, while Sinn Fein's Owen Carron won the by-election caused by Sands' death. The hunger strike was called off in October when the new Northern Ireland Secretary, James Prior, announced that all prisoners could wear their own clothes. The Republican cause had a new crop of corpses to avenge.

Like everything to do with the long tragedy of the Troubles, the reality was rather more complicated than it first seemed. In February 2005 Richard O'Rawe, the IRA spokesman in the Maze during the hunger strike, revealed that he and the IRA's prison council had accepted concessions offered by the Government on 5 July 1981, just before the fifth prisoner, Joe McDonnell, died. However, they were overruled by the IRA army council, which wanted to maintain public sympathy in the run-up to Carron's by-election victory, so allowing five more prisoners to waste away. According to O'Rawe the concessions were offered to Gerry Adams through an unidentified intermediary known as the 'Mountain Climber'. The concessions, including the abolition of prison uniforms, more visits and the segregation of prisoners along political lines, went much further than the final settlement. O'Rawe wrote: 'The army council acted in an inexcusable manner. A generous interpretation is that they disastrously miscalculated on all fronts. A more sceptical view would be that perhaps they didn't miscalculate at all.'[2] That was vehemently denied by Sinn Fein, but the allegation still has the power to cut deeply.

In Republican circles, however, martyrs are martyrs and someone had to pay for so many protracted and sordidly painful deaths. The IRA army council prepared its attack on the top tier of the British political establishment while continuing its war on many fronts, both military and political.

Thatcher's top priority before the hunger strikes was to destroy INLA, who had murdered her friend, Airey Neave. With the criminal investigation going nowhere, there was inevitable pressure to allow anti-terrorist forces to take the law into their own hands. According to Raymond Murray, historian of the IRA in Ireland, assassination operations were conducted under the umbrella codename 'Ranc', with intelligence personnel allegedly using their contacts with Protestant paramilitaries to carry out covert death sentences. Murray claimed: 'Working through the SAS and picking up their own allies, the UDA once more, Ranc engineered three assassination operations. Since it lacked hard evidence for the Neave killing, soft targets were chosen.'[3] In that scenario, widely believed on both sides of the Irish Sea, the first to die was a founding member of the Irish Independence Party.

John Turnley was a 44-year-old councillor in Larne and a confirmed Nationalist despite a Unionist background and previous service as a British Army officer. Although he was not a member of INLA, he was connected through his work on the National H-Blocks Committee. In June 1980 his car was rammed as he was driving his family to a public meeting in Carnlough. He was shot nine times with a sub-machine gun and a pistol. Four UDA men were charged with his murder and two brothers were sentenced to life. One of them, Robert McConnell, claimed from the dock after his conviction – when he had nothing to gain – that he had been supplied with army issue weapons by two SAS NCOs. He claimed that 'Information on Turnley and others were fed through me by British intelligence.'[4]

The second target allegedly was Miriam Daly, an outspoken militant Republican and campaigner against conditions in the Maze. On 26 June her ten-year-old adopted daughter came home from school in Belfast and found her lying face down in a pool of blood. She had been bound hand and foot, and six bullets from a 9 mm semi-automatic pistol fired into her, a cushion being used to muffle the noise. It looked like a professional 'hit'. No one was convicted of her murder, although it was claimed by the UDA.

The third alleged victim was Ronnie Bunting, a senior INLA leader and former internee. After interrogation in August he claimed that detectives had boasted that they could arrange for three bullets in his head. In the early hours of 15 October, masked men broke down his front door in a quiet Andersonstown cul-de-sac. Bunting and his wife Suzanne leapt out of bed and were gunned down. He died on the landing. His wife was shot in the shoulder, armpit and, as a *coup de grâce*, the mouth. Their friend Noel Lyttle was fatally shot as he lay on a bed in another room alongside the Buntings' infant son, who was found screaming in his cot. No paramilitary organisation ever claimed responsibility. The layout of the house was well known to the police, who had frequently raided it. The raid was well planned and carried out by 'cool, calm' men who knew what they were doing. Security experts reckon it was carried out by the same UDA squad that killed Miriam Daly, using intelligence provided by one or other of the security services.

Defence correspondent Mark Urban, however, is unconvinced: 'Like many other rumours surrounding the intelligence services in Ulster, the "Neave revenge" thesis cannot be comprehensively disproved, but it must be said that the evidence to support it is feeble and circumstantial.'[5]

In November 1981 the Anglo-Irish Inter-Governmental Council was set up following improved relations between Thatcher and the Irish premier, Charles Haughey. Any hopes of a new era of reconciliation were shattered first by Ian Paisley's efforts to set up a 'third force' along the lines of the B Specials, and then by the assassination of the Unionist MP for South Belfast, Robert Bradford.

Bradford, 40, was a hard-line Unionist, a Methodist minister and a Queen's University soccer blue who had represented South Belfast since 1994. He was ferocious in his condemnation of the Sunningdale Agreement and, indeed, any concessions to the non-Unionist traditions. He was even more ferocious in his verbal attacks on the IRA and had been instrumental in exposing various Provo fund-raising activities at home and abroad. An IRA spokesman said after his murder outside a community centre in Belfast:

He was an ultra-reactionary Loyalist who was vitriolic in his sectarian and racist outbursts against nationalism. Such people are responsible for motivating purely sectarian attacks on ordinary nationalists, and while they do not personally pull the trigger they provide the ideological framework for the UDA and UVF gunmen who do the killing.[6]

Bradford's widow saw things differently: 'The following Saturday was a horrific day for me as I relived every moment of the previous one. I stood alone in the cemetery, weeping silently, trying to understand.'

The Protestant community reacted with fury and sadness. Bradford had been a very public face of their traditions and had been planning to accompany Paisley to the United States to present their version of the 'truth about Ulster'. Services were held in almost every town and village in Ulster on the day of his funeral to 'mourn not him alone but all the victims of terror, and to show the Government that its security policy was found wanting'.[7] Paisley organised a day of action in favour of armed self-defence forces and 5,000 men marched military-style to the town square at Newtownards.

In 1982 INLA proved it was still a force to be reckoned with by shooting dead a prominent Loyalist and, in December, by killing 17 people, including 11 soldiers, in a bombing in Ballykelly. But the IRA was again in the ascendancy, more powerful and effective than when Thatcher had taken office. Victims included three soldiers in West Belfast, 11 soldiers killed in bomb attacks on military bands in London parks, and Lenny Murphy, leader of the UVF 'Shankill Butchers' who had murdered Catholics at random. The following year's 'successes' included the shooting dead of judge William Doyle as he left a Catholic church in Belfast, the death of four UDR members in a landmine attack in County Tyrone, the detonation of a 1,000 lb bomb outside Andersonstown police station, the escape of 38 IRA prisoners in a mass break-out from the Maze, the murder of UUP assembly member Edgar Graham at Queen's University, Belfast, and the IRA Harrods bomb in London's Knightsbridge, which killed five and injured 80.

But the IRA was not having it all their own way. Their most spectacular failure was an aborted plot to murder the Prince and Princess of Wales.

A trusted IRA Volunteer was told to travel to England and plant a bomb in toilets immediately behind the royal box timed to go off on 20 July, during a gala in London's Dominion Theatre to raise money for the Prince's Trust. Groups performing included two of Princess Diana's favourites, Duran Duran and Dire Straits. Arrangements were made to collect 50 lb of Frangex and 17 timers with a capacity for a 32-day delay system. The Volunteer did a reconnaissance and entered the Dominion while *The Return of the Jedi* was being screened. The Volunteer recalled: 'The cleaners were at work and I simply walked through the open door. It was as simple as that. No one took a single bit of notice of me.' He entered the royal box unchallenged. 'It was a small, flimsy, wood-constructed balcony on the left-hand side of the stage – and about 15 feet away, separated from it by two doors, was the men's toilet. A bomb containing 25 pounds of Frangex would kill or injure anyone within a radius of about 60 feet. I knew that it was possible to kill Charles and Diana ...' But the Volunteer the IRA commanders had chosen for the operation was Sean O'Callaghan, by then the most effective IRA informer in the history of the Troubles. O'Callaghan wrote much later: 'It was a brilliant and horrific plan. The IRA leadership were still desperate to strike at the heart of the British Establishment in revenge for the death of the hunger strikers. If Charles and Diana had been murdered by the IRA, Anglo-Irish relations would sink to a new low. The fall-out for the Irish community, particularly in London, can only be guessed at, something the IRA leadership would have regarded as a bonus.' A complicated, and ultimately successful, operation was launched to abort the operation without blowing O'Callaghan's cover.[8]

1983 also saw the jailing of 22 people for a total of more than 4,000 years on the evidence of IRA super-grass Christopher Black, while the June general election saw the Unionists winning 17 of the 27 Northern Ireland seats at Westminster. And in March 1984 Gerry Adams, now president of Sinn Fein and an elected Westminster MP, was wounded in Belfast by UFF gunmen. Republicans claimed that British intelligence had known of the attack in advance. Further IRA setbacks included the acquittal of three RUC officers for the murder of an unarmed IRA man, and the September seizure of 7 tons of arms and ammunition bound for the IRA from the vessel *Marita Ann* off the Irish coast. But by then the Brighton operation was well under way.

The man who had signed in as Roy Walsh stayed in room 629 of the Grand Hotel from 14 to 17 September and set a primed 30 lb bomb hidden behind a bathroom panel close to what the following month was to be the prime ministerial suite. The mechanics of the plot were similar to those intended in the failed bid to kill the Prince and Princess of Wales. The bomber was 33-year-old Patrick Magee. Belfast-born, he was brought up from the age of two in Norwich but returned to Belfast in 1969. His grandfather was an IRA man but Magee did not join the Provos until after he was arrested and beaten up by British soldiers. 'I felt a sense of anger, real anger. I felt I just couldn't walk away from this,' he said many years later.[9] He got involved in the lower end of Provo activities and was interned without trial for two years. He emerged committed to armed struggle and, it was suggested, received training at a Libyan terrorist camp.

He was long gone by Thursday, 11 October, the last full day of the Party conference. The Tories were in euphoric mood under a leader who now seemed unassailable. The 1982 Falklands War victory had transformed her from the most unpopular prime minister in living memory to the Iron Lady. The following year she had been returned to Downing Street with a massive 144-seat majority and the Opposition seemed to be in its death throes. She was surrounded by her own, adoring folk, including acolytes she had recently promoted to her Cabinet. Political reporters were heading towards their last night of a three-week party conference circuit, having shifted from the hopeless gloom of Labour the previous week to Tory triumphalism. That lunchtime, over a drink with veteran Tory MP Walter Clegg in the Old Bell, Clegg told me: 'Have you noticed that nothing dramatic ever happens at Brighton.' That night, into a long session at the main downstairs bar of the Grand I was introduced to 59-year-old Sir Anthony Berry, MP for Enfield Southgate, and Muriel Maclean, wife of the Scottish Tory chairman. Berry, an MP for 20 years, was the younger son of former *Sunday Times* owner Lord Kemsley, and he had himself been assistant editor of that paper. They seemed very affable and it was a convivial evening. Unusually, the bar closed before 2 am and I headed for my seafront hotel 100 yards away.

Thatcher was still working on ministerial papers when at 2.50 am Cabinet Secretary Robin Butler brought her a report on the Liverpool Garden Festival. She recalled in her memoirs:

A loud thud shook the room. There was a few seconds' silence and then there was a slightly different noise, in fact created by falling masonry. I knew immediately that it was a bomb – perhaps two bombs, a large followed by a smaller device – but at this stage I did not know that the explosion had taken place inside the hotel. Glass from the windows of my sitting room was strewn across the carpet. But I thought it might be a car bomb outside.[10]

Her adjoining bathroom was more badly damaged and a police officer later told my colleague David Healy that she had escaped death 'by seconds', something Thatcher herself denied. (Healy, deputy political editor of the Press Association, had arrived late on the scene and encountered the officer in a gents urinal. 'I could have kissed him,' he told me later.)

Only the incessant fire alarm disturbed the unlikely calm of the next few minutes. Denis Thatcher, who had been asleep in the bedroom, dressed and picked up a spare pair of shoes, which he later gave to Charles Price, the US ambassador, who had lost his. Butler took charge of the government papers and Mrs Thatcher picked up her speech from her shaken staff. Cabinet ministers and their spouses emerged, 'unkempt, anxious but quite calm', and 16 minutes after the explosion they began to leave the hotel, but the exit route was blocked. A little later they descended the main staircase. 'It was now that I first saw from the rubble something of the seriousness of the blast,' Thatcher wrote. 'The air was full of thick cement dust: it was in my mouth and covered my clothes as I clambered over discarded belongings and broken furniture towards the back entrance of the hotel. It still never occurred to me that anyone had died.'[11]

There were immediate deaths, many victims crushed in their beds: Sir Anthony Berry, now the third sitting MP to be assassinated during the Troubles; 45-year-old Roberta Wakeham, wife of the Conservative Chief Whip; North West Area chairman Eric Taylor; Jean Shattock, wife of the Western Area chairman. Muriel Maclean would die of her injuries some weeks later. John Wakeham's legs were shattered; another 33 were injured.

The world woke up that morning to live TV pictures of Norman Tebbit, the Trade and Industry Secretary, being dug out of the rubble. He and his wife Margaret had fallen several storeys in their bed. Mrs Tebbit was paralysed from the neck down. The arc lights needed by the rescue services to locate and bring out such casualties were provided by BBC and regional ITV crews. Their lights were my first impression when I reached the scene, having slept through the blast. The second was one of disbelief as I looked up at the Grand's façade which looked like a

9. The Brighton bomb (PA Photos)

cake sliced through by a giant knife. The central eight-floor section had
collapsed into the basement, although firemen later said that many lives
were saved because the hotel's sturdy Victorian construction stopped
the whole building falling. The dawn rose beautifully over a placid sea.
In those pre-mobile phone days queues of journalists formed at the
few available payphones. A little later I saw Sir Walter Clegg helped

out of the rubble, his clothes shredded and his features bloody from hundreds of splinter cuts.

BBC radio journalist Robert Tapsfield, staying next door in the Metropole, was on the scene much earlier. Twenty years on he recalled:

> I woke up and thought something had just fallen off the bedside table. But then the phone rang and I realised it was a bomb. The scene was chaos. The emergency services were everywhere, and there were senior politicians just wandering around. I saw Sir Keith Joseph looking rather ruffled, walking along the promenade in his dressing gown and slippers. The security people really should have whisked him off somewhere, because there could have been another bomb. That's what would happen now.[12]

The diarist Alan Clarke wrote that day:

> Amazing TV footage. The whole of the façade of the hotel blown away. Keith Joseph (indestructible) wandering around in a burgundy-coloured dressing gown, bleating. The scene was one of total confusion, people scurrying hither and thither, barely a police officer to be seen. But what a coup for the Paddys. If they had just had the wit to press their advantage, a couple of chaps with guns in the crowd, they could have got the whole Government as they blearily emerged ...

Ambulanceman Chris Ford, one of the hundreds of emergency service personnel who took part in the rescue operations, later recalled:

> I was relatively inexperienced but I was among those to go right into the heart of the hotel. The fire brigade had everything running in a very orderly, controlled fashion very early on, and the hotel seemed strangely quiet, almost eerie. Panic stations were over incredibly quickly but there was still, three hours on, a dense mist ... There was still a lot going on and we were routinely asked to be silent and stand still so the firemen could listen for voices. We could see Lord Wakeham in the rubble and while the firemen were doing the physical work, I worked to get a line and drips into him.[13]

Thatcher, much of her Cabinet and other hotel escapees were taken to Brighton central police station where they were served cups of tea. The Thatchers and close staff were then taken at speed in a police convoy to nearby Lewes Police College for the rest of the night. After sleeping fitfully and fully dressed for about 90 minutes Mrs Thatcher saw the television images of Tebbit in the rubble and then heard that Anthony Berry and Roberta Wakeham were dead. 'I knew that I could not afford to let my emotions get control of me,' she said. 'I had to be mentally and physically fit for the day ahead.' Ignoring initial security advice, she declared that she would return to Brighton and that the conference would start promptly at 9.30. In the meantime the local Marks & Spencer store had opened early for those Tories who did not have a change of clothes, although some arrived in the previous night's evening wear, their hair caked with dust.

Thatcher arrived to a thunderous ovation and sat on the platform to listen to the first debate which, by chance, was on Northern Ireland. One observer noted:

> She showed extraordinarily few outward signs of shock, and still fewer of fear. Moving through crowds of reporters, she registered an unreal but impressive calm. It was as if such terrible deeds were only to be expected from her wicked enemies, and they must not be seen, even by so much as a flicker of an eyebrow, to have touched her ... no hair out of place and the picture of exaggerated insouciance, it was as if she almost relished this most extreme of challenges to fortitude.[14]

Mid-morning she left to rewrite her speech in a private room. She removed much of the earlier draft, saying later: 'This was not a time for Labour-bashing but for unity in defence of democracy.'

John Wakeham was still trapped in the rubble, unaware that his wife was dead and that many others were missing. When Thatcher rose to deliver her speech she devoted a relatively short time to the night's horrors but struck the right note with her audience, both in the conference hall adjoining the Grand, and outside. 'The bomb attack,' she said, 'was an attempt not only to disrupt and terminate our conference. It was an attempt to cripple Her Majesty's democratically elected Government. That is the scale of the outrage we have all shared. And the fact that we are gathered here now, shocked but composed and determined, is a sign not only that this attack has failed, but that all attempts to destroy democracy by terrorism will fail.'

She was then driven to the Royal Sussex County Hospital to visit the injured. Wakeham was still unconscious. The consultant, former Tory MP Tony Trafford, and an El Salvadorean doctor with experience in crush injuries, battled successfully to save his legs. Tebbit regained consciousness during her visit and they exchanged a few words. His face was so bloated by injury that she barely recognised him. She also talked to Margaret Tebbit in the intensive care unit. 'She told me she had no feeling below the neck and as a former nurse she well knew what that meant,' Thatcher recalled. Labour leader Neil Kinnock expressed 'horror and outrage'; the queen was 'very shocked'.

On hearing of the prime minister's narrow escape, the IRA issued a statement: 'Today we were unlucky, but remember, we only have to be lucky once; you will have to be lucky always. Give Ireland peace and there will be no war.'

*   *   *

Once the last casualties had been removed from the Grand Hotel, the police investigation began. Detective Constable Dave Gaylor was one of 100 personnel in the initial team sifting through the wreckage. He recalled: 'There was this big hole right down the middle yet there was a real hush. All the rubble was placed in dozens of dustbins and then examined. I remember seeing plates of half-eaten food where people had jumped out of their seats and run out.' He then helped check the identities of everyone – guests, hotel staff, delivery staff – who had called in at the hotel in previous weeks. 'It was a case of working backwards using a process of elimination,' he said. 'There were people we hoped would ring us before we contacted them. People who perhaps should not have been there. Mr and Mrs Smith, we used to call them. We continued checking out everyone's stories and identities until we were left with one suspect.'[15]

That suspect was 'Roy Walsh', whose real identity was revealed when a palm print on a hotel registration card matched a print taken from Patrick Magee in the 1960s when he was arrested in Norwich as a juvenile. Detectives decided not to issue a public alert, fearing that their prey would go to ground, but waited in the hope that Magee would reappear on the mainland. Police trailing another IRA suspect, Peter Sherry, arrested Magee in June 1985 at an IRA safe house in Glasgow. He was planning more bomb attacks on 16 targets in London and more seaside resorts. He and four other members of an IRA active service unit were arrested and on conviction he received eight life sentences for planting the bomb, exploding it and five counts of murder. The eighth life sentence was for a separate conspiracy to bomb other targets the following summer. Mr Justice Boreham recommended that he serve a minimum of 35 years, a tariff which if served would have seen him released when he was 70. The judge said: 'You intended to wipe out a large part of the Government and you nearly did.' Magee gave a clenched fist salute as he was led away to start his sentence.

In gaol Magee achieved a first-class Open University degree on the English fiction spawned by the Troubles. He was controversially moved from an English to an Ulster gaol and, in August 1997, he married novelist Barbara Byer, his pen-pal. He was released in 1999 under the Good Friday Agreement after serving 14 years. Downing Street admitted that his premature freedom was 'very hard to stomach'.

In November the following year Magee came face to face with Jo Tuffnell, the daughter of one of his victims, Sir Anthony Berry, filmed by BBC's Everyman team. She said that within days of her father's murder she wanted the strength to overcome bitterness, and on Magee's release made repeated attempts to meet him. He finally agreed, although he remained a committed Republican and still believed that Berry, as a junior minister in the Thatcher administration, was a 'legitimate' target. But on camera he told her: 'Meeting you reminds me that he was also a human being and he was your father and that's all lost. I think it's very important to be confronted by the consequences – with your pain.'

They met several more times over the following year as Magee became an active member of Irish conciliation groups, helping to arrange similar encounters between former paramilitaries and their victims. Mrs Tuffnell worried that her own search for reconciliation would be seen as disrespectful to other Brighton victims. But former MP Harvey Thomas, also pulled from the Grand Hotel rubble, told her that her father would be proud of her efforts. She said that hearing Magee's story was part of her healing process.

Magee said: 'I wouldn't ask them to forgive. Why should they? Just the understanding is all I could hope for.'

*   *   *

Magee believed that the Brighton bomb he had set helped push the Thatcher Government towards negotiations with Sinn Fein and the IRA: 'After Brighton, anything was possible, and the British for the first time began to look very differently at us.'[16] An IRA spokesman spelt out their reasons for targeting the Cabinet: 'Our objective is to wear down their political resolve. They would have said "We lost Airey Neave, Lord Mountbatten, Margaret Thatcher, etc. – is it worth it?"'[17]

Such a scenario was disputed by the Iron Lady. But behind her public shows of defiance her reaction to such a close scrape with death and the loss of friends was more human. Her biographer Hugo Young wrote:

> She was as terrified, according to friends, as any human being would expect to be. How could anyone shake off the knowledge that she, she in particular and above all, was the target? The event moved her far more deeply than her somewhat routine public expressions of contemptuous bravado might have indicated. When she returned to Chequers and a beautiful autumn weekend, she was said to have wept copiously, on reflecting that 'this was a day I wasn't meant to see'.[18]

And the IRA, bolstered by arms shipments from Libya, were in a strong position to fight on.

16
The Troubles to Ian Gow

'we will never, never surrender'

The dirty little war rumbled on. The British Army, RUC and intelligence battled paramilitaries on all sides. The Provisional IRA fought them, the Protestant paramilitaries, their own breakaway factions and informers within their own ranks. Protestant paramilitaries battled their traditional enemies, each other and, increasingly, the forces of law and order, which they had always believed were – tacitly at the very least – on their side. More and more politicians were seen as legitimate targets as the rhetoric of the chamber matched the violence outside.

In October 1984 an SAS ambush of an IRA gang preparing to kill an RUC officer at Tannamore accidentally killed an innocent bystander while the terrorists escaped. In December another gunfight between the SAS and the IRA near Kesh saw one man killed on each side. Later that month two Provos were killed in an SAS ambush at Gransha psychiatric hospital, Londonderry. In February 1985 three IRA men were shot dead by soldiers in Strabane and nine RUC officers were killed in an IRA mortar attack in Newry. In May four RUC officers were killed by an IRA bomb in Killeen. Loyalists attacked police homes across Northern Ireland forcing scores of RUC families to leave, following the re-routing of parades designed to provoke Catholic communities. And John Stalker, deputy Chief Constable of Greater Manchester, investigated allegations of an RUC 'shoot to kill' policy aimed at Republican suspects.

But in November 1985, to the horror of extremists on all sides, Mrs Thatcher and the Irish Republic's Garret FitzGerald signed the Anglo-Irish Agreement. Regarded as a breakthrough, it gave the Irish

Government a 'consultative' role in Northern Ireland's affairs, boosted cross-border security co-operation, established a joint secretariat at Maryfield and set up permanent intergovernmental machinery.

The newly appointed Northern Ireland Secretary Tom King was attacked by furious Loyalists at Belfast City Hall and 10,000 screamed their anger in a city centre demonstration. Closer to home, the Agreement sparked the resignation of Treasury minister Ian Gow, the prime minister's former ultra-loyal parliamentary private secretary. He believed the deal was one-sided, giving Eire substantial influence in the North with no meaningful concessions in return. The following month the first intergovernmental conference was held, and all 15 Unionist MPs resigned to force by-elections. A Unionist day of action in March halted industry and disrupted public services. Peace through co-operation seemed an empty promise.

The 1980s continued as they has begun, with assassination and attempted assassination – by bomb and bullet – featuring in the headlines. In January 1987 DUP politician David Calvert was wounded by INLA gunmen. In April the Province's second most senior judge, Lord Gibson, and his wife, Cecily, were killed by an IRA car bomb at Killeen. Gibson was the trial judge who had cleared three RUC officers of the killing in 1982 of three IRA men near Lurgan, one of the incidents which resulted in the 'shoot to kill' inquiry. He spoke of bringing terrorists to 'the final court of justice'. On 25 April the couple were driving back from holiday via an Irish port and were escorted to the border by the Gardai. The RUC were not there to meet them, having suspended VIP escort duties on the border road following several fatalities among their own ranks. A 500 lb bomb was detonated at the side of the road. The following month eight IRA members and one civilian were shot dead in an SAS ambush as they raided an RUC station at Loughall. In November an IRA bomb shattered a Remembrance Day service in Enniskillen, killing eleven Protestants. March 1988 saw events which highlighted Ulster's own macabre dance of death. Three IRA volunteers were shot dead by the SAS in Gibraltar. In Belfast's Milltown cemetery their funerals were disrupted by UDA member Michael Stone hurling hand-grenades. He killed three and injured dozens more. And two plain clothes soldiers who gate-crashed the IRA funeral in West Belfast of one of Stone's victims were brutally attacked by enraged mourners and shot dead.

The rest of the year saw an IRA bomb kill six soldiers at a Lisburn 'fun run'; three members of one family killed by an IRA bomb intended for a judge; eight soldiers killed in an IRA bombing at Ballygawley. The following year saw an IRA bomb kill eleven military bandsmen at Deal in Kent and more low-level, but tragic, mayhem.

But the Thatcher Government had embarked on a series of secret contacts with Sinn Fein and the IRA, increased co-operation with the Republic, and other political initiatives designed to achieve a ceasefire ahead of a more permanent peace. Peter Brooke, the latest in a long line of Secretaries of State, signalled acceptance that the IRA could not be beaten by military means alone. Sinn Fein's Gerry Adams saw that as an admission that open negotiations with his party, and through them the IRA, were inevitable, and Martin McGuinness, like Adams a former IRA leader, said that Brooke was the first Northern Ireland Secretary 'with some understanding of Irish history'. Brooke, however, insisted that there could be no talks while the IRA continued its campaign of violence. When Adams said that a ceasefire was possible if Britain agreed to talks about eventual withdrawal from Northern Ireland, he was rebuffed. The Northern Ireland Office, ignoring much of what had already happened in secret, said: 'We do not negotiate with terrorists.' The cautiously optimistic mood turned sour, as the Provos would soon demonstrate with a mainland terror offensive in the run-up to summer.

Bombs were planted at the Territorial Army base in London, an RAF base, the Conservative-dominated Carlton Club, the London Stock Exchange and, ominously, the home of leading Tory Lord McAlpine. The IRA was ready to strike at the heart of the Conservative establishment.

*   *   *

Ian Reginald Edward Gow was born in Harley Street in 1937, the son of an eminent consultant physician. Educated at Winchester he performed his national service in the 15th and 19th Hussars, rising to the rank of major. He served in Malaya and was then posted to Northern Ireland at a time of renewed IRA activity in the late 1950s. The introduction of internment on both sides of the Ulster border stamped out a spate of violent attacks. But the co-ordinated action with the Eire Government increased the determination of Protestants in the North not to be absorbed by the South. Gow, stationed on the border at Omagh, was strongly influenced by such sentiments. After leaving the army he qualified as a solicitor in 1962 and, after several unsuccessful bids, was elected Conservative MP for Eastbourne in February 1974. He forged close links with Ulster Unionists at Westminster and was a friend of Enoch Powell, who sat on the Unionist benches after the October 1974 election. But his most influential contact was Airey Neave, who masterminded Mrs Thatcher's elevation to the party leadership and who was appointed Shadow Northern Ireland Secretary. Neave chose Gow, a kindred spirit, as his deputy, a post he held until Neave's murder.

Gow was the obvious candidate to replace him, but Thatcher chose Humphrey Atkins, who ditched many of Neave's policies and attitude. She made Gow her parliamentary private secretary immediately after her election victory. Gow, who had not voted for Thatcher in the leadership contest, put aside any disappointment he may have felt and threw himself into the job. Rather than being a mere handbag carrier, he became her eyes and ears in Parliament and Whitehall to such an extent that opponents within the party called him 'super-grass'. James Prior, who succeeded Atkins, claimed that Gow undermined his efforts by giving 'utterly disastrous, hard-line Unionist advice' to Mrs Thatcher.[1] Thatcher, however, appreciated his 'combination of loyalty, shrewdness and irrepressible sense of fun'.[2] In June 1983 Gow was appointed Minister for Housing and, to the surprise of many, his Thatcherite, free-market views took second place to more practical, humane considerations. Although he backed the sale of council houses, he objected to the Government's veto on councils spending the cash raised as they saw fit. Two years later, he was promoted to minister of state at the Treasury and appeared to be heading towards a Cabinet post until, after just two months, he resigned in protest at the Anglo-Irish Agreement, saying that he would never accept the involvement of a 'foreign power' in the administration of the Province. On the backbenches he served on the watchdog public affairs committee and took the chairmanship of the Conservative Northern Ireland committee. He spoke frequently and with great passion on the Troubles and on behalf of Unionist traditions, and in other debates he was a traditionalist and a high Anglican. He joined the right-wing John Biggs-Davison in founding the Friends of the Union, a pressure group that brought together opinion-formers in Westminster and Ulster. *Times* political editor Robin Oakley reported: 'It was typical of his sea-green incorruptibility that he then upset his friends amongst the Ulster Unionists by lending his support to the campaign for Conservative candidates to stand in Northern Ireland seats, saying that national parties should fight across the nation. Principle once again came before convenience.'[3] Another commentator wrote: 'Bald and bespectacled, he had in his dress, bearing and manner a slightly old-fashioned air.'[4]

The Provo army council was well aware of Gow's hard-line views and connections and his name was found on a hit-list discovered in Clapham. He refused to take much notice and his address was published in *Who's Who*, a publication scrutinised by IRA active service units newly arrived on the mainland. Sussex police, like all other forces, had warned MPs of the dangers they faced due to the IRA's renewed England campaign but Gow's constituency agent, Anne Murray, revealed that he never checked his car. 'He drove me to the office for the weekly surgery every Saturday mornings and I never saw him take any security precautions,' she said.[5] If anything he stepped up his rhetoric, and introduced a backbench bill to end early remission for terrorists after the IRA bomber Gerrard Kelly was released from the Maze after serving just half of a five-year sentence. In June 1990 he called for the prosecution of Granada TV producers who refused to identify a man interviewed for *World in Action* who claimed to be one of the 1974 Birmingham pub bombers. Later that month he condemned as 'futile and odious' the murder of a nun and three policemen in the Province, saying: 'The message that must go out from all decent people is that we will never, never surrender to people like this.'

On 30 March he got into his car at his home, The Dog House, in the village of Hankham, near Pevensey, just outside his Eastbourne constituency. At 8.39 am he switched on the ignition and began to move out of the car port. A 5 lb bomb with a tilt switch underneath his car exploded. The force of the bomb blew out both car doors and buckled the roof. Gow died 10 minutes later from massive injuries just after an ambulance crew arrived. He was 53. One of the first on the scene was garage mechanic Mark Stewart, who rushed to the sound of the explosion. 'Somebody was coming out of the house and said Mr Gow was still alive, but he was in such a state,' he said. 'There was nothing we could do. You just want to do something but there was nothing that you could.' Gow's body was left in the vehicle for several hours until bomb squad officers arrived. Fragments were collected and anti-terrorist officers, dog handlers and army bomb disposal officers checked for evidence and other devices.[6]

Later that day Thatcher spent an hour consoling Gow's widow, Jane, at her home. When the prime minister saw the car wreckage she turned away, visibly distressed. She told reporters that she could offer her bereaved friend no words of comfort. 'One can only be with her for a time and express one's sorrow and grief that way.' She also expressed her sense of personal loss: 'Ian was a true friend and colleague in all weathers, the first to offer comfort. We find it difficult to realise that he is no longer with us.' Thatcher insisted that the murder would not affect the Government's determination to combat terrorism: 'If Ian could speak to me now he would say that we fight that battle against them and we will bring them to justice.' She urged all MPs to be extra vigilant. 'It is only when we have a tragedy like this in a quiet village that we perhaps think seriously about safety,' she said. That night she accompanied Jane Gow and the Gows' two sons to a special service in a local church where Jane was an organist and her husband had been a church warden. Father Jonathan Graves said afterwards: 'There was not a single person in the church who was not upset.'[7]

Commander George Churchill-Coleman, head of Scotland Yard's anti-terrorism branch, appealed for anyone in the village to report any strangers seen in the previous days and weeks. He said that the bomb, designed to explode as soon as the vehicle moved, could have been planted on the Sunday evening or overnight. 'There must have been people here carrying out a reconnaissance operation either on foot or in a vehicle,' he added.

Near-neighbour Eileen Horsfield said: 'The community is very shocked. Mr Gow was a very nice, jolly man. It's terrible for his family but such a shock to everyone. One of the most frightening things is that there must have been terrorists in this village, strangers who managed to get in without being noticed to plant their bomb.'

As well as Thatcher, a steady stream of visitors called at the Dog House. They included the Democratic Unionist leader Ian Paisley, who was holidaying in Sussex. He said: 'It was a devilish attack. These people have no regard for religion or morality. They have no regard for decency. This act shows that they will sink to any depths to carry out their hellish and barbaric deeds.'[8] Labour leader Neil Kinnock said: 'No one must be daunted by these murderers. Ian Gow's killers proved their weakness in the face of democracy, not their strength.' The US State Department condemned the 'senseless murder' and affirmed that the US would continue to work with the UK to fight against international terrorism. And news outlets repeatedly broadcast a clip from Gow's speech in the Chamber after the TV cameras were first installed: 'Terrorism flourishes where those who perpetrate it believe that one day terror will triumph. That is why all of us need to give no hint that it ever will.'

Thatcher was deposed within a few weeks of her friend's murder, brought down by her stubbornness, the poll tax and the 'treachery' of colleagues – all issues unrelated to Northern Ireland. In one narrow area, however, the IRA did play a part in her downfall by removing the archetypal Thatcherite fixer from the scene when she needed him most. Her political demise was triggered by a devastating resignation speech by her former Chancellor, Sir Geoffrey Howe, and her subsequent re-election campaign was 'grotesquely mismanaged', according to the Tory writer and insider Bruce Anderson: 'Had Ian Gow still been alive, the first ballot campaign would have been properly run. Ian was also a close friend of Geoffrey Howe; even if he had not been able to prevent [Howe] from resigning, he might have persuaded him to make a less destructive speech.'[9]

One of Gow's later obituarists reckoned it was unlikely his murderers intended to hasten the departure of the Iron Lady: 'Presumably, given the victim's long and continuing friendship with Thatcher, the murder was an act of pure vindictiveness. It certainly did not force a change of government policy. At most, the manner of his death forced on Gow's civilised opponents the belated realisation that, for all his frailties, he had been a brave and charming man.'[10]

17

The Attack on John Major and Beyond

'A brief interruption'

The War Cabinet called by John Major to discuss Saddam Hussein's invasion of Kuwait and Allied plans to eject him had been in session for ten minutes. Treasury Chief Secretary David Mellor, his back to the room's large windows, was reporting on his tour of the Gulf States when there was the unmistakeable sound of an explosion, followed by the sound of glass cracking and an inrush of cold air. Major said: 'I think we had better start again somewhere else.'

10 Downing Street had been the target of a mortar bomb attack by the IRA. It was the closest they had come to wiping out the top tier of Government since the Brighton bomb.

* * *

The downfall of Margaret Thatcher had brought signs of some sort of peace in Northern Ireland: for the first time in 15 years the IRA declared a three-day Christmas ceasefire. It was not to last.

In February 1991 Gerry Adams dismissed speculation of a more permanent cessation of hostilities, but added that Sinn Fein was prepared to take political risks. Northern Ireland Secretary Peter Brooke responded that there would be no place at the negotiating table for Sinn Fein until the IRA renounced violence.

On Thursday, 7 February a van stopped in Whitehall diagonally opposite the gates of Downing Street. In the few minutes it was stationary no one noticed the hole cut in its roof. Inside were crude but effective mortars bolted to the van's bed. The first bomb sailed through the air with an audible 'whoosh' and landed in the rose garden at the back of No. 10, 15 feet from the building. The explosion left a crater, scorched the rear wall and shattered upper windows, including those of the Cabinet room. Two more bombs were fired, leaving the van blazing. Both over-shot the garden and landed near the police post on Mountbatten Green. They failed to explode but burst into flames and burnt, according to one witness, 'like bloody great Roman candles'.[1]

Those inside the Cabinet room were saved from carnage by the toughened glass which shattered not into shards but in sheets, which then sagged against heavy blast curtains six feet from Attorney General Sir Patrick Mayhew. Most ministers instinctively ducked, some crouched beside their chairs. The silence was broken by Major's laconic comment. Defence Secretary Tom King, a former Ulster Secretary, told the 15 men in the room not to gawp out of the windows. They took his advice and quietly filed out. One official said later: 'You don't go and look ... you get out.' The others who escaped death or maiming that day were the Chancellor Norman Lamont, Energy Secretary John Wakeham, still suffering from the 1984 bomb, Trade and Industry Secretary Peter Lilley, Foreign Secretary Douglas Hurd, Chief of Defence Staff Air Marshal Sir David Craig, Cabinet Secretary Sir Robin Butler, foreign affairs adviser Sir Percy Craddock, the prime minister's personal secretaries, Andrew Turnbull and Charles Powell, press secretary Gus O'Donnell, and note-taker Len Appleyard. Within ten minutes of the blast the meeting had reconvened in the neighbouring Cabinet Office, with Hurd outlining plans for a weekend visit to the Gulf region. The Cabinet minutes simply recorded: 'A brief interruption to the war committee of the Cabinet took place.'

Outside all hell had broken loose, with the van still ablaze and the police anxiously trying to cordon off Whitehall. As most people ran away from the oily smoke, Westminster political reporters raced towards it. My personal recollection is of confusion followed, once the cordon was in place, by a calm unnatural for the heart of London on a weekday morning.

Later that day Commander George Churchill-Coleman, head of Scotland Yard's anti-terrorism branch, denied that there had been any breach of security, saying that police officers had approached the van as soon as it stopped: 'It was a daring, well-planned, but badly executed attack.' It was also 'cowardly', using inaccurate weapons which could have caused widespread death and injuries, more than the four actual minor injuries suffered by those nearby. But the bomb had come close to wiping out the Cabinet, and the culprits had got away. An IRA statement issued in Dublin boasted that they had breached the heightened security in place around Westminster and Whitehall since the start of the Gulf conflict. It added: 'Let the British Government understand that, while nationalist people in the six counties are forced to live under British rule, then the British Cabinet will be forced to meet in bunkers.'[2]

Major told the Commons that the latest attack, like others before it, would not shift the Government's Northern Ireland policy by 'one single iota'. He went on: 'Our determination to beat terrorism cannot be beaten by terrorism. The IRA's record is one of failure in every respect and that failure was demonstrated yet again today. It's about time they learned that democracies cannot be intimidated by terrorism and we treat them with contempt.'[3] The queen altered a prepared speech to condemn those responsible and underline her premier's message that the bombers would never succeed in undermining Britain's democratic system. Thatcher, in Los Angeles for Ronald Reagan's 80th birthday, telephoned Major as soon as she heard of the attack. She said afterwards: 'I'm glad to hear he and all members of 10 Downing Street are safe. Nothing is totally safe today from terrorist attack.'[4]

The months that followed appeared to confirm her bleak verdict. A man was killed by an IRA bomb at Victoria Station, another bomb was planted at Paddington Station and yet another on the rail line into the City of London caused massive disruption. Peter Brooke published his three-strand approach to all-party talks and opened up a dialogue which was boycotted by Sinn Fein. But in August former IRA commander Martin McGuinness said that Sinn Fein was ready to 'risk everything ... for a real peace agenda'. He was quickly followed by Adams, who claimed he wanted to see an end to all acts of violence. The long war had exhausted all sides and there appeared to be a growing realisation that the gun could no longer accompany the ballot box. Such hopeful signs were shattered by a resumption of the IRA's mainland campaign.

The early 1990s again saw a cycle of abortive talks, secret negotiations, short-lived ceasefires followed by carnage on both sides of the Irish Sea. In London, targets included the Baltic Exchange area of the City of London, Heathrow Airport, Canary Wharf, the Hyde Park Hilton, underground stations and West End bars. Outside the capital the murder of two boys in an IRA explosion in Warrington provoked widespread fury.

But pressure for peace was building, not least from the new US president, Bill Clinton, who saw himself as an envoy for such an elusive peace, and the Irish prime minister, Albert Reynolds, and president, Mary Robinson. The SDLP's John Hume acted as a conduit between the UK Government, the Unionists and, through Sinn Fein, the IRA. It was claimed that in secret talks with the Major administration the IRA had sent a message that 'the conflict is over'. In December 1993 Major and Reynolds signed the Downing Street Declaration, which included a commitment that the people of Northern Ireland would decide its future and demanding a permanent renunciation of violence by the IRA. Although there were many more lethal hiccups in the peace process which added to the casualty lists on all sides, international pressure grew ever more intense, leading to the August 1994 IRA ceasefire. That in turn paved the way for the Good Friday Agreement brokered by Tony Blair after Labour's 1997 general election landslide victory. It meant that the main Protestant and Catholic parties had an opportunity to share power in a new Stormont administration, provided both sides renounced the pursuit of politics by violent means. For the IRA and Sinn Fein the bitterest pill to swallow was the key clause which stated: 'It would be wrong to make any change in the status of Northern Ireland save with the consent of the majority of its people'; for the Ulster Unionists it was the prospect of power-sharing with implacable enemies, the IRA's arsenal and the early release of convicted terrorists.

The Agreement proved a major breakthrough, although opinion is still divided over the motivation of so many paramilitaries to renounce the bullet and the bomb. Many, of course, were genuinely tired of decades of slaughter and were happy to embrace the trappings of ministerial authority. But it is also true that by then British security forces had so thoroughly infiltrated the terrorist groups that they were increasingly ineffective. During the 1980s it is estimated that around 30 super-grasses were recruited from the IRA, INLA and the loyalist UVF.[5]

The peace that followed was only comparative. IRA hard-liners broke away to form the Real IRA. In June 2000 that splinter group deployed a new and highly accurate mortar against London's Hammersmith Bridge. Security forces identified it as the work of a Dundalk 'engineer' who had defected from the Provos just months before. He had perfected his skill, it was alleged, by helping to make the mortars used in the Downing Street attack.[6]

The scale of British infiltration of the IRA was dramatically exposed in December 2005 when Denis Donaldson, a top Sinn Fein official and former terrorist, revealed in a television interview that for 20 years he had been a British agent. His confession came after the case against him for being part of an alleged Republican spy ring in Stormont had collapsed. Donaldson had been imprisoned in the Maze during the mid-1970s and became close to Bobby Sands. When he emerged his IRA credentials were impeccable and he swiftly advanced through the Republican hierarchy, becoming a key man in Adams' inner circle. He was sent to raise funds in the United States and such terrorist hotspots as Libya, Syria and South America. But he was tailed by an MI5 squad who noted his predilection for short-lived sexual liaisons. Expert opinion remains divided over whether he was 'turned' by the exposure of a particular affair to his Catholic family, or the threat of gaol for one family member. The truth is probably a combination of both, plus other factors, including self-preservation. He went on MI5's payroll – although he insisted his payments were modest – with orders not to flaunt his extra income. His subsequent double life would have stretched the nerves of most men. Reporter Joe Gorrod said: 'Donaldson was the perfect double agent. He had a gift for blending into any company without raising any suspicion. He gained the trust of hard-bitten IRA men who did not trust their own grannies.'[7] Donaldson became a well-known figure on the American fundraising circuit and a key player in the movement away from the bullet and towards the ballot box. Following the Good Friday Agreement he was appointed Sinn Fein administrator in the party's Stormont offices. But when those offices were raided by the police in 2002 Donaldson was one of several officials accused of running a spy ring in the heart of the Province's devolved government. The Unionists declared they could no longer trust Sinn Fein and power-sharing was suspended. After the case against Donaldson was dropped Donaldson confirmed that he had been a British agent: 'I was recruited in the 1980s after compromising myself during a vulnerable time in my life.'

The Republican movement was deeply shocked and Adams claimed that Donaldson spoke out because he was about to be exposed by police officers bent on deflecting attention from the murky circumstances of the raid and the collapse of the subsequent case. Previous informers had faced an IRA death sentence, but such action would have thrown further doubt on the Republicans' commitment to peace. Donaldson disappeared from circulation, accepting 'banishment' to a small family cottage without electricity or running water in an isolated area of County Donegal. He refused the offer of police protection. He was tracked there in March 2006 by a Sunday newspaper reporter, Hugh Jordan, who said: 'He looked like a hunted animal. He was extremely depressed. The nerves in his eyes were trembling. He did not see his life to be in danger, but felt the only future he had was where he was, living in that dreadfully sordid situation.'[8]

Some time during the night of 3 April 2006, Donaldson heard a noise outside. Dressed in his pyjamas, he rushed to bolt the only door but it was kicked in and shotgun blasts knocked him backwards. There was nowhere to run. The gunman reloaded two shotgun cartridges. Donaldson held up his arms and the blasts almost severed his right hand before hitting him in the chest and face. The killer, or killers, then drove away. Donaldson's body was found the following afternoon by a neighbour who was surprised that he did not come out and give her his customary wave when she tooted her horn as she drove past.[9]

The IRA denied any involvement in his assassination. Adams said: 'It has to be condemned. We are living in a different era in which everyone could share. This killing seems to have been carried out by those who have not accepted that.'[10]

They are not alone. Nationalist and Protestant paramilitaries and criminal gangs continue to undermine the rebuilding of the social, moral and physical fabric of the Province. Power-sharing proved too fragile for some Unionists. The issue of decommissioning of weapons continues to be thorny. Intimidation, punishment beatings, protection rackets and other activities which are a legacy of the Troubles continue to blight lives. But compared with the previous continuous carnage, every day without a death is a small victory.

Such little victories cannot be taken for granted. Michael Stone, the Loyalist killer who attacked mourners in Milltown Cemetery, provided a strange double postscript to the Troubles.

In November 2006, 18 years after committing that massacre and six after being released under the Good Friday Agreement, Stone revealed how close he had come to murdering Ken Livingstone, the London mayor. During the mid-1980s, while running the Greater London Authority, Livingstone had espoused Irish Republicanism, as had many English lefties despite the carnage inflicted on civilians in the capital. His invitation to Adams and McGuinness to County Hall across the Thames from Parliament caused widespread anger. Scotland Yard alerted him that he was on a Loyalist hit-list. They were right. The Loyalist paramilitary high command decided that Livingstone should die and picked Stone, an established assassin and a freelance operator for the three main terrorist groups, to carry out the hit. Stone recalled: 'Livingstone was the enemy. He was hated with a passion by Loyalists. He was giving support to people we were at war with and that made him a legitimate target. I was called to a meeting and given his name. I was told to "have a look at him". It meant "clip him".' A Scottish Loyalist contact gave him a room and a job as a barman in a Scarborough hotel, where Stone studied a dossier on Livingstone. It revealed that Livingstone used the London underground and walked short journeys. 'They had done a good job,' said Stone. 'They knew everything about him, where he lived and how he moved about. There were plenty of pictures of him.'[11]

Stone, then 29 with shoulder-length hair, decided to disguise himself as a jogger with a 9 mm Beretta tucked into his tracksuit. He travelled to London to carry out a 'dry run' of the Livingstone hit.

> I followed him into Westminster Tube Station, jogging behind him. He's a fast walker, so it was easy. I decided I would run up beside him when he was on the steps going down, fire one shot into the back of his head, then a double-tap into his torso – to make sure. He'd go down head first and I'd turn around and jog out of the station, towards the Embankment, and drop the gun into the river. We had a safe house set up in London and I was going to head for there. The idea was to lie low for a couple of weeks. Then, when things quietened down, I was going to travel to Scotland and

return to Northern Ireland with Rangers fans who had been to Glasgow to watch the game.

Stone returned to Scarborough where he practised with his gun in the hotel cellar. Three days before the planned hit, Stone began to suspect that the plot had been compromised by an informer. His contacts in Belfast agreed to a postponement. 'It was unravelling,' Stone said. 'The whole thing was suddenly very iffy. From what I learned later, if I had gone ahead I would probably have been ambushed by Special Branch. I was very frustrated. Livingstone represented a high-profile and worthwhile target.'[12]

In October 2006 anti-terrorist police interrogated Stone about the Livingstone plot but released him without charge. Stone then went public about his involvement, convinced that otherwise he would be blackmailed by former terrorist colleagues.

His story took an even more surreal twist the following month as the Stormont Parliament was engaged in a key debate on power-sharing. Stone burst through the front door carrying a pistol and a knife and shouting 'No surrender!' He was overpowered by two security guards, one a woman, and charged with the attempted murder of Gerry Adams, Martin McGuinness and others. Tony Blair said: 'No step forward in Northern Ireland is easy.'

Some dismissed Stone as a publicity-seeker or someone who simply could not suppress the hatred within him. But his actions, bizarre, murderous and suicidal, could provide a metaphor for the assassin within the body politic.

18
The Attempt on Tony Blair

'Bloody hell, we can't do this'

A Puma military helicopter idled on the tarmac at Petrovec airport in Skopje, the Macedonian capital, on a hot, dusty day in May 1999. The pilot patiently awaited his VIP passengers, British prime minister Tony Blair and his wife Cherie Booth, whom he was to take on a short hop to the Brazde refugee camp 10 miles from the Kosovo border, where 29,000 ethnic Albanians were sheltering from the ethnic cleansing ordered by Yugoslav president, Slobodan Milosevic. The conflict was still raging and security was ultra-tight. Nearby, beside their Lynx helicopter, a British press party was quietly smoking, checking their equipment or running through their stories. Downing Street press supremo Alastair Campbell sauntered from the prime minister's flight and ordered the reporters and photographers aboard. They clambered into their seats and strapped themselves in as the rotors started to turn.

Moments before lift-off Campbell ran back shouting: 'Out. Get out, we're not going. Get out of the helicopter, we're not using them.' A cameraman, who suspected it was a ruse to stop him filming, queried the order. Campbell replied: 'I couldn't give a toss if you get blown up ... it's the prime minister I'm worried about.'

The incident showed that Blair was not immune from the threat of assassination.

* * *

Milosevic had by his own, violent logic good reason to hate the British premier. Britain had been deeply involved in the convoluted and vicious politics of the Balkans since the fall of communism, and Blair had already proved himself determined to uphold UN mandates designed to impose some degree of peace and stability.

Serbs and Albanians had coexisted in Kosovo for centuries and the Serbians regarded it as the birthplace of their nation. In 1913 the province was incorporated into the Yugoslav federation but for the rest of the twentieth century the two ethnic groupings competed for control. In 1974 Kosovo was designated an autonomous province, but the death of the Yugoslav president, Josip Tito, saw mounting pressure for independence. Milosevic took advantage of Serbian resentment and, on becoming president in 1989, began to strip Kosovo of its autonomy. A passive resistance movement failed to reverse his purges and the Kosovo Liberation Army, an ethnic Albanian guerrilla group, stepped up attacks on Serb targets. That sparked brutal reprisals which, as the crisis mounted and the UN appeared reluctant to intervene directly, led in turn to all-out ethnic cleansing. Thousands died and hundreds of thousands more fled to neighbouring Albania, Macedonia and Montenegro as Serbian troops drove them from their homes. In September 1998, NATO gave Milosevic an ultimatum to halt the ethnic cleansing and the following March he rejected an internationally brokered peace deal signed by the Kosovo Albanians.

On 24 March 1999 NATO launched air strikes on Serbian military targets. One analyst wrote of 'Operation Horseshoe':

> NATO's military planners appear to have calculated when the air campaign began that the 'permissive environment' they wanted might be achieved by intensive air attacks, by both high-level bombers and low-level ground attack jets. The idea was that this assault would paralyse the Serb military's transport, communications and supply of ammunition, and that the low-flying fighter-bombers would batter the tanks, artillery pieces and troop units so badly that the Serb forces would be disabled as an effective fighting force. Then, NATO forces would be able to occupy Kosovo without real resistance.[1]

It did not go to plan. NATO attacks were severely hampered by bad weather and difficulties in pinpointing precise targets. And the air strikes enraged Milosevic. An Albanian resident of one Kosovo town recalled: 'With the bombs, the Serbs turned on the people. They started to burn Stimlje and shoot with different weapons.' An aid worker in the same town said: 'For five days without stopping, every night, they shot and burned and beat people in the street and the people ran until Stimljie was nearly empty. The earth was burning, from the ground and from the sky, and it seemed there was nowhere to hide.'[2]

As such scenes were repeated across Kosovo, the air bombardment had precisely the opposite effect to that intended by NATO. Rather than toppling the Milosevic regime, it united Serbs behind their leader and behind military operations in the province. Serbian troops were given a free hand to shell villages. Thousands more ethnic Albanians were herded onto trains and expelled across the Albanian border. Huddled in hastily erected refugee camps they told grim tales of massacre, rape, arson and mass looting. Within just a few weeks before and during the air war, over 800,000 had been driven out of the province, another half a million or so had fled into the mountains and at least 10,000 were dead.[3]

On 6 April Milosevic announced a unilateral ceasefire, but NATO intensified its aerial attacks. A few days later Milosevic announced he was ordering a 'partial withdrawal' of Serbian forces, claiming that they had completed operations against KLA 'terrorists'. He was also engaged in subtle diplomatic efforts to weaken Western resolve and bring about a pause in the air bombardment, knowing that, once halted, NATO would find it difficult to resume the onslaught. All such efforts failed and Milosevic resorted to bluster. Towards the end of April he told Western journalists that he was waging 'a life and death issue of national honour and sovereignty'. He added:

> We have never thought we could defeat NATO, an alliance of some 700 million people armed with the most advanced and sophisticated weaponry in the world. But you [the American people] are not willing to sacrifice lives to achieve our surrender; we are willing to die to defend our rights as an independent sovereign state.[4]

Later he dismissed the air campaign, saying: 'They are not even scratching us in Kosovo, they are just hitting the civilians.'

This was the arena the Blairs and their entourage flew into on 3 May. Blair's visit, the first by a senior Western leader since the air strikes began, was to stiffen the resolve of NATO and its member nations, weakened by civilian casualties and by Milosevic's apparent determination. He also wanted to ensure that the Macedonian Government would stay on side, and he wanted to see at first hand both the growing numbers of refugees and British forces – over 4,000 members of the NATO Rapid

Reaction Corps – commanded by General Mike Jackson. Security considerations were paramount and the accompanying press pack were only told on arriving at RAF Northolt that they were going 'somewhere in the Balkans'. On landing, just after noon, Blair described the NATO campaign as a 'battle for humanity'. The temperature was a sweltering 40 degrees Celsius as Blair was driven, with the Chief of the Defence Staff General Sir Charles Guthrie, to 4 Armoured Brigade HQ at Skopje. There, performing mainly for the cameras, Blair chatted to Challenger tank crews about NATO's planned invasion and climbed into a Warrior fighting vehicle. Jon Smith, the Press Association's political editor, said: 'Tanks. Warriors. Even a Milan anti-tank guided missile system. If Milosevic had had any doubt about NATO's willingness to send troops into his country, the TV pictures were also designed to remove them from his mind.'[5]

Milosevic was certainly watching those broadcasts in the bunker beneath his Belgrade residence, which had been wrecked by a NATO cruise missile. So too was General Nebojsa Pavkovic, the Yugoslav Third Army's Chief of Staff in charge of 200,000 Serbian troops and police in Kosovo at the time. What conversation passed between them is still a matter of controversy, but two years later, when facing war crimes trials, Pavkovic received orders 'from the top' to assassinate Blair as he was being flown by helicopter to the next stop on his schedule.

Pavkovic, married to a cousin of Milosevic's wife, claimed he had the weapons system Orkan (Hurricane) in place 30 miles from Skopje airport, which was just within range. The multiple launcher was capable of firing rockets at 1,200 m a second and releasing 288 bomblets, enough to envelop Blair's helicopter and those nearby as they took off. It had been developed in a joint project with Saddam Hussein's regime and was reckoned to be wildly inaccurate, although Pavkovic claimed that his had been upgraded and had proved effective on previous operations. Chris Foss, of *Jane's Defence Weekly*, said that it would have taken the first missile 110 seconds to strike in the air above the airport. 'The Orkan is an area weapon: you fire one and, if it's near the target, you open up with the lot.'[6]

Pavkovic told journalists:

> We had the possibility to do it and we had the political decision to strike at the airport when Blair was coming. We knew from our intelligence sources when exactly he was coming. As commander of my army I had the open

door to do it. I had the political decision to use the [Orkan] system and I got them reinforced to do that. I was under pressure to do it since NATO was destroying Yugoslavia.[7]

He believed that any such attack would have been legitimate under international law because British and NATO troops were massing on their borders with a clear intention to invade. But he finally decided against it because, he claimed, he feared 'massive' civilian casualties would result if he brought down the helicopters at the airport. He also feared that such an attack would remove any hope of Macedonia, an historic Slavic ally, switching their support to the Serbians. He also claimed that he had a similar opportunity to kill Hillary Clinton, wife of the US president, when she visited the area a few days later. It must be remembered, however, that Pavkovic's claims emerged as he was facing extradition to The Hague to face a war crimes trial two years after the event. It can be assumed that he wished to put the best spin on why he aborted the assassination attempt. Pavkovic's critics in Serbia claimed he was desperate for good publicity and wished to distance himself from Milosevic. A NATO source quoted by the *Sunday Times* said that any attack on Blair would have changed the rules of engagement: 'We'd have dismantled Serbia brick by brick. I think the more they thought about it, the more they thought, "Bloody hell, we can't do this".'[8]

What remained unclear at the time of writing is this: if the mission was dropped, why was Blair's helicopter flight cancelled that weekend? NATO sources later insisted they had no knowledge of the plot, but a cancellation for routine security considerations seems too much of a coincidence. A Ministry of Defence spokesman in Macedonia, Paul Sykes, said: 'We were taking appropriate security measures, but obviously we're not prepared to say what they were.' Downing Street said that a plot to murder Blair was plausible. An official said: 'The assumption was that the prime minister was a target.' Later, officials confirmed that their main fear during the Blairs' visit was an attack on his helicopter by shoulder-launched rockets known to be carried by Yugoslav special forces who had infiltrated the Macedonian highlands. But again it seems to stretch credulity that the Blair helicopter was halted at precisely the moment of his greatest vulnerability to Orkan simply because of a more widespread alert concerning inaccurate Scuds.

After barking his orders to the press party, Campbell explained: 'The Macedonians have told us the Serbs have picked up our movements and have started moving a missile unit to shoot us down.' Jon Smith recalled: 'We now had a lot of ground time while the programme was re-scheduled. Unlike one or two of our colleagues, I had no doubt that the threat was real. Our phones, therefore, remained switched off. A fleet of 4 × 4s were assembled to drive us straight to the refugee camp and we scrambled in.'[9]

When they reached the camp there was mayhem. The Blairs were mobbed by refugees, the children chanting, 'Tony, Tony, Tony.' The prime minister promised them all they would be able to return to their homes. Cherie Booth brushed away tears. The scenes were repeated when the convoy moved on to the Kosovo border crossing at Blace. Smith recalled: 'As soon as Blair arrived, the already jumpy Macedonian border guards began aimlessly thrashing around, pushing, shoving, barging cameras out of the way, toppling over crush barriers.' The Blairs, to the horror of his protection officers, then wandered into no man's land within range of Serbian snipers. Face to camera, Blair pointed to the Serbian hills and said:

> We must redouble our commitment to these people. I have just been speaking to them about the torment they have been through, people who have seen loved ones killed, who have had money taken from them, who have seen the most unbelievable brutality carried out across the border. We have taken this action because we refused to allow a policy of ethnic cleansing and racial genocide to be carried out and succeed here on the doorstep of the European Union.

Finally, his protection team were allowed to bundle him out of the danger area.

The air bombardment continued and became increasingly effective, with 200 attacks against 150 targets destroying half the Yugoslav air force's MiG-29 fighters, oil refineries and much of Milosevic's early warning radar systems. Eventually, in early June, he withdrew all forces from Kosovo. NATO troops moved into the province as the United Nations set up a Kosovo Peace Intervention Force. General Pavkovic claimed he wanted to fight to the end: 'My soldiers were crying when Milosevic gave in. I told Milosevic that we can continue, and he told me, "I know you can stand more, but Serbia cannot".'

Milosevic made him chief of general staff of the Yugoslav Army and decorated him. Pavkovic returned the favour by changing sides in the presidential elections and civil disturbances which finally toppled the Milosevic regime in 2000 after ten years of untrammelled power. In August 2004 Milosevic told his war crimes trial in The Hague that the Serbs had been the victims of a plot by the US and Europe to break up the former Yugoslavia for their own ends. 'They supported a totalitarian chauvinistic elite, terrorists, Islamic fundamentalists, neo-Nazis whose objective was an ethnically pure state, that is a state without any Serbs,' he said with no hint of irony.

In the post-Milosevic era Pavkovic performed numerous U-turns to remain in favour with those in power on any one day, all the while cultivating the media and building up his personality cult. He stressed his devotion to democracy and the importance of bringing Yugoslavia into the international community. Following rumours that he could be indicted for war crimes, Pavkovic then backed the wrong person in Belgrade's power struggles and was arrested as part of a supposed crackdown on organised crime. After three months he was released and played cat and mouse with the Belgrade authorities after his war crimes indictment was confirmed. He finally gave himself up in April 2005, claiming it was a 'noble gesture' which proved his commitment to democracy. He described his surrender as his 'last sacrifice to his country'.[10]

He was charged, with three other generals, with four counts of crimes against humanity and one of violating the laws and customs of war.

*   *   *

The question remains: was there a serious plot to assassinate Blair? Both Milosevic and Pavkovic were vainglorious and cruel men who had their backs to the wall. Milosovic in particular may have seen the NATO missile attack on his own home as an attempt on his life, which justified a similar response against a Western leader who, as luck would have it, had put himself within range of such retaliation.

Moreover, both were products of the Balkans where assassination had been long regarded as a political tool. All previous Serbian leaders, save for King Peter I and Marshal Tito, had been deposed by death or exile. In 1903 the pro-Austrian King Alexander and Queen Draga were assassinated following a wave of popular unrest over corruption and financial mismanagement. Twenty-six conspirators blew open the palace doors with dynamite, cutting off electricity and telephone wires, and searched the darkened rooms for two hours before finding the royal couple hiding in a closet. Their bodies were stripped, mutilated and thrown from their bedroom windows. Their successor, King Peter, proved to be a fine, liberal ruler. In the minds of many Serbs, whose parents and grandparents remembered the murders, assassination was an honourable tradition. And it was a Serbian, Gavril Princip, who assassinated Archduke Franz Ferdinand and his wife Sophie in Sarajevo, an event which set off a train of events which led inexorably to the First World War. Such precedents must have occurred to Milosevic as he sheltered in his bunker while bombs and missiles rained down. Dictators on the brink of annihilation always believe they can destroy their enemies.

Milosevic spent four years in a cell charged with 66 counts of genocide, crimes against humanity and war crimes in Bosnia, Croatia and Kosovo. The trial in The Hague was drawing to a close when he was found dead in his bed on 11 March 2006. Less than a week earlier the former Croatian Serb leader Milan Babic, a star witness in the trial, had committed suicide in his cell. Former peace envoy Lord Owen said of Milosevic's death: 'People everywhere will feel cheated. It is a tragedy that justice has not been able give the verdict.'[11]

19
Conclusions

'call it blood lust ...'

In March 1974 the IRA's mainland terror campaign was reaching its height: with deadly pub bombings in Birmingham and Guildford, Britain was on high terror alert. Therefore, it was not surprising that when news filtered in of a gunman's attack on a limousine carrying Princess Anne, then fourth in line for the throne, on 20 March, it was seen as part of a long-feared terrorist onslaught against the royal family. The princess was unharmed and the attacker, Ian Ball, apprehended, but four people were shot and both palace and government aides suspected a more widespread Republican plot.

Such suspicions were shared by the queen, then on a tour of Indonesia. Her ambassador in that country, Sir Willis Combs, wrote urgently to Prime Minister Wilson: 'Viewed from this distant island, it seems to me that it is important to establish whether this horrible business was just the act of a nutcase or something more serious.'

The drama had begun when the 23-year-old princess was being driven down the Mall by her chauffeur, Reg Callender, alongside her husband, Captain Mark Phillips, a lady-in-waiting and her bodyguard, Inspector Jim Beaton. A Ford Escort driven by Ball overtook their Rolls-Royce, cut in front and forced it to stop. Anne, Captain Phillips and the lady-in-waiting were thrown to the floor. Ball leapt out brandishing a pistol and fired several shots, one of which came within inches of hitting the princess and wounded her bodyguard. Inspector Beaton fired one shot, but his gun jammed. He threw himself over the back seat to shield the couple and was shot twice more. Ball pointed his gun directly at Princess Anne and said: 'I want you to come with me for

a day or two because I want £2 million. Will you get out of the car?'
She looked him in the eye and refused, telling him: 'Bloody likely! I
haven't got two million.'[1]

Ball then tried to pull Anne out of the car, but Captain Phillips
wrestled to keep the passenger door shut. A witness described it as a
'deadly tug-of-war'. Constable Michael Hills was shot as he arrived
on the scene. So too was the chauffeur. *Daily Mirror* journalist Brian
McConnell, who had been travelling in a taxi behind the royal car,
confronted the panicky gunman, saying: 'Don't be silly, old boy, put the
gun down.' He too was shot for his pains. The princess later reported:
'It was all so infuriating. I kept saying I didn't want to get out of the
car – and I wasn't going to get out. I nearly lost my temper with him.
But I knew if I did, I'd hit him and he'd shoot me.'[2]

Her ordeal lasted six minutes as security forces rushed to the scene.
According to an equerry, Colonel John Miller, who witnessed the finale,
Princess Anne's actions prevented further bloodshed. In a report to
Downing Street he wrote: 'It seems that Princess Anne then decided
that if she made as if to get out of the door on the opposite side of the
car, Ball would go round there and could be apprehended.' Ball fell for
the stratagem, dashed round the limousine and was brought down by
a flying tackle from a police officer.[3]

Ball was found to be carrying a ransom note addressed to the queen.
He was quickly identified as a 26-year-old petty thief with a history
of mental illness – not a likely terrorist – nevertheless, Special Branch
launched a fruitless search for Irish Republican links. Sir Robert
Armstrong, Wilson's principal private secretary, wrote to the queen's
private secretary, Sir Martin Charteris, to allay her fears. His letter, kept
secret for 30 years, read: 'It is of course impossible to be absolutely
sure but all the indications are that this man was operating entirely on
his own and without political motive. He had obviously worked out
the details of his idea with care and attention to detail but the whole
framework was lunatic. So we have no reason to believe anything other
than that this was the work of an isolated nutcase.' He added: 'It is still
worrying because of the risk that such infections may spread.'

Ball admitted attempted murder and attempted kidnap. He was
detained indefinitely under the Mental Health Act and remains in
Rampton secure hospital in Nottinghamshire. Inspector Jim Beaton

was awarded the George Medal and Brian McConnell the Queen's Gallantry Medal for their courage.

The point of retelling this incident here is that the initial reaction of the authorities sums up the dilemma which faces those investigating or analysing any assassination bid: 'just the act of a nutcase or something more serious?'

As we have seen, the murder of Spencer Perceval and Edward Drummond, and the attempts on Queen Victoria's life, generally fell in the former category. The case of Drummond's killer, indeed, led to changes to the insanity laws. In such instances the motives emanating from damaged minds tended to focus on an outraged sense of personal injustice, real or perceived, a grudge against society in general personified by a head of state or prime minister.

At least some of the attempts on Victoria's life were an early manifestation of the celebrity assassin. Before mass-produced photography, only the very greatest in the land were instantly recognisable. Even major politicians were relatively anonymous in the early part of the nineteenth century, resulting in several botched attempts and tragic cases of mistaken identity. A visage as famous as the queen's was a tempting target to those whose ego or insanity demanded a victim of renown. Mass media, the social revolutions of the mid- to late twentieth century, and the switch from princes to pop stars in terms of public awe and deference contributed to the elevation of talented individuals to world-wide icons. It took some time for it to be realised that such icons – flesh and blood, flawed and famous – would become the target of the jealously deranged.

In the age of celebrity, political and personal grievances have been overtaken by the desire to be more famous than the famous – by killing the object of widespread adulation – and thereby become an object of adulation, or at least horrified fascination, oneself. It is one way to get noticed.

John Lennon was arguably one of the most famous people on the planet. With the Beatles, he was the object of desire for millions of fans. Since the break-up of the group his lyrics had been pored over and analysed by millions more, their meaning given extra kudos by legions of pop-conscious academics. His peacenik campaigning, confused and naive though it was, made him a leading figure in efforts to halt the Vietnam War.

On 8 December 1980, he left his luxurious apartment in the Dakota building overlooking New York's Central Park with his wife, Yoko Ono, to spend the evening at a recording studio. Before getting into the waiting limousine he was approached by a 25-year-old Texan, Mark Chapman, who asked him to autograph his copy of Lennon's 'Double Fantasy' album. He complied. When he returned several hours later Chapman was waiting for him. It is likely that Lennon did not notice his assailant until five bullets slammed into his back. He staggered a few steps into the vestibule before collapsing. He was rushed by police car to St Luke's Roosevelt Hospital where he died. He was aged 40.

BBC correspondent Tom Brook was the first British radio reporter on the scene.

> As soon as I arrived I knew something was horribly wrong. A group of about 20 were gathered outside the apartment building. They looked agitated and confused. A short time later I listened to a report on my small radio confirming that Lennon had indeed died. Within the hour the Dakota became a makeshift shrine. Fans in a state of disbelief, many of them crying and bearing candles, began to fill the street. I remember one woman, surrounded by a crowd chanting Lennon's 'Give Peace a Chance', commenting that his death had hit her hard, it made her feel like she had been punched in the stomach. Personally I didn't have time to respond emotionally ...

Later he had difficulty keeping his emotions in check: 'I had grown up with Lennon's music. I was a fan and I suddenly realised that his passing was truly shocking news. For my parents' generation the assassination of President Kennedy in 1963 was a truly seismic event. But for baby-boomers Lennon's passing had far more emotional significance.'[4]

The cause of so much grief was the archetypal nobody, a loner and a self-important fantasist who felt betrayed by someone he had never known. Chapman made no attempt to avoid arrest. He stood looking at Lennon until a doorman took the gun from his hand and kicked it into the road. Chapman then sat down and began reading his well-thumbed copy of *The Catcher in the Rye*. The initial police report said there had been no robbery and that Lennon had been shot by a 'deranged' person. Chapman was sentenced to 20 years to life for murder. In prison, and at subsequent parole hearings, he claimed that far from killing in a fit of pique or a moment of madness, he had been planning the assassination for three months. He had also considered killing other celebrities he regarded as 'phonies'. He had travelled to New York to kill Lennon once before, but could not go through with it. He went to Hawaii where he was angered by a book containing pictures showing Lennon's lavish lifestyle. Chapman said that such opulence mocked his own struggles, both internal and external: 'It was just a tremendous compulsion of feeling just this big hole. Of being what I thought was a big nobody, a big nothing, and I couldn't let it go. And it just keeps going very strongly, and I couldn't stop it.'

Chapman was a lonely and compulsive rock fan who had learnt lyrics by heart since his early teens and heard messages in them. Such messages had led to an increasingly erratic cycle of attempted suicide and treatment for paranoid schizophrenia. In a taped interview with journalist Jack Jones, he said that he had hoped to find his own identity by killing Lennon. 'There was a successful man who kind of had the world on a chain, so to speak, and there I was, not even a link of that chain, just a person who had no personality. And something in me just broke.'[5] In 2000, when he became eligible for early release, Chapman enraged fans by claiming that, if he were still alive, Lennon would want him freed. He told a 2004 parole board that he had wanted to 'steal' Lennon's fame by doing something which meant everyone would know *his* name. To some extent he had succeeded, he said, then added: 'People hate me now instead of, you know, something positive. So that's a worse state. I'm a bigger nobody than I was before.'

The parole board told him he had 'a clear lack of respect for life': 'During the interview, your statements for motivation acknowledge the attention you felt this murder would generate. Although proven true, such rationale is bizarre and morally corrupt.'[6]

Another classic 'lone nut' case was the attempt to murder President Ronald Reagan. On 30 March 1981, John Hinckley, a 26-year-old Texan, gunned down Reagan outside the Washington Hilton, also wounding a press secretary, a police officer and a secret service agent. As Hinckley was wrestled to the ground, Reagan was bundled into his limousine and taken to hospital with a bullet lodged near his heart. He went on to make a full recovery, as did the two officers. Press secretary James Brady was left permanently paralysed. Hinckley was found not guilty of attempted murder by reason of insanity and remains incarcerated in St Elizabeth's psychiatric hospital a few miles from the White House. His lawyers persuaded a jury that Hinckley had been psychotic at the time and therefore not accountable for his actions.

In a reverse of Britain's McNaughton Rules, Congress rewrote the US insanity laws to prevent similar outcomes in assassination cases.

During the investigation and trial, it emerged that Hinckley, who had severed all connections with his prosperous family, had modelled himself on Travis Bickle, the psychopathic outsider in the ground-breaking 1970s film *Taxi Driver*. The character, played by Robert de Niro, considers killing a politician but instead murders the pimp of a twelve-year-old prostitute, played by Jodie Foster. After the assassination attempt on Reagan an unmailed letter to Foster was found in Hinckley's hotel room. It read: 'Jodie, I would abandon this idea of getting Reagan in a second if I could only win your heart and live out the rest of my life with you.' Hinckley had been a celebrity stalker, trying to visit the actress as she studied at Yale University, and sending her love letters and tapes of himself singing love songs.[7] Doctors judged him to be a psychotic with a narcissistic personality disorder and suffering from deep depression. Despite claims that his condition was much improved, his obsession with murder continued behind the locked doors of the institution. During the mid-1980s he formed a close relationship with another inmate, a much older woman who had shot and killed her ten-year-old daughter. And in 1987 authorities discovered he had been writing to the notorious serial killer Ted Bundy. A search of his room found 57 photographs of Foster and, the following year, more correspondence was found in which he praised Adolf Hitler and the mass murderer Charles Manson. A psychiatrist told a court hearing, at which Hinckley was seeking to be granted outside excursions, that he displayed a love of 'secretiveness and deception'. Another hearing in 2000 heard that he had a 'continued interest in violently themed books and music'. Patti Davis, Reagan's daughter, said: 'I don't believe for a second that he is no longer mentally ill.'[8]

Mental instability was given as the cause of two attempts made on the life of Reagan's predecessor, Gerald Ford. On 5 September 1975 Lynette ('Squeaky') Fromme, a former groupie of Charles Manson's mass murdering clan, took aim at the president in Sacramento, but was seized before she could fire. Seventeen days later in San Francisco, Sara Jane Moore, a 45-year-old housewife, fired two shots at him. The first shot only narrowly missed the president; the second wounded a bystander. Moore was deemed to be suffering from a personality disorder which led her into 'extremist' politics. Both women remain in prison serving life sentences.

Mental illness, however, has long been used by the authorities, whether repressive or benign, and the general public as a term to categorise the political assassin or terrorist. Professor Maxwell Taylor writes:

> The acts committed by the terrorist are in a sense extra-normal. They are unusual in our society, although not unique. The nature of the violence ... greatly influences our view, and we feel that the terrorist is not just extra-normal, but abnormal. We see his behaviour as pathological and therefore he is in some sense mentally ill. By taking this perspective, we also tend to place the terrorist within a clinical context, because in our society this is how we conventionally deal with mental illness.[9]

Branding dissidents, of whom the assassin or terrorist is the most extreme form, as mentally ill has been used by totalitarian regimes to deny legitimate grievances. In such cases the locked asylum ward and electroconvulsive treatment have been as effective as the prison cell or torture chamber.

The spectre of assassination has also spawned a thriving conspiracy theory industry. It grew from attempts to show that Lee Harvey Oswald was a 'patsy' for the killing of President Kennedy in Dallas in 1963. That theory has been comprehensively taken apart, as have the more recent claims that Diana, Princess of Wales was killed by the British secret services on the orders of the Duke of Edinburgh. But such theories multiply on denial. Any rebuttal, no matter how factually comprehensive, is seen as proof of a cover-up. The Internet has allowed such theories, previously slow to disseminate, to become instantly global, lending them a bogus air of authority. There are currently at least 2,000 websites devoted to John Lennon, many of which insist he was assassinated as part of a vast conspiracy involving the FBI, US presidents, the Mafia and Cuban exiles, just like the wilder theories surrounding the assassination of President Kennedy. Such fantasies allow the lonely and the obsessive to indulge their own theories and link up with the like-minded.

Back to real life. Assassination as a tool of the genuinely crushed and dispossessed is considered alien to Britain. In retrospect it is astonishing that, with the exception of the doomed Despard and Cato Street conspiracies, it was rarely used to address real rather than imagined grievances from the Industrial Revolution onward when the cruelties inherent in rule by an elite merged with those of capitalism and market forces. Generations faced poverty, famine, insecurity and early death with little or no chance of advancement. But during the long war for universal suffrage, trade unionism and human rights, the riot and the strike were the main weapons of the increasingly literate working classes, not the assassin's bomb or bullet. The carnage was immense, with hundreds killed in the 1830 Battle of Bristol, more dead in the Peterloo Massacre, the Merthyr uprising, the Newport insurrection and Featherstone colliery, scores executed following the Luddite and Captain Swing riots, and thousands gaoled or transported to Australia. But, with a very few exceptions, the killers wore uniforms or a judge's wig. And the fight for social justice involved disparate groups of relatively powerless men and women facing up to the might of state repression and joining together to make common cause, whether through the Reform and suffrage movements or through the new trade unions, rather than by secret societies which attract natural-born killers. Suffrage was won by economic power and the threat of social revolution, not by the death of 'great' men.

The exception, during the second half of the nineteenth century and throughout the twentieth, was driven by Ireland, a place where murder and intimidation had a long history. The Phoenix Park murders were the first successful terrorist act aimed at the representatives of English power but, as we have seen, many more followed. And in Ireland, at least until the removal of the British from the southern counties, a patriotic form of nationalism and a righteous sense of injustice were certainly factors in the making of what we would now call a terrorist.

A typical example from the Irish war of independence is Tom Barry. He was a 16-year-old Cork lad when he joined the British army in 1915, not for any fine ideals, but for adventure. 'I knew nothing about nations, large or small,' he wrote. 'I went to war for no other reason than that I wanted to see what war was like, to get a gun, to see new countries and to feel a grown man. Above all I went because I knew no Irish history and had no national consciousness.' That was awoken in May 1916 when he was serving with the Mesopotamian Expeditionary Force as one of 30,000 troops surrounded by Turkish-German forces at Kut el Amara. His unit was withdrawn to a rest camp and there he read a military communiqué detailing the Easter Rising in Dublin.

On his return to West Cork in 1919 he read avidly the stories of Irish revolt. 'I read the history of the corpses of the famine, of the killings of Irishmen without mercy, the burnings, the lootings and repeated attempts at the complete destruction of a weaker people. In all history there had never been so tragic a fate as that which Ireland had suffered at the hands of the English ...' The following year he became training officer to the Third (West) Cork IRA Brigade fighting those, he was convinced, responsible for so much misery.[10]

He swiftly rose to command the Brigade's Flying Column, plotting the assassination of British officers and judges, leading raids on police and army barracks and ambushing their columns, torching the homes of Loyalists in reprisal for the destruction of Catholic homes, ordering the execution of informants and becoming a renowned guerrilla leader. To the British authorities and the Protestant elite he was a thug, an assassin and a terrorist. But, as he made clear in his frank memoirs, he regarded those he was fighting as the real terrorists – the Black and Tans, the Auxiliaries and the officers and men of the Essex Regiment who were guilty of murder, torture, thuggery, looting, home-burning and wanton destruction.

Barry displayed the raw hatred he felt towards a despised enemy in February 1921 when his column infiltrated the small town of Bandon with orders to 'flush out and shoot' any Essex men they could find. He accidentally bumped into five Black and Tans. They were equally surprised, and a gun fight erupted with Barry aided by another Volunteer. Barry recalled:

> The first to fall was the terrorist who was already swinging his revolver in his hand as he came into view. A second staggered across the road and also fell to the ground. I missed a third with a left-handed snap shot as he sprinted past. The fourth had bolted back to the barracks as the first shot was fired. The fifth, who was yelling unintelligibly, had dropped to the ground unhurt. Now he leapt up and ran around the corner before I could fire at him. Then I was guilty of the most senseless act of my life, for I ran after him. He had seven yards start ... and his revolver was in his hand as he thundered on towards the barracks. I gained rapidly on him, and when only three or four paces behind, I pushed the short Webley revolver I had in my left hand into my tunic pocket, retaining the Colt automatic in the right. I have never understood since why I did not shoot him in that race up North Main Street, as I was never more than a few yards behind him and I could not have missed him if I had pulled the trigger. But call it blood lust arising

out of hate, madness or what you will, I wanted to get my hands on him, hence the freeing of my left hand. It never occurred to me, and apparently not to him, that all he had to do was turn and pull the trigger. Sixty yards from the scene of the gun fight I grabbed his left shoulder with my left hand. Fright-crazed, he squealed and turned like a hare into the nearest door which I passed before turning to follow him. As I ran into the small shop he was entering the kitchen immediately behind. Jumping the low counter gate, I too was in the kitchen a few yards from him, when common sense returned and I fired. His revolver clattered to the ground as he fell dead, but he was shot again to make sure his terrorist days were over.[11]

The man he killed was later identified as Constable Frederick W. Perrier, whom Barry described as a 'ruffian and a bully'.

From the start of the more recent Troubles in Northern Ireland, potential killers were recruited from disenchanted and bloodied members of the civil rights movement and the various radical organisations which sprouted in the late 1960s, especially once the Provisional IRA had split from the more sedate Republican Old Guard. By the 1970s and 1980s, however, the main recruiting ground was the semi-derelict housing estates where youths saw the petrol bomb as an educational tool. That created a semi-literate underclass, which saw criminality, hooliganism and sectarian murder as a legitimate part of the armed struggle, especially when matched with the brutality of trigger-happy soldiers and vicious Loyalist paramilitaries. Given that potent mixture, peace, or the closest to it we can expect, was a long time coming. It also left an ongoing legacy of organised crime and deep hatred, mitigated only by the contrition of some of the most active participants.

In 1971, when he was nine, Protestant Alex Calderwood began hanging round a British army barracks in Belfast's Lower Shankill area. Three off-duty Scottish soldiers were murdered and the young boy was flown, at army expense, to Scotland for their funeral. He later recalled: 'I had to ask questions and one of them was, who killed the three soldiers? I was told it was the IRA. So I once again asked: who's the IRA. And I was told, it's the Fenians, or the Taigs, or the Roman Catholics. So basically, from a very early age, I grew up hating Roman Catholics.' When he was 14 he beat up so many Catholic boys on a cross-community trip to the Netherlands that he was placed in a Dutch mental hospital until the visit was over. Calderwood said later:

From 14 through 16, my life was one of growing up through violence – people were being murdered, the police was being murdered, the army was being murdered, people in my community was being murdered. We just got constant rioting all the time. Sixteen years of age, I looked around me, I saw that a lot of my friends were joining the junior paramilitaries. At that particular time we used to get these blue jackets with wee fur collars on them, so I says I'll have one of them. At least I felt I could belong to something then.

At 17, while walking along the Shankill Road, he saw fellow UDA (Ulster Defence Association) members pinning two Catholic boys against a wall. He took one to a derelict garage and beat him to death with a cinder block. The 20-year-old victim, Alexander Reid, had no connection with the IRA but had got drunk and taken a taxi to the wrong part of Belfast. Calderwood, horrified when his uncle ordered the murder of a Catholic lad he had met in prison while serving a burglary sentence, suffered huge remorse. He turned himself in and paid the penalty – prison and castigation by his family and community. After his release he ran a community youth club on the Shankill Road.[12]

As we have seen, such remorse was not universal. Michael Stone has never regretted his killings, believing himself to be a soldier in a just war. 'I believed I was fighting for a cause,' he said in 2006. 'I was not into gangsterism or self-gain. I did it because I am British and I wanted Northern Ireland to stay British. I never shot a man just because he was a Catholic, as some did. I was never into drugs or crime. I kept out of the pubs and went about the work quietly.'[13]

An 18-year-old IRA Volunteer described shooting at British soldiers in a way familiar to most veterans of conventional warfare: 'You are firing at their uniforms. You do not see faces, you just aim for the uniforms ... They were your enemy, they were trying to kill you, you were trying to kill them. It scared me. I was afraid to admit it even to myself. I did not want to get caught or go to jail and I did not want to die.'[14]

Virtually all the assassins and would-be assassins featured in this book are male. The IRA and other terrorist organisations have employed women who are prepared to kill and die, but, with some exceptions, they have been used in logistical support roles. This may be more to do with sexist assumptions by the operational leaders of terror organisations than reluctance by the women themselves to become assassins.

An exception to the general rule was displayed in relatively recent history with the most militant Suffragettes battling for the right to vote. The collective memory has them engaged in illegal but essentially non-violent protest: chaining themselves to railings, defacing artworks, throwing themselves under race horses. The reality is that a minority engaged in arson, sabotage, attempted horse-whippings, aborted kidnappings and the like, which bear the hallmarks of an embryonic terrorist organisation. In September 2006 documents released by the Public Records Office showed that some were involved in a serious plot to kill the prime minister, Herbert Asquith.

In 1909 two would-be assassins practised their pistol fire at miniature shooting ranges in London. One, described as a little woman wearing a tam-o'shanter, had been firing a Browning pistol for six weeks. A letter suggesting that their aim was to shoot Asquith as he left the Commons was handed to Asquith's sister-in-law, a member of the Women's Freedom League, who deplored the escalation of violent tactics. She informed the authorities. They concluded that the woman intended to use the long-standing Suffragette picket of Parliament as a cover for her attempt. But after weighty deliberations they concluded that it would be safer to allow the picket to continue so that it could be closely watched. An official briefed:

> It seems to me we have grounds for believing, though of course not evidence, that there is something amounting to a conspiracy to murder. If there is an unknown woman who has made up her mind to shoot, it will be easier to prevent the act if she is one of the pickets. Each of the pickets at the entrance to Palace Yard, where the PM drives in, will be watched by several constables standing close to her, and if she draws out a revolver, will be instantly seized and stopped. But if she is turned away from her post at the gate, and instead walks up and down between the Houses of Parliament and Downing Street at the hour when the PM may be expected to drive down, though the chance of her getting near the carriage is somewhat less, the chance if she does of her getting a shot is very much greater.[15]

It is believed that the supposed assassins realised that they were being watched, and so abandoned the plot. Their identities have never been conclusively known. Fellow Suffragettes described them as 'half insane' because of the level of injustice they had witnessed.

Now we are facing a different sort of assassin, the suicide bomber, the descendant of the original Middle East cultist promised heavenly bliss for his or her murderous sacrifice. Many of those have proved to be women, ready to massacre others and die themselves. The causes are many and this is not the place to argue the merits or otherwise of the 'war on terror'. But they undoubtedly include the West's response to the 9/11 blitz on New York and Washington, the invasion of Afghanistan and Iraq, the ongoing civil wars, the al-Qaeda network financed largely by Saudi oil billions, the rise of Islamic fundamentalism and the disaffection of young Moslems born and raised in Britain. As in Northern Ireland, a poverty of expectation makes such youngsters putty in the hands of fanatics. The Moslem comedienne Shappi Khorsandi said: 'It is young men a bit lost, like white neo-Nazis. Terrorists are never 37-year-olds caught up in life and mortgages.'[16]

The historian Louise Richardson's shorthand description of the terrorist mindset cannot be bettered: 'revenge, renown, reaction'. Revenge is the reward for grievance, real or imagined. Renown is illustrated by the 900 million worldwide TV audience for the live killing of eleven Israeli athletes at the Munich Olympics or the words of an IRA bomber after his first outrage: 'I was no longer an insignificant teenager. I became heroic overnight. I felt drunk with power.' Reaction is the response of the state to such atrocities, whether by withdrawal, as the Americans did from Lebanon and Somalia, or repression on a scale which will cause the wider population to rebel against the Government's policy,[17] or at least provide a sense of injustice which recruits more to accept the gun or the bomb.

That raises the question of whether the assassin, terrorist or paramilitary can ever be defeated by repressive measures. Tony Blair argued convincingly that the loss of some personal liberties, whether through extension of detention without charge, the introduction of identity cards or massively increased surveillance, are prices worth paying to safeguard the most important liberty – that of a person to go about his or her business without being killed and to maintain the security of the nation. The same argument, however, was deployed against Reformers, trade unionists and Suffragettes by previous administrations who feared that the fabric of society would be destroyed by such revolutionary notions as universal suffrage and a society which protected all its citizens. Repression breeds terrorism, as was graphically shown by internment without trial in Northern Ireland.

Experienced security operatives know that better than politicians and can – albeit rarely – curb knee-jerk responses which they feel can be counter-productive. Shortly after the 7 July 2005 London bombings, Blair issued a twelve-point strategy to counter Islamic extremism in Britain. High on the list was the outlawing of the radical group Hizb ut-Tahrir which campaigns for Britain to become a caliphate subject to Sharia law. Later, Blair gave a personal assurance to Pakistan's President Musharraf that the ban would go ahead. But in December 2006 it was shelved after weeks of discussions between Downing Street, law officers, security services and police. Blair was warned that a ban would serve as a recruiting agent if the group appealed. And evidence collected so far has not justified a legal veto. Rob Beckley, of the Association of Chief Police Officers, said: 'We think that such a move would be counter-productive and not in the spirit of the Government's anti-terrorism legislation. It is not an offence to hold extreme views.'[18]

There is also the moral issue of whether the security forces can use the tactics of terrorism to defeat terrorists. An Israeli death squad sent out to hunt down and murder the Munich killers had few moral qualms at the start of the operation, and many by its abortive end. After the 1972 Munich massacre Israel's premier Golda Meir said: 'I promise you that we will hunt down those that have blood on their hands ...' A team of Mossad agents was despatched across Europe killing suspected PLO terrorists using the same weapons as the assassin, the hollow-nosed bullet and the bomb. Former Mossad deputy head David Kinche recalled:

> We wanted to make them afraid of being a terrorist. We were using psychological elements very, very strongly ... We wanted to make them look over their shoulders and feel that we are upon them. We tried not to do things just by shooting a guy in the streets, that's easy. But by putting a bomb under the mattress of a guy to go off when he falls asleep or by putting a bomb in his phone, this was a message that they can be got at anywhere, at any time and therefore they have to look out for themselves 24 hours a day.[19]

A series of blunders, the suspicion that some of the victims had nothing to do with Munich, arrests of Mossad agents and the 'collateral damage' deaths of innocent civilians led Israel to call off the mission after killing nine on their hit list. The operation, though cathartic for the families of the Munich victims, did nothing to counter terrorism or protect Israel's borders. Former Mossad agent Efraim Halevy said:

'Except in very unique cases, deterrence ultimately doesn't work. And there is no way of successfully deterring terrorists if they are bent on carrying out their acts, because their whole system of evaluating life is different to ours.'[20]

But equally the assassin has achieved nothing in recent history, apart from prolonging collective agony. The two most astounding assassinations of the nineteenth century achieved the precise opposite of the assassins' aims. John Wilkes Booth, the actor son of an alcoholic and mentally fragile Maryland farmer, killed Abraham Lincoln in 1865 in the belief that it would allow the Confederacy to negotiate an honourable end to the Civil War and prevent the emancipation of slaves. Instead, the North won an unconditional victory – the remnants of the Confederate army surrendered a few days after the assassination – and the slaves were freed. His murderous act was seen as sheer villainy and ensured, rather than prevented, Lincoln's legacy. In 1881 a Polish student Ignaty Grinevitsky, a member of a terrorist group the People's Will, threw the bomb which killed both himself and Tsar Alexander II. Grinevitsky had believed that only the death of Alexander could end the long cycle of vicious repression in Poland. In fact, Alexander was embarking on a radical programme of reforms, including the abolition of the secret police, granting freedom of the press, liberalising education and the introduction of locally elected representatives in a step towards constitutional rule. His brutal death saw his successor, Alexander III, reverse all reforms and reintroduce rule by repression and fear. A successful revolution would have to wait 36 years. At the beginning of the twentieth century two bullets were said to have killed 10 million: those fired by 19-year-old Gavrilo Princep. They killed Archduke Franz Ferdinand and his wife Sophie in Sarajevo in 1914, and are credited with setting in motion an unstoppable series of events which culminated in the First World War. But, as Miles Hudson put it: 'The fears, antagonisms, prejudices and deep-rooted jealousies in Europe at that time would have inevitably resulted in armed conflict sooner or later.'[21]

The impotence of assassination is certainly true through much of Ireland's history. T. H. Corfe wrote of the effect of the murders of Lord Cavendish:

> The men of sane vision on both sides, the men who believed in a new Ireland to be made by Irish men working in co-operation with English men, were

given no chance, however slight, to work out their plans. That this was so, that the momentary glimpse of a harmonious future for Ireland so quickly vanished, was a result of the actions of the Irish Nationalist Invincibles and of the murders in Phoenix Park, a classic demonstration of the utter futility of assassination as a political weapon.[22]

The murder of Field Marshal Sir Henry Wilson in 1922 remains the highest ranking military casualty and is another case in point. Hudson writes: 'Wilson's death did not alter the pattern of antagonism or change the status quo very much ... It changed nothing and proved to be merely an irritant at a difficult moment, if anything stiffening the resolve of the assassins' enemy, Great Britain.'[23] Much later, the IRA's attempt on Margaret Thatcher's life did not force her to the negotiating table or cause any loss of nerve among the British people. It was the desperately long attrition rate, the general war-weariness on all sides of the Ulster divide, and the prospect of European and US finances which kick-started the peace process. A case can be made that terrorism, in its widest sense, did allow the IRA and its political wing to bomb their way to the negotiating table. But the essential puerility of individual assassination as a political cure-all proved ineffectual and, indeed, counter-productive.

The contrast between the 'long haul' in Northern Ireland and the knee-jerk responses of Blair and Bush to Islamic terrorists and alleged terror states is vivid. The veteran commentator Simon Jenkins writes:

> When the IRA tried to kill the British Cabinet in 1984, Margaret Thatcher left the matter to the police and calmly asked Marks and Spencer to replace lost clothes so that her party conference could continue. There is evidence that the approach worked. The IRA bombing campaign won it only enemies in mainland Britain, while the 1990s ceasefire brought swift political gains ... Yet al-Qaeda has been accorded near-mystical status. When Rudy Giuliani, the mayor of New York, told its citizens after 9/11 to disregard 'these murderers', stay normal and go back to business, he was ignored. Britain is little better, with ricin, smallpox and dirty-bomb scares trumpeted from Downing Street and Scotland Yard. Politicians invited by al-Qaeda to erode liberty, persecute minorities and subvert commerce seem happy to oblige.[24]

The assassin, the terrorist and the suicide bomber thrives on over-reaction. The erosion of everyone's liberties is the aim. Modern democracies must understand that or we shall all be the losers.

Notes

1 Introduction

1. Paul Wilkinson, *Political Terrorism* (Macmillan, London 1974), p. 46.
2. Paul Elliot, *Warrior Cults: A History of Magical Mystical and Murderous Organizations* (Blandford, London 1995), pp. 91–2.
3. Ibid., p. 103.
4. Lacey Baldwin Smith, *Treason in Tudor England* (Jonathan Cape, London 1986), p. 1.
5. Ibid., pp. 30–1.
6. Ibid., p. 276.
7. *Dictionary of National Biography* (Oxford University Press, Oxford 1889 edition), pp. 266–8.
8. Saul David, *Prince of Pleasure: The Prince of Wales and the Making of the Regency* (Little, Brown, London 1998), p. 73.
9. *Madame D'Arblay Diary and Letters*, edited by her Niece, Charlotte Barrett, Vol. III (Bickers and Son, 1842), p. 46.
10. David, *Prince of Pleasure*, p. 74.
11. Christopher Hibbert, *George III: A Personal History* (Penguin Books, London 1998), pp. 227–8.
12. Ibid., p. 229.

2 The Despard Plot

1. *The Newgate Calendar*, www.exclassics.com/newgate/ng465.htm.
2. Mike Jay, *The Unfortunate Colonel Despard: Hero and Traitor in Britain's First War on Terror* (Bantam, London 2004), pp. 216–17.
3. Oxford University Press factsheet, 1995, pp. 1–3, taken from James Bannantine's *Memoirs of Edward Marcus Despard*.
4. Jay, *The Unfortunate Colonel Despard*, p. 257.
5. Ibid., p. 273.
6. *The Times*, 8 February 1803.
7. Jay, *The Unfortunate Colonel Despard*, p. 284.
8. *The Times*, 8 February 1803.
9. Ibid.
10. *The Newgate Calendar*.
11. Ibid.
12. Ibid.
13. Ibid.
14. Jay, *The Unfortunate Colonel Despard*, p. 9.
15. Ibid., p. 10.

3   Death of a Prime Minister

1. *Dictionary of National Biography* (Oxford University Press, Oxford 1889 edition), pp. 101–6.
2. Marjie Bloy, *The Victorian Web*, www.victorianweb.org/history/pms/perceval.html.
3. www.spartacus.schoolnet.co.uk/PRperceval.htm.
4. *Annual Register* 1812, *Chronicles*, pp. 44–61.
5. *The Times*, 13 May 1812.
6. Ibid.
7. www.spartacus.schoolnet.co.uk/PRperceval.htm.
8. *Annual Register* 1812, pp. 46–7.
9. Ibid.
10. *The Times*, 16 May 1812.
11. *Annual Register* 1812, pp. 52–7.
12. Ibid., p. 58.
13. Ibid.

4   The Cato Street Conspiracy

1. www.spartacus.schoolnet.co.uk/PRcato.htm.
2. Ibid.
3. *Sunday Observer*, 3 March 1820.
4. www.spartacus.schoolnet.co.uk/PRcato.htm.
5. www.spartacus.schoolnet.co.uk/PRbrunt.htm.
6. Letter, 18 April 1820, http://www.spartacus.schoolnet.co.uk/PRings.htm.
7. *The Traveller*, May 1820.
8. George Theodore Wilkinson, *An Authentic History of the Cato Street Conspiracy* (pamphlet, London 1820).
9. John Hobhouse, diary entry, 1 May 1820.
10. www.spartacus.schoolnet.co.uk/PRedwards.htm.

5   Queen Victoria – The First Attempt

1. *Annual Register* 1840, p. 258.
2. *The Times*, 10 July 1840.
3. *Annual Register* 1840, pp. 259–61.
4. Yvonne Demoskoff, Royalty Home Page, http://users.uniserve.com/~canyon/queen_victoria.htm.
5. *Annual Register* 1840, pp. 245–6.
6. *The Times*, 11 June 1840.
7. *The Times*, 13 June 1840.
8. *The Times*, 11 June 1840.
9. *The Times*, 11 July 1840.
10. *The Times*, 10 July 1840.
11. Ibid.
12. Ibid.
13. *Annual Register* 1840, pp. 254–63.
14. Yvonne Demoskoff, Royalty Home Page, http://users.uniserve.com/~canyon/queen_victoria.htm.

6 The McNaughton Rules

1. *The Times*, 3 March 1843.
2. No. 10 Downing Street – Sir Robert Peel, www.pm.gov.uk/output/page151.asp.
3. *The Times*, 4 March 1843.
4. *The Times*, 26 January 1843.
5. *Annual Register* 1843, *Chronicle*, pp. 6–7.
6. Ibid., pp. 8–9.
7. *The Times*, 4 March 1843.
8. *Annual Register* 1843, *Law Cases* &., pp. 345–52.
9. Ibid., p. 353.
10. *The Times*, 5 March 1843.
11. *Annual Register* 1843, *Law Cases* &., pp. 358–9.
12. *Official Report*, 13 March 1843.
13. The National Lunacy Inquiry and its Circumstances, www.mdx.ac.uk/www/study/4_05.htm.

7 Queen Victoria – Further Attempts

1. Yvonne Demoskoff, Royalty Home Page, http://users.uniserve.com/~canyon/queen_victoria.htm.
2. *The Times*, 31 May 1841.
3. Yvonne Demoskoff, Royalty Home Page, http://users.uniserve.com/~canyon/queen_victoria.htm.
4. *The Times*, 1 June 1842.
5. *The Times*, 2 June 1842.
6. *The Times*, 18 June 1842.
7. *The Times*, 4 July 1842.
8. Yvonne Demoskoff, Royalty Home Page, http://users.uniserve.com/~canyon/queen_victoria.htm.
9. *The Times*, 20 May 1849.
10. Ibid.
11. *The Times*, 28 June 1850.
12. *The Times*, 12 July 1850.
13. Ibid.
14. Ibid.
15. *The Times*, 1 March 1872.
16. *Annual Register* 1872, pp. 209–13.
17. *The Times*, 20 March 1872.
18. *The Times*, 12 April 1872.
19. Ibid.
20. Yvonne Demoskoff, Royalty Home Page, http://users.uniserve.com/~canyon/queen_victoria.htm.
21. Ibid., p. 11.
22. *The Times*, 3 March 1882.
23. *The Times*, 5 March 1882.
24. *The Times*, 20 April 1882.
25. Ibid.
26. www.mcgonagall-online.org.uk/poems/pgassass.htm.
27. *The Observer*, 12 May 2002.

8   The Wounding of the Duke of Edinburgh

1. Lawrence James, *Warrior Race: A History of the British at War* (Little, Brown, London 2001), p. 265.
2. Justin McCarthy, *A History of Our Times*, 7 volumes (Caxton Publishing Company, London 1908), Vol. IV, pp. 126–8.
3. Ibid., pp. 143–7.
4. *The Times*, 15 December 1867.
5. *Annual Register* 1868, *Chronicles*, p. 25.
6. *Sydney Morning Herald*, 13 March 1868.
7. *Annual Register* 1868, *Chronicles*, p. 27.
8. Ibid., pp. 27–8.
9. T. D. Sullivan, *Recollections of Troubled Times in Irish Politics* (Sealy, Bryers and Walker – M. H. Gill and Son, Dublin 1905), pp. 190–1.

9   The Phoenix Park Murders

1. T. H. Corfe, *The Phoenix Park Murders* (Hodder & Stoughton, London 1968), p. 128.
2. *Dictionary of National Biography* (Oxford University Press, Oxford 1889 edition).
3. Ibid.
4. *The Times*, 9 May 1882.
5. *Annual Register* 1882, English History, p. 62.
6. *The Times*, 9 May 1882.
7. Ibid.
8. *Annual Register* 1882, pp. 64–5.
9. T. D. Sullivan, *Recollections of Troubled Times in Irish Politics* (Sealy, Bryers and Walker – M. H. Gill and Son, Dublin 1905), pp. 200–1.
10. *The Times*, 9 May 1882.
11. Ibid.
12. Sullivan, *Recollections of Troubled Times in Irish Politics*, p. 203.
13. Official Report (*Hansard*), 12 May 1882.
14. *Annual Register* 1882, p. 67.
15. Ibid., p. 69.
16. Miles Hudson, *Assassination* (Sutton Publishing, Stroud 2000), p. 102.
17. Sullivan, *Recollections of Troubled Times in Irish Politics*, p. 206.
18. *The Times*, 22 January 1883.
19. *Annual Register* 1883, English History, pp. 194–5.
20. *The Times*, 19 February 1883.
21. Sullivan, *Recollections of Troubled Times in Irish Politics*, p. 204.
22. *The Times*, 19 February 1883.
23. *The Times*, 22 January 1883.
24. *The Times*, 19 February 1883.
25. Sullivan, *Recollections of Troubled Times in Irish Politics*, pp. 205–6.
26. *Dictionary of National Biography*, pp. 336–41.

10   The Cairo Gang and the Pass of the Flowers

1. Michael Collins, *The Path to Freedom* (Talbot Press, Dublin 1922), p. 134.
2. Ibid.
3. *The Times*, 20 December 1919.

4. *Cork Examiner*, 22 September 1920.
5. Tom Barry, *Guerrilla Days in Ireland* (Anvil Books, Dublin 1962), p. 34.
6. *Cork Examiner*, 4 November 1920.
7. Collins, *The Path to Freedom*, p. 137.
8. *Irish Independent*, 22 November 1920.
9. *The Times*, 22 November 1920.
10. Edward Norman, *A Modern History of Ireland* (Penguin Books, London 1971), pp. 273–4.
11. Barry, *Guerrilla Days in Ireland*, p. 128.
12. Duff Cooper, *Haig* (Faber and Faber, London 1936), p. 328.
13. *The Times*, 23 June 1922.
14. Sir C. E. Caldwell, *Sir Henry Wilson* (Cassell, London 1927), p. 305.
15. James Mackay, *Michael Collins: A Life* (Mainstream Publishing, Edinburgh 1996), p. 211.
16. Meda Ryan, *The Day Michael Collins Was Shot* (Poolbeg, Dublin 1989), pp. 104–5.
17. Ibid., pp. 112–13.
18. Barry, *Guerrilla Days in Ireland*, p. 184.
19. *Irish Independent*, 28 August 1922.
20. Mackay, *Michael Collins: A Life*, p. 215.
21. Miles Hudson, *Assassination* (Sutton Publishing, Stroud 2000), p. 161.

11 The Attempt on Edward VIII

1. *The Times*, 17 July 1936.
2. Ibid.
3. *Daily Express*, 18 July 1936.
4. Ibid.
5. *Daily Express*, 3 January 2003.
6. Ibid.
7. *Guardian*, 3 January 2003.
8. Ibid.

12 British Assassinations Overseas

1. Sir Sydney Smith, *Mostly Murder: An Autobiography* (Guild Publishing, London 1959), pp. 101–2.
2. Ibid., pp. 106–7.
3. Ibid., p. 110.
4. *Hansard*, 7 November 1944.
5. http://en.wikipedia.org/wiki/Lord_Moyne.
6. Samir Raabat, *Egyptian Mail*, 9 December 1995.
7. Ibid.
8. www.britains-smallwars.com/Palestine/index.htm.
9. BBC News, 8 June 2000.
10. *The Times*, 9 June 2000.
11. BBC News, 8 June 2000.
12. BBC News Online, 4 March 2003.
13. Reuters, 3 March 2003.
14. BBC Radio 4 Today programme, 8 December 2003.
15. BBC News Online, 31 December 2003.

13   The Troubles to Airey Neave

1. Gerry Fitt, interview with author, 1992.
2. Sean O'Callaghan, *The Informer* (Bantam Books, London 1998), p. 32.
3. *Guardian*, Weekend Magazine, 4 March 2006.
4. BBC News webpage, onthisday.
5. Margaret Thatcher, *The Path to Power* (HarperCollins, London 1995), p. 398.
6. O'Callaghan, *The Informer*, p. 70.
7. Ibid., pp. 72–3.
8. Ibid., p. 75.
9. BBC News Online, 22 July 2001.
10. *Guardian*, 23 March 1979.
11. *Oxford Dictionary of National Biography* (Oxford University Press, London 2004), pp. 209–10.
12. Ibid., p. 311.
13. Paul Routledge, *Public Servant, Secret Agent: the Elusive Life and Violent Death of Airey Neave* (Fourth Estate, London 2002), p. 271.
14. Ibid., p. 288.
15. *Daily Express*, 31 March 1979.
16. Thatcher, *The Path to Power*, p. 434.
17. Press Association, 30 March 1979.
18. Ibid.
19. Routledge, *Public Servant, Secret Agent*, pp. 15–16.
20. *Daily Express*, 31 March 1979.
21. Routledge, *Public Servant, Secret Agent*, p. 344.
22. Ibid., p. 354.

14   The Murder of Lord Mountbatten

1. *Time Europe*, 15 September 1974.
2. www.victims.org.uk.
3. Frank Melville, *Time Europe* website.
4. Philip Ziegler, *Mountbatten: The Official Biography* (Collins, London 1985), p. 695.
5. Philip Ziegler, *Oxford Dictionary of National Biography* (Oxford University Press, London 2004), p. 557.
6. *Daily Mail*, 12 June 2004.
7. Ibid.
8. Press Association, 27 August 1979.
9. *Belfast Telegraph*, 29 August 1979.
10. Ziegler, *Oxford Dictionary of National Biography*, p. 558.
11. Richard English, *Armed Struggle: A History of the IRA* (Macmillan, London 2003), p. 221.
12. *The Times*, 27 August 2004.
13. *An Phoblacht – Republican News*, 5 January 1980.
14. Ed Maloney, *A Secret History of the IRA* (Allen Lane, London 2002), p. 176.

15   The Brighton Bomb

1. Margaret Thatcher, *The Downing Street Years* (HarperCollins, London 1993), p. 379.
2. *Guardian*, 27 February 2005.
3. Raymond Murray, *The SAS in Ireland* (Mercer Press, London 1990), p. 259.

4. Martin Dillon, *The Enemy Within: The IRA's War against the British* (Doubleday, New York 1994), p. 291.
5. Mark Urban, *Big Boys' Rules: The Secret Struggle against the IRA* (Faber and Faber, London 1992), p. 58.
6. Associated Press, 19 November 1981.
7. *Annual Register* 1981, p. 54.
8. Sean O'Callaghan, *The Informer* (Bantam Books, London 1998), pp. 144–56.
9. *Guardian*, 10 December 2001.
10. Thatcher, *The Downing Street Years*, p. 379.
11. Ibid., p. 380.
12. Matt Adams, *PA News*, 10 October 2004.
13. Ibid.
14. Hugo Young, *One of Us: A Biography of Margaret Thatcher* (Macmillan, London 1989), p. 373.
15. *PA News*, 10 October 2004.
16. *Guardian*, 28 August 2000.
17. Richard English, *Armed Struggle: A History of the IRA* (Macmillan, London 2003), p. 248.
18. Young, *One of Us*, p. 373.

16 The Troubles to Ian Gow

1. James Prior, *A Balance of Power* (Hamish Hamilton, London 1986), p. 191.
2. Margaret Thatcher, *The Downing Street Years* (HarperCollins, London 1993), pp. 29–30.
3. *The Times*, 31 July 1990.
4. Mark Garnett, *The Oxford Dictionary of National Biography* (Oxford University Press, London 2004), p. 91.
5. *The Times*, 31 July 1990.
6. Ibid.
7. Ibid.
8. Ibid.
9. Bruce Anderson, *John Major: The Making of a Prime Minister* (Fourth Estate, London 1991), pp. 157–8.
10. Garnett, *The Oxford Dictionary of National Biography*, p. 92.

17 The Attack on John Major and Beyond

1. *Guardian Unlimited* homepage.
2. Press Association, 7 February 1991.
3. *Hansard*, 7 February 1991.
4. *The Times*, 8 November 1991.
5. *The Times*, 31 July 1990.
6. Ibid.
7. *Daily Mirror*, 6 April 2006.
8. *Daily Express*, 5 April 2006.
9. Liam Clarke, *Sunday Times*, 9 April 2006.
10. Press Association, 4 April 2006.
11. Keith Dovkants, *Evening Standard*, 1 November 2006.
12. Ibid.

18   The Attempt on Tony Blair

1. William Horsley, BBC News, 13 April 1999.
2. Dusko Doder and Louise Branson, *Milosevic: Portrait of a Tyrant* (The Free Press, New York 1999), pp. 259–60.
3. Ibid., p. 261.
4. Ibid., p. 263.
5. Interview with author, February 2006.
6. *Sunday Times*, 1 July 2001.
7. Ibid.
8. Ibid.
9. Interview with author, February 2006.
10. Daniel Sunter, IWPR, 29 April 2005.
11. *Mail on Sunday*, 12 March 2006.

19   Conclusions

1. *The Times*, 22 March 1974.
2. *Daily Express*, 21 March 1974.
3. ITV1, 'To Kidnap a Princess', 26 August 2006.
4. BBC News Online, 2 December 2005.
5. BBC News, 17 November 2005.
6. BBC News Online, 15 October 2004.
7. Roger Parry, *Daily Express*, 26 March 2006.
8. Ibid.
9. Maxwell Taylor, *The Terrorist* (Brassey's, London 1988), p. 74.
10. Tom Barry, *Guerrilla Days in Ireland* (Anvil Books, Dublin 1962), pp. 1–3.
11. Ibid., pp. 105–7.
12. Jonathan Stevenson, *They Wrecked the Place: Contemplating an End to the Northern Ireland Troubles* (The Free Press, New York 1996), pp. 63–5.
13. Keith Dovkants, *Evening Standard*, 1 November 2006.
14. Kevin Toolis, *Rebel Hearts* (Picador, London 1996), p. 126.
15. *Daily Mail*, 29 September 2006.
16. *Sunday Times*, 20 August 2006.
17. Ibid.
18. *The Observer*, 24 December 2006.
19. Richard Girling, *Sunday Times Magazine*, 15 June 2005.
20. Ibid.
21. Miles Hudson, *Assassination* (Sutton Publishing, Stroud 2000), p. 102.
22. T. H. Corfe, *The Phoenix Park Murders* (Hodder & Stoughton, London 1968), p. 226.
23. Hudson, *Assassination*, p. 160.
24. *Sunday Times*, book section, 20 August 2006.

Bibliography

Anderson, Bruce, *John Major: The Making of the Prime Minister* (Fourth Estate, London 1991)

Annual Register (various years)

Arthur, Max, *Northern Ireland Soldiers Talking 1969 to Today* (Sidgewick & Jackson, London 1987)

Bannantine, James, *Memoirs of Edward Marcus Despard* (J. Ridgway, London 1799)

Barry, Tom, *Guerrilla Days in Ireland* (Anvil Books, Dublin 1962; reprinted 1989)

Bennett, Richard, *The Black and Tans* (New English Library, London 1970)

Benson, Arthur and Viscount Esher (eds), *The Letters of Queen Victoria* (John Murray, London 1911)

Bloy, Marjie, *Spencer Perceval* (www.thevictorianweb, 2003)

Caldwell, Sir C. E., *Sir Henry Wilson* (Cassell, London 1927)

Campbell, John, *Margaret Thatcher, Volume 2 – The Iron Lady* (Jonathan Cape, London 2003)

Carr, Matthew, *Unknown Soldiers: How Terrorism Transformed the Modern World* (Profile, London 2006)

Charlot, Monica, *Victoria: The Young Queen* (Blackwell, Oxford 1991)

Clarke, Alan, *Diaries* (Weidenfeld & Nicolson, London 1993)

Collins, Michael, *The Path to Freedom* (Talbot Press, Dublin 1922)

Cook, Chris and Stevenson, John, *The Longman Handbook of Modern British History* (Longman, London and New York 1983)

Corfe, T. H., *The Phoenix Park Murders* (Hodder & Stoughton, London 1968)

Curran, Joseph, *The Birth of the Irish Free State 1921–23* (Alabama University Press, Montgomery, AL 1988)

David, Saul, *Prince of Pleasure: The Prince of Wales and the Making of the Regency* (Little, Brown, London 1998)

Dillon, Martin, *The Enemy Within: The IRA's War against the British* (Doubleday, New York 1994)

Doder, Dusko and Branson, Louise, *Milosevic: Portrait of a Tyrant* (The Free Press, New York 1999)

Elliot, Paul, *Warrior Cults: A History of Magical, Mystical and Murderous Organizations* (Blandford, London 1995)

English, Richard, *Armed Struggle: A History of the IRA* (Macmillan, London 2003)

Feehan, John, *Michael Collins: Murder or Accident* (Mercier Press, Cork 1981)

Garnett, Mark, *The Oxford Dictionary of National Biography* (Oxford University Press, London 2004)

Geraghty, Tony, *The Irish War: The Military History of a Domestic Conflict* (HarperCollins, London 1998)

Gray, Denis, *Spencer Perceval: The Evangelical Prime Minister* (Manchester University Press, Manchester 1963)

Grigg, John, *Lloyd George from Peace to War* (Clarendon Press, Oxford 1964)

Hemmings, Ray, *Liberty or Death: Early Struggles for Parliamentary Democracy* (Lawrence & Wishart, London 2000)

Hibbert, Christopher, *Queen Victoria in Her Letters and Journals* (Penguin Books, London 1984)
—— *George III: A Personal History* (Penguin Books, London 1998)
Hodges, Michael, *Ireland from Easter Rising to Civil War* (Batsford, London 1987)
Hudson, Miles, *Assassination* (Sutton Publishing, Stroud 2000)
James, Lawrence, *Warrior Race* (Little, Brown, London 2001)
Jay, Mike, *The Unfortunate Colonel Despard: Hero and Traitor in Britain's First War on Terror* (Bantam Books, London 2004)
Litton, Helen, *The Irish Civil War* (Wolfhound, Dublin 1995)
Longford, Elizabeth, *Queen Victoria: Born to Succeed* (Perennial Library, New York 1974)
Mackay, James, *Michael Collins: A Life* (Mainstream Publishing, Edinburgh 1996)
McCarthy, Justin, *A History of Our Own Times*, 7 volumes (Caxton Publishing Company, London 1908)
Maloney, Ed, *A Secret History of the IRA* (Allen Lane, London 2002)
McKittrick, David and McVea, David, *Making Sense of the Troubles* (Blackstaff Press, Belfast 2000)
Murray, Raymond, *The SAS in Ireland* (Mercer Press, London 1990)
Norman, Edward, *A Modern History of Ireland* (Penguin Books, London 1971)
O'Callaghan, Sean, *The Informer* (Bantam Books, London 1998)
O'Connor, Matt, *With Michael Collins in the Fight for Irish Independence* (Peter Davis, London 1929)
Oxford Dictionary of National Biography (Oxford University Press, London 2004)
Pare, Robert A., *Dying to Win: Why Suicide Terrorists Do it* (Gibson Square, London 2006)
Prior, James, *A Balance of Power* (Hamish Hamilton, London 1986)
Rhodes James, Robert, *Prince Albert: A Biography* (Alfred A. Knopf, New York 1984)
Richardson, Louise, *What Terrorists Want: Understanding the Terrorist Threat* (John Murray, London 2006)
Routledge, Paul, *Public Servant Secret Agent: The Elusive Life and Violent Death of Airey Neave* (Fourth Estate, London 2002)
Ryan, Meda, *The Day Michael Collins Was Shot* (Poolbeg, Dublin 1989)
Smith, Lacey Baldwin, *Treason in Tudor England* (Jonathan Cape, London 1986)
Smith, Sir Sydney, *Mostly Murder: An Autobiography* (Guild Publishing, London 1959)
Stevenson, Jonathan, *They Wrecked the Place: Contemplating an End to the Northern Ireland Troubles* (The Free Press, New York 1996)
Sullivan, T. D., *Recollections of Troubled Times in Irish Politics* (Sealy, Bryers and Walker – M. H. Gill and Son, Dublin 1905)
Talbot, Hayden, *Michael Collins' Own Story* (Hutchinson, London 1923)
Taylor, Maxwell, *The Terrorist* (Brassey's, London 1988)
Thatcher, Margaret, *The Downing Street Years* (HarperCollins, London 1993)
—— *The Path to Power* (HarperCollins, London 1995)
Toolis, Kevin, *Rebel Hearts* (Picador, London 1996)
Urban, Mark, *Big Boys' Rules: The Secret Struggle against the IRA* (Faber and Faber, London 1992)
Veitch, G. S., *The Genesis of Parliamentary Reform* (Constable, London 1913)
Walpole, S., *The Life of the Rt Hon Spencer Perceval* (Hurst and Blackett, London 1874)
Wilkinson, George Theodore, *An Authentic History of the Cato Street Conspiracy* (pamphlet, London 1820)
Wilkinson, Paul, *Political Terrorism* (Macmillan, London 1974)

Young, Hugo, *One of Us: A Biography of Margaret Thatcher* (Macmillan, London 1989)
Younger, Calton, *Ireland's Civil War* (Frederick Muller, London 1968)
Ziegler, Philip, *Mountbatten: The Official Biography* (Collins, London 1985)
—— contributions to *The Oxford Dictionary of National Biography* (Oxford University Press, London 2004)

Newspapers and Periodicals

Daily Express
Daily Mail
Daily Mirror
Daily Telegraph
Guardian
Irish Independent
The Newgate Calendar
The Observer
Republican News
The Sunday Times
The Times

Index